CU00403447

Heinemann History Scheme

INTO THE TWENTIETH CENTURY

BOOK 3

Judith Kidd
Rosemary Rees
Ruth Tudor

Heinemann Educational Publishers
Halley Court, Jordan Hill, Oxford, OX2 8EJ
a division of Reed Educational & Professional Publishing Ltd
Heinemann is a registered trademark of Reed Educational & Professional Publishing Ltd

OXFORD MELBOURNE AUCKLAND
JOHANNESBURG BLANTYRE GABORONE
IBADAN PORTSMOUTH NH (USA) CHICAGO

© Heinemann Educational Publishers 2001

Copyright notice

All rights reserved. No part of this publication may be reproduced in any material form (including photocopying or storing it in any medium by electronic means and whether or not transiently or incidentally to some other use of this publication) without the prior written permission of the copyright owner, except in accordance with the provisions of the Copyright, Designs and Patents Act 1988 or under the terms of a licence issued by the Copyright Licensing Agency Ltd, 90 Tottenham Court Road, London W1P 0LP. Applications for the copyright owner's written permission to reproduce any part of this publication should be addressed to the publisher.

First published 2001

ISBN 0 435 32596 5

03 02 01
10 9 8 7 6 5 4 3 2

Designed and typeset by Visual Image, Taunton

Illustrated by Paul Bale and Ian Heard

Printed and bound in Italy by Printer Trento S.r.l

Picture research by Sally Smith

Photographic acknowledgements

The authors and publishers would like to thank the following for permission to reproduce photographs:

Associated Press: pp. 93, 98;
Bridgeman Art Library: pp. 13, 58, 83, 195, 196 (top), 200, 204, 209, 229;
Centre for the Study of Cartoons and Caricature: pp. 123, 136 (top), 246;
Corbis UK Ltd: pp. 33, 36 (bottom), 39, 102 (right), 206, 213, 218 (bottom);
David King Collection: p. 136 (bottom);
Fortean Picture Library: p. 196 (bottom);
Hiroshima Peace Memorial Museum: p. 121 (bottom right and left);
Hulton Getty: pp. 43, 55, 102 (both), 106, 152, 203;
Image Bank: p. 162;
Imperial War Museum: pp. 77, 242;
Katz Pictures: p. 138;
Kobal Collection: p. 161;
Magnum/Danny Lyon: p. 36 (top);
Mansell Collection: pp.16, 32;
Mary Evans Picture Library: pp. 12, 20, 23, 60, 116, 150, 158, 205 (top);
Peter Newark's Military Pictures: pp. 107, 113;
Popperfoto: pp. 41 (top, middle, bottom right), 95, 103 (bottom), 160, 168, 194, 217, 232, 234, 238;
Punch: pp. 78, 183;
Tate Gallery: p. 47;
Topham Picturepoint: pp. 41 (bottom left), 74, 81 (both), 88 (both), 103 (top), 104, 121 (top), 169, 212, 218 (top), 237, 245.

Cover photograph: © Imperial War Museum

Written source acknowledgements

The authors and publishers gratefully acknowledge the following publications from which written sources in the book are drawn. In some sources the wording or sentence structure has been simplified.

G Alperovitz, *Atomic Diplomacy: Hiroshima and Potsdam*, Secker & Warburg, 1966: p.216
V Brittain, *Testament of Youth*, Fontana, 1979: p.76
M Chaikin, *A Nightmare in History*, Clairon, 1987: pp.153-4, 170
J R Clynes, *Memoirs*, London, 1937: p.239
B Devlin, *The Price of My Soul*, Deutsch, 1969: p.95
S Everett, *The History of Slavery*, Grange Books, 1996: p.26
R Field, *African Peoples of the Americas*, Cambridge University Press, 1995: p.29
A Frank, *The Diary of a Young Girl*, Penguin, 2000: pp.163-5
G M Fraser, *Quartered Safe Out Here*, Harvill, 1992: p.167
P Gourevitch, *We Wish To Inform You That Tomorrow We Will Be Killed With Our Families*, Picador, 1999: p.109
W Heyen, *Erika: Poems of the Holocaust*, Time Being Press, 1991: p.173
D Hinds, *Black Peoples of the Americas, 1500-1900s*, CollinsEducational, 1992: pp.30, 31, 34
A Hitler, *Mein Kampf*, Hutchinson, 1969: p.148
J & L Horton (Eds), *History of African American People*, Salamander Books, 1995: p.13
The Independent, article by Steve Crawshaw, 27th November 1999: p.176
C Isaacman, *Pathways Through the Holocaust*, Ktav Publishing House, 1988: pp.153, 158
Keesing, *Contemporary Archives*, Keesing's Worldwide, 1989: p.138
T & S Lancaster, *Britain and the World: The 20th Century*, Causeway Press, 1992: p.170
Primo Levi, *If This Is A Man (Survival In Aucshwitz)*, translated by Stuart Woolf, copyright © 1959 by Orion Press, © 1958 by Giulio Einaudi editore S.P.A. Used by permission of Viking Penguin, a division of Penguin Putnam Inc.
W K Marshall (Ed.), *The Colthurst Journal*, KTO Press, 1977: p.20
K Martin, *Father Figures*, Penguin, 1969: p.246
E McCann, *War and an Irish Town*, Penguin, 1974: p.92
The New York Times, January 1944: p.167
E Ringelblum, *Notes from the Warsaw Ghetto*, McGraw-Hill, 1958: p.154
B Rogasky, *Smoke and Ashes*, Oxford University Press, 1988: p.155
S Rowbotham, *A Century of Women*, Penguin, 1999: p.77
J Scott, *Medicine Through Time*, Collins, 1990: p.210
L C B Seaman, *Post-Victorian Britain*, London, 1966: p.241
B M Senior, *Jamaica by a Retired Military Officer*, Negro University Press, 1969: p.20
J Simkin, *Contemporary Accounts of the Second World War*, Tressell, 1984: p.215
N Smith, *Black Peoples of the Americas*, Oxford University Press, 1992: pp.25, 30
The Times, 1968: p.93
V B Thompson, *The Making of the African Diaspora*, Longman, 1987: p.21
M Weber, *Causes and Consequences of the African American Civil Rights Movement*, Evans Brothers, 1997: p.26
E. Wiesel, *Night*, trans. Stella Rodway, Penguin, 1981: p.173

"I Have A Dream", license granted by the Heirs of Dr. Martin Luther King, Jr., by permission of Intellectual Properties Management, Atlanta, GA, ref – www.pbs.org/greatspeeches: p.39
Malcolm X's Audubon address, © Dr Betty Shabazz, under licence authorized by Curtis Management Group, Indianapolis, IA., ref – www.pbs.org/greatspeeches: p.39
Richard Dimbleby transcripts of April 1945 taken from *BBC History Magazine CD-Rom*, BBC Worldwide Limited: p.166
Voices of the Holocaust, The British Library Board, published by The British Library National Sound Archive, 1993: p.111

The publishers have made every effort to trace copyright holders of material in this book. Any omissions will be rectified in subsequent printings if notice is given to the publishers.

Contents

Unit 15: Black peoples of America – from slavery to equality?

You may not consider your life to be especially free. You may moan about having to go to school, wear a school uniform or come home at a certain time. We take our 'freedom' for granted. This unit will investigate a group of people that makes up a large part of American society – African Americans. Their history is one of slavery and a long fight for freedom. We will investigate where most black Americans came from originally, how they ended up in America as slaves with no freedom at all, and how they gradually broke away from slavery. The fight was not easy. Many people argue that freedom has still not been achieved, so we will also think about how far black people in America, indeed all over the world, are actually free from their past and equal to white people. This is the question behind the title of this unit: Black peoples of America – from slavery to equality?

WHAT DOES IT MEAN TO BE FREE? WHAT DOES IT MEAN TO BE A SLAVE?

For many centuries there have been people who have believed that human beings have natural rights as individuals. This means that societies need to have laws to protect people's freedom. These laws might also limit the amount of power rulers and organisations, such as the police and trade unions have. Some societies pass laws to make sure that people are free to make choices about their own lives – about jobs and religions and how to live.

SO HOW FREE ARE YOU?

Make a list of the ways that you could be said to be free. Divide your list into two sections, daily life and society in general. Freedom can mean *free from* things as well as *free to do* what you like. Make a list of things that we try to be *free from* in our society.

Some human rights groups think that even in this country we are not free enough. They argue that inventions such as CCTV and identity cards used by young people limit the real freedom that people have. Do you agree? Can there be many different kinds of freedom?

SLAVERY – AN ANCIENT INVENTION

Slavery has existed since ancient times. It existed in Ancient Egypt, China and Babylonia and it became even more widespread under the Greek and Roman Empires. The word 'slave' comes from the Slavic people who were taken to Germany as slaves in the Middle Ages. The rulers and armies of empires and kingdoms would often make slaves of their prisoners of war. Sometimes people were made slaves as a punishment or they were born into slavery and were bought and sold as slaves. Some slaves were bought and sold as part of the sale of a plot of land. Slavery became slightly less common after the collapse of the Roman Empire although slaves were still popular under the early Islamic and Ottoman Empires. These early slaves were white or black, Muslim or Christian.

Slavery changed during the sixteenth century when a huge trade in mainly African black people was developed by the Spanish and Portuguese. Both Spain and Portugal wanted to gain strong successful empires in the Americas. Slaves were needed to clear and farm new land and make it profitable for the new inhabitants.

What were they?

Islamic Empire
The empire of the Saracens (Arabians) who, in the mid-seventh-century, captured large parts of Africa, Asia and Europe, and ruled there until the Turks overran much of the empire at the end of the thirteenth century.

Ottoman Empire
This was called after Osman who built up the Turkish Empire at the end of the thirteenth century. In 1453 Constantinople was captured by the Turks and became the capital. This also marked the end of the Eastern Roman Empire.

SLAVERY CONTINUES

Although slavery was abolished in America in 1865, and throughout many parts of the British Empire in 1833, many other countries continued to use slaves. It was only banned in Mauritania in 1980 and it still goes on in many places. Human rights organisations report on many different forms of slavery that exist today. Child labour in India and the Sudan and child prostitution in Asia are only two examples. There was a recent campaign in China against the sale of women and children.

Question Time

1 Copy the phrase below and complete it with four different sentences.
To be free means...
Now compare your sentences in groups and discuss which of the different sentences you think describe the most important aspects of freedom. Does everyone in your group agree?

2 Research examples of slavery that still exist today. Human rights organisations, such as Amnesty International and Anti-Slavery International, have information on recent campaigns. What sorts of slavery still go on today?

AFRICAN ROOTS – WHERE DID MOST BLACK AMERICANS ORIGINATE?

Most black Americans can trace their roots to West Africa. This area is just one part of the huge continent of Africa, which is made up of many different environments: rainforests, ice-capped mountains, grasslands and deserts, and many different tribes and peoples. In the Middle Ages, West Africa itself was made up of many different complex societies. Most people lived in villages or small towns within separate kingdoms, each with their own traditions and cultures. Their wealth was mainly based on the trade of gold from the gold mines in West Africa, as well as leather, ivory and copper. They traded with each other and with the Islamic Arabs who had taken over most of North Africa. The Arabs wanted gold in return for spices, salt and luxury goods. They also traded in slaves.

Activity Time

1 Look at a modern map of Africa and the maps on page 7 to find out some of these things about the continent:

a How big it is (compared to Britain).

b What different types of climate and environment there are.

c Where the old kingdoms were (think about what people need to survive).

d Find modern Nigeria, Cameroon and Northern Angola. By the eighteenth century the majority of slaves were taken from these areas. What does this tell us?

2 In the nineteenth century, many African countries were colonised by European countries. In the twentieth century many of these countries gained their independence. Since becoming independent some modern African countries have called themselves after ancient African kingdoms. Why do you think this is?

SOME EARLY WEST AFRICAN KINGDOMS

Ghana (fifth to eleventh century)
This kingdom is not the same as the modern country called Ghana. The old kingdom was based on the gold trade and situated in between the gold mines near the coast and the salt mines in the Sahara Desert, so that it could control the trade to the north. It was a large and developed kingdom, with a court and an army. Its people were farmers and traders. It later became part of the Kingdom of Mali.

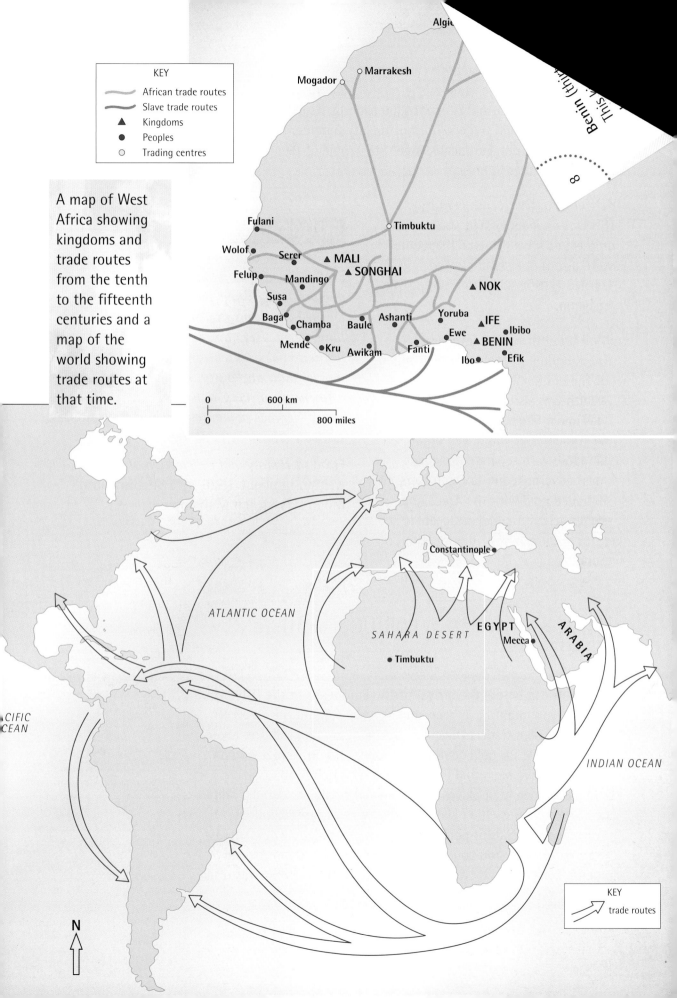

KEY
~ African trade routes
~ Slave trade routes
▲ Kingdoms
● Peoples
○ Trading centres

A map of West Africa showing kingdoms and trade routes from the tenth to the fifteenth centuries and a map of the world showing trade routes at that time.

Algi...

○ Marrakesh
Mogador ○

Benin (this ...
this is ...

8

○ Timbuktu

Fulani ●
Wolof ●
Serer ●
Felup ●
Mandingo ●
Susa ●
Baga ●
Chamba ●
Mende ●
Kru ●
Awikam ●

▲ MALI
▲ SONGHAI
▲ NOK

Ashanti ●
Baule ●
Yoruba ●
Ewe ●
Fanti ●
▲ IFE
Ibibo ●
▲ BENIN
Ibo ●
Efik ●

0 | 600 km
0 | 800 miles

ATLANTIC OCEAN

Constantinople ●

SAHARA DESERT   EGYPT   ARABIA
● Timbuktu   Mecca ●

CIFIC
CEAN

INDIAN OCEAN

N

KEY
→ trade routes

(teenth to nineteenth century)
...ingdom is not the same as the modern country either.
It existed in the area that is now called Nigeria. Its people were
farmers, hunters and traders. During the late nineteenth and early
twentieth centuries, Europeans knew the people of Benin for their
art and sculptures in brass.

Ife (tenth to fourteenth century)
This was an independent state in the
area we now call Nigeria. Its people
were also farmers and hunters and
learned artistic skills from the people
of Benin.

Mali (twelfth to fifteenth century)
The Kingdom of Mali took over much
of the old Kingdom of Ghana. Its
wealth was also based on gold, but it
was much larger, containing as many
as 400 cities. It was a well organised
kingdom with separate provinces,
local governors and tax collectors.
It traded gold with the Arabs and
slaves across the Indian Ocean. It
later became part of the Kingdom of
Songhai.

SOURCE 1

In Timbuktu there are many shops of craftsmen and merchants. There are many doctors, judges and priests, and other learned men that are maintained at the king's cost. Here are bought manuscripts or written books which are sold for more money than any other merchandise. Gao is a town full of very rich merchants and many Negroes come here to buy cloth from Barbary (North Africa) and Europe.

From *A History and Description of Africa* written in about 1526 by a Spanish-born Moor, Hassan ibn Mohammed.

SLAVERY IN AFRICA: A PORTUGUESE TURNING POINT?

As an African before the arrival of the Europeans in the fifteenth
century, you might have been sold as a slave. From the eleventh
century Muslim traders travelled to Africa bringing salt and luxury
goods to trade for gold, leather and slaves. If you were a woman,
you might have been sold into a harem of a rich Arab or an
Ottoman leader. Male slaves were sold to be soldiers in India and in
the Islamic Empire. Other slaves would work as farm labourers,
government officials or porters on caravans (trade journeys) across
the Sahara Desert. You could even become a slave to an African
emperor. Slavery had existed for centuries in Africa. What was it like,
and what were the chances of becoming a slave?

HOW PEOPLE BECAME SLAVES IN EARLY AFRICA

- Prisoners taken in battle between different kingdoms were kept as slaves to work for a set period or until a ransom was paid.
- People were kept as slaves as a punishment for a crime.
- Women and children were sold as slaves during a famine or drought to ensure that they stayed alive.
- People were exchanged for luxury goods from the Islamic Empire or India and taken away as slaves.

One of the most famous African rulers was Mansa Kankan Musa. He ruled the Kingdom of Mali, an area rich with gold mines, until he died in 1337. He used the gold to build up the capital Timbuktu with schools and palaces as well as mosques like the one at Jenne.

Mansa Musa was a strict Muslim. He is perhaps most famous for going on pilgrimage to Mecca, the Muslim holy city, and to Cairo. He took over 8000 men with him on the long journey, including 500 slaves, each of whom carried a gold staff to show off Mansa Musa's wealth. One hundred camels carried sacks of gold which he gave as presents to rulers in Egypt. The whole journey took over two years.

SOURCE 1

This city (Jenne) is great, flourishing and prosperous. Here gather the merchants who bring salt from the mines of Teghaza and those who bring gold from the mines of Bitou. It is because of this fortunate city that the caravans flock to Timbuktu from all points of the horizon.

A description of the city of Jenne by Es-Saídi, a government official who was born in Timbuktu in 1596.

THE TREATMENT OF SLAVES

Different tribes treated slaves in different ways. Sometimes, a fixed time was set as a period for slavery, for example four to seven years. Slaves could often work to buy their freedom and the children of slaves did not automatically become slaves. The treatment of slaves in Africa was influenced by the spread of the Islamic religion and culture in this period. The Islamic Arabs believed that slaves should be well treated, properly fed and looked after when they were unwell. They believed that it was acceptable to release slaves.

SOURCE 2

They do no more work than any other person, even their master. Their food, lodgings and clothing are almost the same, although they are not allowed to eat with free men.

A member of the Benin people describing their slaves.

Activity Time

❶ Why do you think that some prisoners of war were kept as slaves in a kingdom rather than killed or sent back home?

❷ Can you think of any advantage of having foreign slaves as soldiers in your army rather than local men?

❸ Think of several different reasons why Mansa Musa took slaves with him on his famous pilgrimage.

❹ Design an information sheet to collect evidence about slavery. Include a column for information about slavery after 1440, which you will fill in later. The example below is in the form of a chart. There are four questions to answer. Add another question of your own.

SLAVERY IN AFRICA	Before 1440	After 1440
Who were slaves sold to?		
Where would they work?		
How long were they slaves for?		
How were they treated?		

THE PORTUGUESE ARRIVE

During the fourteenth and fifteenth centuries sailors and adventurers from European countries began to explore the newly discovered countries and they started to see how they could use the land and resources. It was the Portuguese who first 'discovered' the West African coast in 1444, but it was another 40 years before the slave trade with Africa was developed. The winds that drove their ships did not let them reach the West African coast and if the winds dropped then the waters were often too shallow for them to sail up to the shore. But the Portuguese sailors managed to find a clever way of tacking (zig-zagging) against the winds, and used smaller boats to reach the shore. They began to stop more on the coast of West Africa. They traded a little with the Kingdom of Benin, but at first only really used Africa as a stop-over on the way to India and the Orient.

THE 'DISCOVERY' OF THE AMERICAS

In the 1490s Portugal and Spain both began to claim land in the newly discovered Americas. In order to increase, defend and farm the new colonies, they needed to settle people on the land. The Portuguese and Spanish, and also the French, competed with each other to discover and claim new territory in South, Central and North America, as well as in the Caribbean Islands. European soldiers killed many Native Americans who stood in their way and many others were taken as slaves. Settlers began to mine these new lands for silver and gold, and establish sugar and tobacco plantations. The demand for workers increased rapidly. During the sixteenth century the Spanish and Portuguese began to capture Africans and ship them over to the Americas. By 1570 there were about 20,000 slaves in Mexico alone, mainly working in the silver mines. The Europeans also employed what were called indentured servants, some of whom came from Britain and Europe, but many also came from Africa. Indentured servants had their journey to the new colonies paid for and in return they agreed to work for a certain number of years. After working for this period they would be free. Many of the first black Americans were therefore not officially slaves at all. They developed their own trades and in some areas they could vote. However, the treatment of these servants by the Europeans soon changed, and over the years the number of indentured servants declined.

As people began to see how much profit could be made in the American colonies, other European countries were quick to claim land in the Americas. They also needed a workforce and began to trade in slaves. As sugar, cotton and tobacco became more popular in Europe the demands for slaves to work on the plantations became even greater. In 1619 the first black slave arrived in a British colony.

What does it mean?

Colony
An island or land which was not independent, but was ruled by another country.

A TRADE IN LIVES

The number of slaves traded by the early Europeans on the coast of West Africa was not high. Slaves were seen by Europeans more as a status symbol for their owners than a necessary part of their owners' workforce. But as the demands for workers on the plantations in the Caribbean Islands and the Americas grew, so did the whole slave trade. Europeans travelling to West Africa stopped trading gold and ivory and just traded in slaves. They set up forts on the coast of West Africa where slaves were collected ready for the journey across the Atlantic. The Europeans were more powerful than the Africans. They had firearms and could use force to capture as many people as their ships would hold.

This painting shows a 'barracoon' in Sierra Leone. This was where many slaves were held before being shipped across the Atlantic. They were often chained up by the neck or legs.

While indentured servants were still used, the new type of slaves were not indentured servants. So many men and women were needed in the Americas that slaves would be kept for life. Children of slaves became slaves automatically. There was no escape, except for those who could make enough money to buy their freedom. The new type of slavery also meant that for the Africans who were taken overseas to the Americas, there was no chance of return.

Question Time

❶ Find out which areas the European traders called:

  a the Windward Coast
  b the Ivory Coast
  c the Gold Coast
  d the Slave Coast.

❷ What have you read so far that shows that Europeans had different ideas about slavery?

CHANGING ATTITUDES

As the numbers of slaves traded for a profit rose, the white traders' attitude towards the slaves changed. Business men were making so much money on the sugar and cotton plantations that they could afford to lose some slaves on the journey, there were plenty more available. Europeans began to think of the slaves as a cargo and as savage people who needed saving from their un-Christian lives in Africa. Once in the colonies, any rights the slaves had previously had were soon taken away. This change of attitude meant that slavery would grow and grow and the treatment of slaves would get worse.

WHAT DID THE AFRICAN RULERS DO?

Some Africans fought the Europeans, but they didn't stand much chance of winning unless they had guns. However, they could only get rifles and gunpowder by trading slaves for them. Some African kings thought that the only way to stop their people being caught as slaves was to become the slave catchers themselves and trade slaves from other kingdoms to the Europeans. The Europeans did deals with local rulers who organised the collection of slaves in their area. This often meant carrying out raids inland.

SOURCE 4

To take a black man from the wilds of Africa was a humanitarian and Christian task for it changed a savage and a heretic into a person capable of gaining from the benefits of Western civilisation.

An extract from a 1950s history book showing attitudes towards slavery.

SOURCE 5

This painting from 1833 shows a ship's captain bargaining for slaves with African slave dealers in Sierra Leone. Slaves are being branded and herded into boats to ferry them to the ships.

Once the Africans got firearms a whole new series of internal wars were started. Kingdoms fought with each other over the capture of slaves. One example is the King of Dahomay who set up his own army of men and women to fight against the Europeans, but eventually turned slave catcher to survive.

Historians disagree in their estimates of the number of Africans transported across the Atlantic into slavery by the Europeans. One estimate is that between around 1490 and 1890 15 million Africans were delivered to the Americas. An equal number died on the African coast before they set off and around 40 million slaves died on the voyage.

THE EFFECTS OF THE SLAVE TRADE ON AFRICA

The slave trade affected Africa for many years, even after the Europeans made trading in slaves illegal in the nineteenth century. Slave traders continued to sell people to countries like Arabia up to the twentieth century. Some Africans became focused on the slave trade, and neglected their other traditional trades. The ancient overland trade routes were abandoned in favour of coastal trading stations built to house the captive slaves until ships arrived. Along the old routes (see the map on page 7) craftsmen and merchants lost their livelihoods as European goods were exchanged for slaves.

Throughout the African societies, everyone was affected. The Europeans introduced firearms and alcohol and indirectly encouraged tribes in the different kingdoms to fight against each other for slaves. Villagers fled from the raiding parties looking for captives to remote areas where the land was poor. Fear and famine spread with the continual warfare. Kings who had protected their people now became kidnappers, while the Europeans encouraged the wars between kingdoms as prisoners were sold as slaves.

The Europeans brought new food crops to Africa, such as corn, which would grow in some areas, but any positive effects were far outweighed by the negative effects of the slave trade upon African people and society.

SOURCE 6

The Africans became the architects of their own ruin. The most rewarding occupation became war to get slaves. It was only then that permanent insecurity, endless raids and the misery and famine that come with them, became established features of African society.

Written by an historian of Africa in 1982.

Question Time

❶ Look at the 'barracoon' shown in Source 3. How might a man who ran the compound have interested a new trader in what he had there? What might he have said? What might he have shown the trader?

❷ Why do you think that historians have argued over the numbers of slaves involved?

SOLD INTO SLAVERY: WHAT WAS THE REALITY OF THE ATLANTIC SLAVE TRADE?

As we have seen on page 11, the first black Americans were not slaves, but worked as indentured labourers, for a fixed period of time, in exchange for payment for their passage, accommodation and food. Some of them gained their freedom and became settlers in different parts of the Americas.

THE TRIANGULAR TRADE

As the number of European settlers in South, Central and southern North America increased, so the need for labourers to work in the mines and on the plantations grew. The settlers and merchants could see a way of getting cheap labour from Africa and making money through selling back in Europe the much desired sugar, coffee and tobacco from the plantations. The large workforce needed could be 'captured' in Africa and taken across the Atlantic to the Americas. The great demand meant that the trade in enslaved Africans was very profitable, and by the seventeenth century many European nations joined in what became known as the Triangular Trade.

This map shows the 'Triangular Trade' route taken by slave ships.

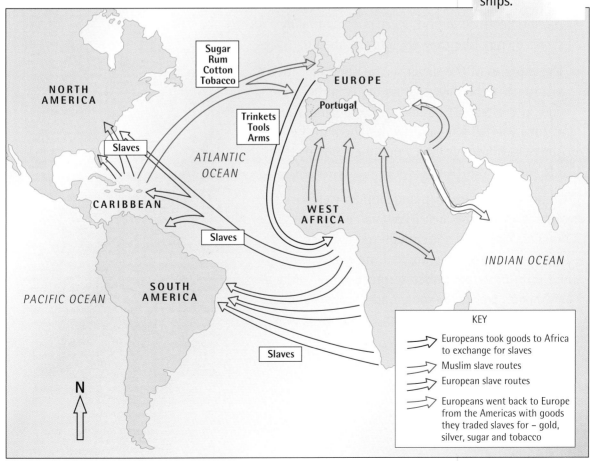

KEY

⇒ Europeans took goods to Africa to exchange for slaves

⇒ Muslim slave routes

⇒ European slave routes

⇒ Europeans went back to Europe from the Americas with goods they traded slaves for – gold, silver, sugar and tobacco

The Triangular Trade was between Europe, Africa and the Americas.

- Ships with European goods sailed to Africa. There the goods were exchanged for human beings, the ships packed full with as many enslaved Africans as possible.
- The slaves were taken to the Americas and sold there to the settlers.
- With the profits the merchants bought cargoes of sugar, rum, tobacco or cotton and set sail to sell their cargo in Europe for more profit.
- The crossing from Africa to the Americas was known as the Middle Passage.

THE MIDDLE PASSAGE

Ships from Europe arrived on the west coast of Africa with cargoes of guns, alcohol and tools to use to bargain for slaves. These men, women and children would have been captured, possibly by their own rulers, marched to the coast and kept in prisons in the forts built along the coast by the Europeans or their African agents. At these trading posts, conditions were poor and many slaves died before they were taken aboard.

The captains of the slavers (ships specially fitted out to carry the slaves across the Atlantic) were only interested in fit and healthy-looking slaves, as they wanted a good price for them in the Americas. Those rejected would be killed or taken into slavery in Africa.

On board the ships men and women were separated, and the men were chained by the ankle in pairs. There was not enough room in the hold for the slaves to stand up, and the overcrowding and filth meant that disease spread quickly. Many died, some jumped overboard and some mutinied and tried to take over the ship. This journey took between five and eight weeks.

SOURCE 1

This picture shows the space each slave had on a slave ship. It was published by Thomas Clarkson, an anti-slavery campaigner.

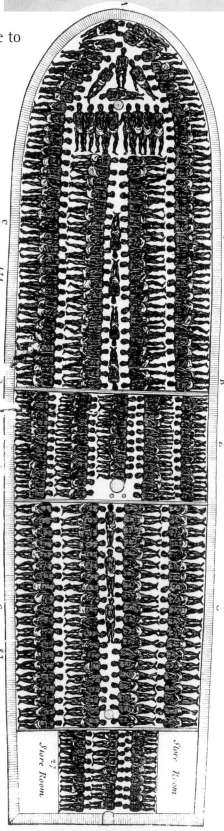

Question Time

❶ Copy the map on page 15 which shows the Triangular Trade. Label on it the types of goods that were traded as well as the main countries and routes involved.

❷ Why do you think the slave ships were crammed so full?

❸ Source 1 was used by abolitionist campaigners like Wilberforce and Clarkson in Britain. It has also become almost a symbol for the terrible conditions of the Middle Passage.
a Why do you think that it is such a powerful symbol?
b Do you think it is likely to be accurate?

Different jobs in different areas
This map shows the major slave centres and how the slaves were used.

NORTH AMERICA

Domestic servants

Farming
Plantations
Domestic servants

ATLANTIC OCEAN

CARIBBEAN

Plantations
Craftsmen
Servants

CENTRAL AND SOUTH AMERICA

PACIFIC OCEAN

Mining
Farming

ARRIVAL IN THE AMERICAS

If slaves actually survived the journey across the Middle Passage they would be sold again to plantation owners and other Europeans in the Americas. Just before arrival the sailors would clean the slaves up, rubbing oil on their skins to make them look healthy, and try to conceal signs of sickness so they could sell them for as much money as possible. When the ship docked, the slaves were sold by private treaty with planters or middle men who would sell them on. Some were sold in a 'scramble' (see Source 2) or at public auction. Husbands and wives, parents and children were separated forever as potential buyers inspected them as if they were animals at market. Once bought they were branded (had a number or a mark burned onto their skin so people could see who owned them), and then most of them would be taken to farms or plantations to work in the fields.

SOURCE 2

On a signal given (the beat of a drum) the buyers rushed into the yard where the slaves were confined like sheep in a pen, and chose the ones they liked best. The noise and the clamour, and the eagerness shown on the faces of the buyers, increased the fear of the terrified Africans. In this way, relations and friends were separated, most of them never to see each other again.

Olaudah Equiano describes a 'scramble' in his account of his life, written in 1789. The price of the slaves would have been agreed before hand and the buyers then grabbed as many slaves as they could. Olaudah had been transported from Africa and was sold in a 'scramble' in Barbados.

Question Time

❶ What are the main similarities between the types of jobs that slaves were expected to do all over the Americas?

❷ By the eighteenth century many European countries had developed industrial machinery. Why do you think that the Europeans preferred to use slaves rather than machines on the plantations?

HOW WERE SLAVES TREATED?

Slaves came to be the basis for all the wealth in the colonies. They produced the goods that their owners sold for a huge profit. But this did not mean that they were well-treated.

Not so much profit was to be made from using the slaves taken to the Northern States of America as they tended to work as servants more than as labourers. This meant that they were often better cared for, as they would be expensive to replace. Many slaves were also taken to work on the plantations in the Southern States where conditions were harsh (see Source 3).

In the Caribbean, the plantation owners were so wealthy and slaves were so readily available that the slaves could be easily replaced. Slave owners would not think twice about literally working a slave to death or using torture or death as a punishment. They thought of slaves as their possessions rather than as human beings. Slaves outnumbered Europeans by at least five times, and the owners were worried about keeping control. They ruled the islands with fear, punishing slaves so harshly that they thought no one would dare to think of rebelling.

SOURCE 3

The whip used by the overseers on the cotton plantations is different from all other whips that I have ever seen. The staff is about twenty inches (50cm) in length, with a large and heavy head, which is often loaded with lead and wrapped in cat gut.

Charles Ball was a slave who escaped and then wrote his autobiography published in 1836.

The inequalities of slavery

Slaves could not:

- marry
- earn a wage
- own property
- keep their own name
- choose where to work or live
- give evidence in a court case against a white man
- worship in their own way
- meet together in groups
- learn to read and write
- protect their children or friends from cruelty or punishment
- refuse to do anything for their owner (including sexual acts).

Some Europeans tried to turn slaves against each other by putting some slaves in charge of others. Slaves with certain jobs or backgrounds became more important than those who just worked in plantation fields. The diagram below shows the different levels in slave societies, with the most important level first.

Different jobs	Different backgrounds
Slave drivers (bosses)	Mulattoes (mixed race, usually a slave mother and a white father)
Skilled slaves, e.g. carpenters	
Domestic servants	Slaves born in the Americas
Field workers	Slaves born in Africa

The majority of slaves suffered at the hands of their masters and overseers, who, as long as there was a constant supply of replacement slaves arriving from Africa, only wanted to get as much work out of them as possible. A small minority of domestic slave owners ensured that their slaves were well looked after, educated and even allowed to earn money to buy their freedom. Some white men, who had children by slave women, took pains to look after their mixed-race children (mulattoes). But these cases were very few. As the price of slaves went up over the years, owners wanted to extend the slaves' working lives rather than work them to death.

SOURCE 4

This picture shows a slave being whipped by another slave.

SOURCE 5

Much money is made by a steady negro by the sale of provisions, tobacco and corn and by the rearing of pigs and poultry.

Some slaves were given the chance to earn money. In some cases their wages would be stolen by their owner. This extract is from a book on Jamaica written by a military officer in 1835.

SOURCE 6

None of the evils of slavery are more horrible than the treatment of females. They were obliged to give in to prostitution, to equal labour with males and to become the breeders of slaves at the will and pleasure of their masters.

From the journal of Major J B Colthurst published in 1847. Colthurst was a special judge sent to the Caribbean from Britain.

SOURCE 7

The slave may be 'used up' in seven years – used as a breeder, as a prostitute, to serve drink and as a subject of surgical experiments – but the law says that he may not be used as a clerk.

William Goodell writing in 1854 about American slavery.

Question Time

1 a What evidence is there in Source 4 that there was a hierarchy of slaves (some slaves were treated better than others)?
b Does this painting make life on the plantations look realistic or romantic? Explain your answer carefully.

2 Does Source 5 suggest that some slaves had opportunities to improve their lives?

3 Find out more about how slaves were treated. Remember to use key words, such as *plantations*, in your searches.

4 Would it be fair to say that
a Slaves suffered as much mentally as they did physically?
b Female slaves suffered more than males?
Explain your answers using all your knowledge and the sources.

5 Look back to the chart you made on page 10. Fill in the second column about slavery after 1440 with as much detail as you can.

FREEDOM: HOW WAS IT ACHIEVED?

Slavery was an unfair system but some slaves managed to fight against it and gain their freedom. Some slaves resisted quietly by working slowly or by sabotaging (deliberately damaging) crops and property. This often resulted in whipping. Other slaves took greater risks. In Jamaica, for example, there were 250 rebellions. Before the official abolition of slavery in North America in 1865 some individuals managed to beat the system and lead the way for others. Here is the story of some of those people.

WHAT WAS THE UNDERGROUND RAILROAD?

The Underground Railroad was the system which helped slaves to escape to the Northern States of America from the Southern States. It was set up in about 1787 when a Quaker called Isaac Hopper, who was against slavery, began to organise a system of safe houses and contacts to look after escaped slaves.

As many as 3000 escaped slaves, free black people and white people worked on the railroad, including helpers known as 'conductors', like Harriet Tubman, who risked their own lives to hide and lead the slaves to their freedom. As many as 50,000 slaves escaped this way.

HARRIET TUBMAN (1820–1913) – AN ESCAPED SLAVE WHO RISKED HER LIFE FOR OTHERS

Harriet Tubman escaped at the age of 29 from slavery in Maryland where she was born, when her owner died. She became a conductor for the Underground Railroad and was later a nurse and a spy for the Northern side in the American Civil War. She made 19 different trips from the South, going north to the safety of Canada. She saved 300 slaves. Slaves were hidden in covered carts with false bottoms and driven between the Underground Railroad 'stations' where they were fed and hidden during daylight hours before moving on. They often had to hide in forests, cross rivers and climb mountains. Slave owners offered a reward of $40,000 for Harriet's capture, but she was never caught. After the war Harriet ran a home for elderly African Americans until she died in 1913.

TOUSSAINT L'OUVERTURE IN HAITI – FROM REBEL SLAVE TO GOVERNOR

Toussaint L'Ouverture was born a slave in 1743, the grandson of an African king. His grandfather had been captured as a slave and taken to the island of Saint Domingue (a French colony which became known as Haiti after it had gained its independence). Unusually, Toussaint was taught to read and write by his 'godfather' and he studied Latin, geometry and French. He was then put in charge of all the other slaves on the plantation. He was an obvious choice for leader of a slave revolt and finally took action as the French Revolution supported freedom for slaves. He gathered together 3000 slaves and organised a rebellion against French rulers in 1791. In 1792 the rebels then beat the British who had invaded to try and take control. In 1798 Toussaint became Governor of Saint Domingue.

SOURCE 1

The journey was so hard over the rugged mountain passes, that often the men who followed her would give out, and foot-sore, and bleeding, they would drop on the ground, groaning that they could not take another step. They would lie there and die, or if strength came back, they would return on their steps and seek their old homes again. Then the revolver carried by this bold and daring pioneer, would come out, while pointing it at their heads she would say 'Dead niggers tell no tales; you go on or die!' And by this heroic treatment she compelled them to drag their weary limbs along their northward journey.

From *Harriet Tubman - The Moses of her People,* by Sarah Bradford, 1886.

What does it mean?

Godfather
An older slave who kept an eye on younger slaves whose families had been broken up by the slave owners.

Napoleon took back Saint Domingue for the French between 1801–3, but in 1804 Haiti became independent. Toussaint had led the only society to overthrow the slave owners successfully. He died in a French prison in 1804.

REBELLION ON BOARD THE *AMISTAD*

Although the slave trade had been banned by North America, Spain and Britain by 1820, thousands of Africans were smuggled into the Southern States illegally. In 1839 the slaves on one illegal slave ship, the *Amistad*, revolted. They killed the captain and the cook, set the rest of the crew adrift in a small boat and tried to force the Spanish slave traders to sail to Africa. They were led by Cinque, son of a West African chief. The Spaniards followed Cinque's orders to sail east by day but by night sailed towards the North American coast. The boat was spotted by the American navy as it neared the coast. The navy rescued the Spanish from the Africans and arrested Cinque and all the Africans for murdering the captain. The case went to court. There were newspaper articles and arguments about it all over America.

The Africans said that they were not slaves but free Africans who were being held prisoner by the Spanish traders. The Queen of Spain demanded that the ship and all its cargo including the slaves should be returned to Spain. The jury agreed with the Africans. They should be freed and returned home to Africa. An appeal heard by the Supreme Court agreed with the decision. The slaves had won, and returned to Africa in 1841.

Question Time

❶ What do these three stories of rebellion have in common?

❷ Who do you think contributed most to the fight for freedom for slaves – Harriet Tubman, Toussaint L'Ouverture or Cinque?

❹ Carry out research about other individuals who managed to gain their freedom. One good example is Olaudah Equiano. Another is Henry Brown. Find out about his famous box. Include subheadings such as 'Background', 'Struggle' and 'Why they were important?' in your research notes.

THE SLAVERY DEBATE – WHAT DID PEOPLE THINK?

A map of North America showing the different attitudes towards slavery in the Northern States and the Southern States.

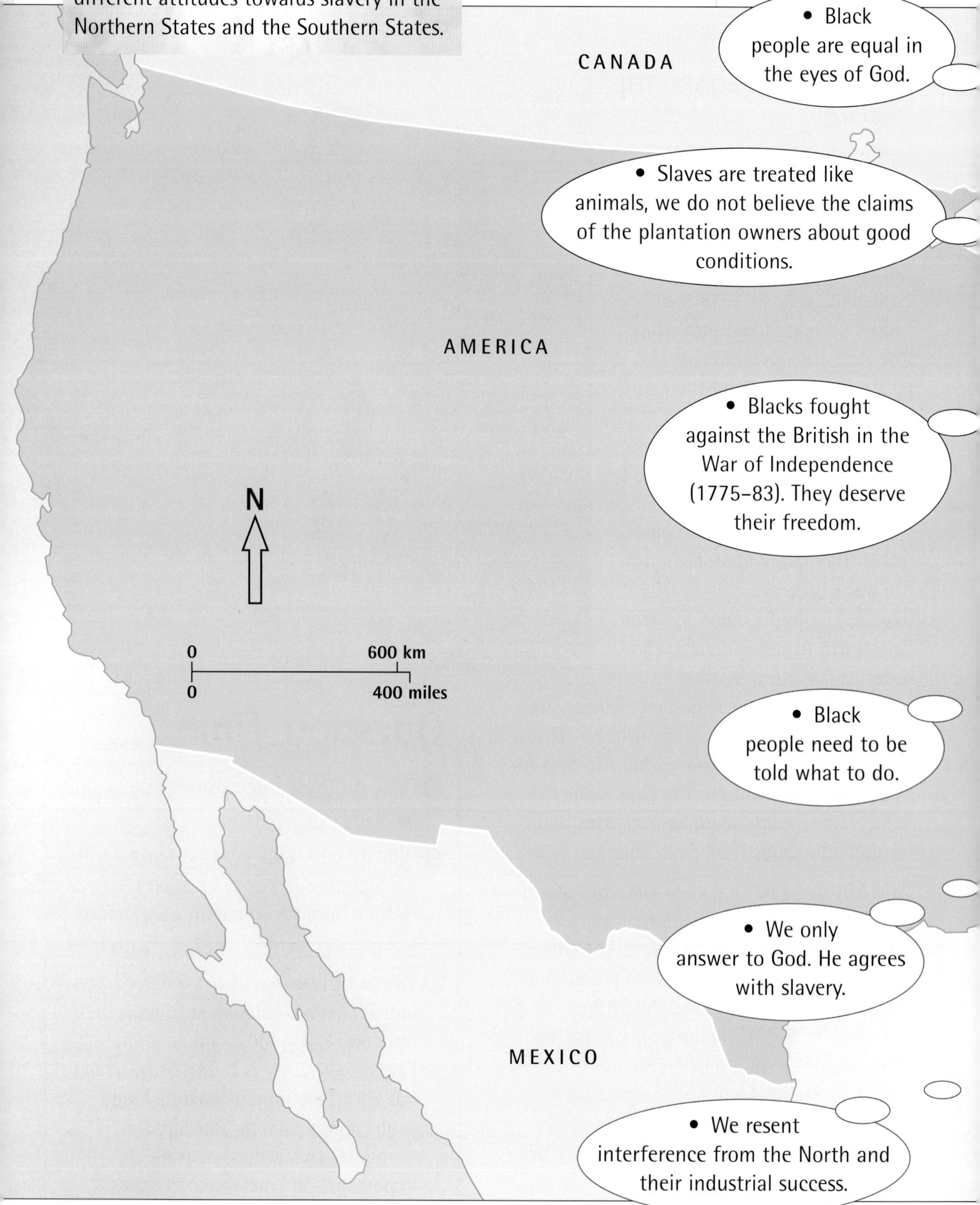

CANADA

AMERICA

N

| 0 | 600 km |
| 0 | 400 miles |

MEXICO

- Black people are equal in the eyes of God.

- Slaves are treated like animals, we do not believe the claims of the plantation owners about good conditions.

- Blacks fought against the British in the War of Independence (1775–83). They deserve their freedom.

- Black people need to be told what to do.

- We only answer to God. He agrees with slavery.

- We resent interference from the North and their industrial success.

- America is a country for the free so slaves should be free.

- Perhaps black people should be sent back to Africa to live separately.

Northern States – richer and more industrial

- The economy would collapse without slavery – we would all suffer.

- Slaves are happy to work, they have all they need and do not have to look after themselves.

Southern States – poor and dependent on the cotton plantations

- We want the right to keep slavery even if the rest of America bans it.

- Where would the blacks go if it weren't for the slave plantations?

- We can make much more profit now we have new machines, called cotton gins – we need the slaves to work them.

ATTITUDES TOWARDS SLAVERY

The Declaration of Independence of 1776 had promised to protect the civil liberties of the people of America. Yet by 1861 the number of slaves had increased from about 700,000 to four million. Four out of the first five Presidents of America were slave owners themselves. Slavery was one of the causes of the American Civil War (1861–5). Most of the North agreed with the abolitionists who wanted to abolish (ban) slavery. The South was anti-abolitionist and wanted to keep slavery.

SOURCE 3

What, to the American slave is your fourth of July? I answer; a day that shows to him, more than other days in the year, the gross injustice and cruelty to which he is a constant victim. To him your celebration is a sham ... your shouts of liberty and equality, hollow mockery.

Frederick Douglass (a former slave and anti-slavery campaigner) in a speech at a Fourth of July (Independence Day) celebration in 1852.

SOURCE 4

When Harriet Beecher Stowe published a novel giving an unpleasant picture of Southern slavery, Southerners sprang fiercely to its defence. Fourteen novels disagreeing with Stowe were written in three years, and many other writers fell over themselves to point to the hypocrisy of the North, describing the 'hardships of factory labour' and the Northerners' eagerness to keep escaped slaves to work for them. George Fitzhugh created a stir when he compared the oppressed conditions of the British working class with the sheltered life of plantation slaves.

Adapted from Suzanne Everett's *T e History of Slavery*, published in 1996.

SOURCE 5

I am not, nor have ever been in favour of bringing about the social and political equality of the white and black races ... but in the right to eat the bread without leave of anyone else, which his own hand earns, a black person is equal and the equal of every living man.

Abraham Lincoln, President of USA from 1861–5, said this in a speech in 1858.

Question Time

1 Look at the map on pages 24-25. How many of the ideas of the Southern States are based on economic or practical reasons? How many of the ideas of the North are based on moral reasons (right and wrong)?

2 Use Source 5 to explain whether the North wanted total equality for black and white people.

3 It is harder to find evidence of anti-abolitionist attitudes than it is to find speeches and articles criticising slavery. Why might this be?

4 Prepare a report on a meeting of community leaders to decide whether to abolish slavery in your state. Your state is in the South and your meeting should be based on a vote after all the arguments have been heard. Different groups are represented at the meeting: plantation owners, freed slaves wanting to stay in the South, Church groups, a powerful landowner who is a politician in Washington, a black abolitionist group, a white anti-slavery group and local workers. Your report on the meeting should be for the local or national newspapers.

AMERICA DIVIDED

From 1777-1858 19 Northern States banned slavery and became 'free' States. Southern States were desperate to keep slavery and did not want the Federal (central) Government to force them to change. As more people campaigned to abolish slavery, the tension between North and South increased.

The timeline shows that the courts could not really decide about the slavery laws. One court case was used by the South as a victory for slavery.

THE DRED SCOTT CASE

Although many black people turned to violence to fight injustice, increasing numbers of black people went to court to try to win freedom legally. One of the most famous court cases was held in 1857. It shows, also, how America became divided over slavery.

Dred Scott was a slave who had moved around with his family as his master moved homes. Scott saved enough money to buy his freedom, but his master refused to accept it. So Scott used the money to sue his master, saying that living in states that did not accept slavery made him and his family free. A local court agreed with him, but the state court overruled the decision. Scott appealed to the Supreme Court, which turned him down. The highest court in America said that the Declaration of Independence was never meant to include black people as equal citizens. It also said that it was illegal to take away slaves from their owners. This meant that in practice slavery could not be banned, slave owners could take their slaves with them into free states and black people had no rights.

Question Time

❶ Why do you think that the Dred Scott case increased the split between abolitionists and pro-slavery campaigners? In your answer mention how both sides would react to the outcome of the case.

❷ Choose two of the events from the timeline and explain how they increased the division between North and South.

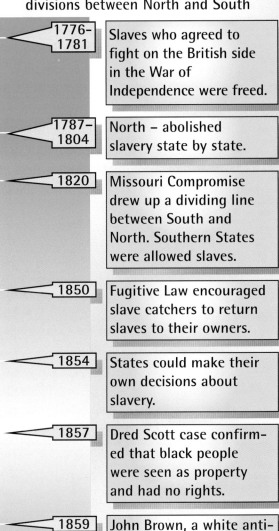

Timeline of events which increased divisions between North and South

1776–1781 Slaves who agreed to fight on the British side in the War of Independence were freed.

1787–1804 North – abolished slavery state by state.

1820 Missouri Compromise drew up a dividing line between South and North. Southern States were allowed slaves.

1850 Fugitive Law encouraged slave catchers to return slaves to their owners.

1854 States could make their own decisions about slavery.

1857 Dred Scott case confirmed that black people were seen as property and had no rights.

1859 John Brown, a white anti-slavery campaigner, tried to start an armed slave rebellion. He was caught and executed, but the South was worried that it might be invaded.

1860 The new President of the USA, Abraham Lincoln, was a Republican. The South assumed that all Republicans were abolitionists, see page 28.

November The 11 Southern States broke away from the North to create the Confederate States of America.

WAS THE CIVIL WAR FOUGHT TO FREE THE SLAVES?

In April 1861 the North invaded the South to force the 11 Confederate states back into the Union. What followed was a bloody war where more soldiers died than in all the wars America has been involved in during the twentieth century. It ended in March 1865 and five days later President Lincoln was assassinated. The war represented a power struggle between Southern plantation owners and Northern industrialists, but how much was slavery the root cause?

Southern States' rights

- The Southern States feared losing power when Lincoln and the new Republican Party came into office in 1860. They felt that their way of life was threatened by everything the Republicans stood for.
- They wanted to pass their own laws, keep taxes low and keep their right to have slaves.
- The South wanted any new state admitted to the Union to have a choice over slavery and other issues.
- Fearing that Lincoln would remove their rights, 11 States broke away from the United States of America and formed the Confederate States of America in November 1860.

Saving the Union

President Lincoln's main aim was to keep America together. Many Republicans were anti-slavery but Lincoln considered protecting slavery if this compromise would save the Union of North and South. As the war progressed, Lincoln allowed slavery to become a more central issue. He needed men to fight for the Union and so began to push for emancipation (freedom) of the slaves.

SOURCE 6

In aiding the Federal Government, we are aiding our own liberty. We do not say that the North is fighting on behalf of the black man's rights, as such – if this was the single issue, we even doubt if they would fight at all. But ... in struggling for their own nationality they are forced to defend our rights.

Written by the editors of the Anglo-African newspaper published in New York.

Economic divisions

- The economies of North and South developed in different ways. The industrial North wanted the taxes on goods brought in from foreign countries (import taxes) to be increased to protect their own manufactured products from foreign competition.
- The agricultural South depended upon trade and so strongly opposed import taxes.
- Southerners resented their dependence on Northern industries and business, and thought that Northerners had received better treatment from the government.
- Southerners feared that the Republicans would make the economic divisions greater still.

Anti-slavery movement

Support for the abolitionists was high in the North. In 1832 the Anti-Slavery Society was set up with white and black people as members. Meanwhile encouragement to end slavery came from other countries, for instance laws passed in 1833 banned slavery throughout the British Empire. Even though it was against the law to hide runaway slaves, many Northern States refused to return esaped slaves to the South. Northern industrialists also supported abolition as they wanted freed Southern slaves for labour in their factories.

SOURCE 7

My main aim in this struggle is to save the Union. If I could save the Union without freeing any slave, I would do it. If I could save it by freeing all slaves, I would do it. If I could do it by freeing some and leaving others alone, I would do that ...

President Lincoln speaking in 1862.

SOURCE 8

The iron gate of our prison stands half open. One gallant rush for the North will fling it wide open, while four millions of our brothers and sisters shall march out into liberty.

Frederick Douglass wrote this in a newspaper article to persuade black people to join the Union army in 1863.

SOURCE 9

Our Confederacy is founded upon the great truth that slavery is (the black persons') natural and normal condition.

Alexander Stephens, a Confederate leader, said this in a speech in 1861.

THE IMPORTANCE OF BLACK SOLDIERS

Slaves started joining the Union army illegally, so their right to fight was made official in 1863 with the Emancipation Proclamation. This declared that slaves in any rebel state were to be freed and that they could join the Union army. Ten per cent of the Union army was made up of black soldiers and 37,000 black Union soldiers were killed in the war. At first black soldiers were paid less for doing more work than the white soldiers. This changed by the end of the war, but black men fought in separate regiments. Some historians say that black men were only allowed greater freedom because they were needed to fight. The South refused to let black men into the army and realised too late that this was a mistake. This ban was lifted in March 1865, but by the end of the month the South was finally beaten.

Question Time

❶ What do Sources 6–9 tell us about people's motives (reasons) for fighting in the American Civil War?

❷ How could war be said to be a factor helping to free the black people in America? Mention the War of Independence and the Civil War in your answer.

❸ Was the Civil War fought to free the slaves? Answer this question in the form of some extended writing. Use the suggestions below if you like, but try to add some of your own. Write each point in a different paragraph.
a Introduction – when was the war and who was on each side?
b The main aims of each side.
c How people on the same side fought for different reasons.
d The most important reasons for the war.
e How important was the issue of slavery?
f The effect of war was freedom for the slaves, whether or not it was the main reason.

FROM EMANCIPATION TO SEGREGATION: HOW FREE WERE BLACK PEOPLE?

By 1870 the fourteenth and fifteenth Amendments to the American Constitution had given black people equal civil rights and the right to vote. Black people were full of hope. They could now legally own land, vote, and marry and raise a family without the fear of being separated. The period after the Civil War is known as 'Reconstruction' and it brought major problems for poor people, white and black. For 80 years after the end of the Civil War, America faced problems of recovery, industrialisation, economic boom and depression. Despite changes to the law, the freedom of black Americans depended on which state they lived in. Many states, particularly in the South, chose to persecute black people and limit their rights. This section will consider several major influences on the lives of black people to see how free they really were.

SHARECROPPING

Sharecropping was the system that the Southern landowners developed to adjust to the changes brought about by emancipation. The plantations were still owned by the same people as before, and black people were needed to work the land for their old slave masters. The freed slaves obviously needed work. Landowners would not be able to pay their workers until their crops had been harvested, so a system was devised which allowed black people to work the land and keep a third of the crops as their wages. This meant that they relied on good harvests and would often get heavily into debt waiting to be paid. Freedom did not seem that different from life before the Civil War for many workers in the South.

SOURCE 1

Ol miss and massa (master) was not mean to us at all until after the surrender and we were freed ... They got mad at us because we were free and they let us go without a crumb of anything ... We wandered around for a long time. Then they hired us to work and man, we've had a hard time then and I've been having a hard time ever since.

Frank Filkes, an ex-slave, wrote this account in the 1930s.

THE FREEDMEN'S BUREAU

The Freedmen's Bureau was an organisation set up by the government in 1865 to deal with the many problems freed slaves might face. It was responsible for education and health care and some branches set up orphanages and helped find work for ex-slaves. The schools increased literacy amongst black people to 20 per cent by 1874, but states often used the widespread illiteracy as an excuse to limit black people's rights. If you couldn't read or write then you couldn't vote (although the literacy of white people was not checked). The effectiveness of the Freedmen's Bureau was limited, especially after the army left the South, and the States governed themselves.

JIM CROW LAWS BRING SEGREGATION

Many Southern States felt that emancipation had been forced on them. Between 1890–1910 they limited the rights of black people by passing their own laws which meant that black people were forced to live separately from white people. This was called segregation. The laws were called Jim Crow Laws after a line in a plantation song. Black people were forced to use separate hotels, transport, churches, theatres, schools and hospitals and were treated as second class citizens. In states where the laws were not changed, violence and intimidation were used to scare black people away from voting and leading free lives.

MARCUS GARVEY'S PLANS FOR LIBERIA

What impression do you get of the man in Source 2? He is Marcus Garvey. Garvey was born in Jamaica and set up the Universal Negro Improvement Association in 1914. He moved to America in 1916 and set up branches there. This organisation wanted to bring together black people from all over the world and celebrate their heritage. He promoted 'black nationalism' to encourage black people to be proud of their race and African roots. He wanted black people from America to move to an African country called Liberia. 'Africa for the Africans' was one of his messages. This was not a new idea as 100 years earlier the American Colonisation Society had come up with the same idea in order to get rid of free black people. Garvey actually set up a shipping line to take people to Liberia, but the ships were not seaworthy and in 1923 he was sentenced for fraud. He declared himself the leader of the black people and campaigned for their rights. Many of his ideas and his slogans, such as 'Black is Beautiful', were used by civil rights leaders in later years.

SOURCE 2

Marcus Garvey wore a magnificent uniform and represented hope for many black people.

THE KU KLUX KLAN

The Ku Klux Klan (KKK) was set up in 1865 as a secret society of white extremists who aimed to persecute other ethnic groups and make sure white people kept control of society. They used brutal violence and lynching against black people in the Southern States. 'Lynching' means killing someone, sometimes by hanging, who had not committed, or had not been proven to have committed, a crime.

Although banned in 1872, the organisation continued and became popular again several times in the twentieth century, and in 1920 its membership reached over five million. The group is famous for dressing in white robes and hoods so that members were not recognised (see Source 3). It was difficult to stop their violent campaigns as judges and policemen were often in the Klan themselves.

In order to escape the hardship and extreme discrimination of the South, many black people migrated to the industrial cities of the Northern States. Between 1916 and 1920, for example, half a million black people moved to the North. Although jobs could be found in the cities, housing and education was inadequate and urban slum areas, called ghettos, rapidly developed. Although segregation was not legal in many Northern States, it was an accepted part of life.

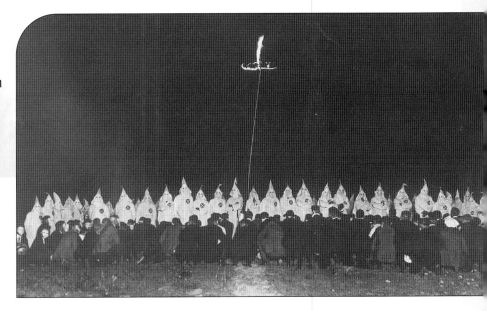

SOURCE 3

This photograph from 1940 shows Ku Klux Klan members at a cross-burning ceremony.

THE TWO WORLD WARS

America entered the First World War (1914-18) in 1917 and black soldiers fought as part of America's troops, although they were in units segregated from the white soldiers. When America entered the Second World War (1939-45) in 1941 black men were trained to be pilots, although they still could not join the Marines or be an officer in the Navy. Fewer than one per cent of black soldiers became officers. However, both wars represented a turning point for black people. For men and women not fighting, the world wars gave new job opportunities and many more black people migrated to the industrial North to work in factories.

Question Time

❶ Why did Garvey's idea of 'Africa for the Africans' seem the best solution for many black people living in America in this period?

❷ Why do you think that the Ku Klux Klan became so popular in the Southern States?

When white soldiers returned from war and wanted their jobs back, black people often were sacked or were the subject of violent attacks. In 1946 there were outbreaks of violence against black soldiers which reminded many people of the problems which still existed.

CIVIL RIGHTS AND SELF-HELP ORGANISATIONS

Several groups had been founded, all of which brought the situation of black people to the attention of the government and society. The Niagara Movement (1905) later became part of the National Association for the Advancement of Coloured People (NAACP), founded in 1910. The National Urban League worked to help black people who had migrated to the cities. Churches also formed powerful groups that campaigned against segregation. By 1945 these groups began to put pressure on federal and state governments and the courts to take positive action for black people.

However, black people sometimes disagreed amongst themselves about the best approach to use to improve their civil rights. In the early twentieth century, Booker T Washington and W.E.B. Du Bois both became influential black leaders. Washington set up an institute to provide training in practical skills such as carpentry and farming. He believed that by peacefully improving the economic position of black people they would gain power and achieve equality. Du Bois was one of the founders of the NAACP to campaign for civil rights. He disagreed with Washington by arguing that they needed to campaign for civil rights first, and only when these were won could they hope to become socially and economically equal with white people.

SOURCE 4

The negro race in America ... needs help and is given hindrance, needs protection and is given mob violence, needs justice and is given charity, needs leadership and is given cowardice and apology, needs bread and is given a stone. The nation will never stand justified before God until these things are changed.

From a statement made by the Niagara Movement in 1905.

What does it mean?

Civil Rights
The rights of citizens to political and social equality and freedom.

Question Time

1. Read Source 4. Explain in your own words the point that the NAACP is making.

2. Carry out research to find out more about the lives of black people at the turn of the century. For example you could find out about the New York area of Harlem where black artists, writers and jazz musicians like Ella Fitzgerald and Duke Ellington became famous. You could find out more about individuals such as W.E.B. Du Bois or Booker T Washington to see how they disagreed over the way forward for black people. Tell the rest of your group about what you find.

Activity Time

1 Using the information you have read, design a board game for a younger student based on the theme of snakes and ladders. You will need to design your board to show the situation for black people after the Civil War. You could have different sections based on different events or changes. You need to decide which of the events from the previous pages represent progress (a ladder) for black people and which represent regression, or a backward move (snake). Make snakes and ladders cards which show each event and explain how each would be a step forward or backward. Add some more events if you can. Include some of the most important events on the design of the board itself.

2 Which events were difficult to decide on? Why do you think that is?

3 Do you think that there were more positive or negative changes for black people between 1865 and 1945?

4 Copy and fill in this summary box:

From emancipation to segregation
Black people were emancipated in.......
How black people's lives changed after emancipation:

1

2

3

Segregation means ...

Life was still difficult for many black people because ...

FROM SEGREGATION TO CIVIL RIGHTS: DID THE CIVIL RIGHTS MOVEMENT BRING FREEDOM FOR BLACK PEOPLE?

BLACK PEOPLE IN AMERICA IN THE 1960s

We have seen that freedom and equality for black people was still limited up to the end of the Second World War. Black people often lived in the poorest parts of cities and had the worst paid jobs. Remember that black and white people were supposed to have equal civil rights, which means that they should have been treated equally in every way. Did the 1950s and 60s bring improved civil rights?

There were violent reactions to the black civil rights movement and, despite the increasing number of campaigns in the 1950s, segregation in schools, transport and other facilities also meant that inequality between black people and white people still continued. For instance 57 per cent of houses lived in by black people were sub-standard and black people's incomes were significantly lower than those of white people.

SOURCE 1

Black protestors in 1964 are treated brutally after a demonstration in Massachusetts.

SOURCE 2

The March on Washington to demand racial equality in 1963 was organised by several different civil rights organisations and white labour and church leaders. It was attended by hundreds of thousands of peaceful protestors. Martin Luther King made his famous 'I have a dream' speech at this march (see page 39).

TAKING ACTION

In the 1950s and 60s black people continued to campaign for civil rights in many different ways. They continued to argue over the best way to bring change, as they had done in the time of Booker T Washington and W.E.B. Du Bois. Groups held marches and rallies like the one in Washington in 1963, staged peaceful sit-ins, boycotted white shops and transport systems and deliberately rode on segregated buses. Look at these different real life stories from the 1960s.

Septima Clark – beating the system. This woman managed to use education to beat the racist system in an area where black people could not vote unless they passed a literacy test. During the 1950s and 1960s she taught many people to read and write and pass the test, giving them a chance to be involved in politics.

Rosa Parkes – bus boycott heroine. Rosa Parkes was a 42-year-old seamstress from Montgomery, Alabama. Rosa was a campaigner for the NAACP and a member of the SCLS, the Southern Christian Leadership Conference, which was one of the main organisations for black churches in America. After a long day at work in December 1955, she sat down on the bus home and broke the state law by refusing to give up her seat to a white person. The law also said that black people had to enter the front door of the bus to pay, and then leave to enter again by the back door near to the seats for black people. Rosa was arrested and charged, receiving a lot of attention from the press. Black leaders in Rosa's town formed the Montgomery Improvement Association. They called for a mass boycott of the bus system which was carried out until the Supreme Court declared the bus segregation law illegal in 1956. Rosa went on to make speeches at many civil rights rallies and set up the Rosa and Raymond Parkes Institute for Self Development, which was a school for black children in Detroit.

Little Rock, Arkansas – Police protection to attend school. The town of Little Rock hit the headlines in September 1957 when nine black children were to be sent to the previously all-white High School. The town had de-segregated several parks and libraries and employed black and white people in its police force. The Governor of Arkansas protested about the proposal for black children to attend the school and mobs surrounded the school. The Governor thought that black and white children should be educated separately, but this would be breaking the federal law. The police had to guard the children on their first day. Riots followed and President Eisenhower sent in federal troops to make sure that the children were allowed to go to school. The real problems for the children started when the guards had left them and the constant bullying from white children began. The children became heroes and heroines for all black children in the South.

SOURCE 3

There were lots of kids doing what we did. We weren't unusual but we got the attention. We couldn't fight back or we'd be expelled, which might mean the end of integration. It was a daily torment for us and our parents. But we had to make integration work.

Elizabeth Eckford was one of the nine black children who started at Little Rock High School in 1957.

Alabama Children's Crusade – a message in numbers. In Alabama a huge campaign was set up to force de-segregation which included sit-ins and a Children's Crusade. In May 1963 a large group of black children marched into the white area of town and were arrested for breaking the law. After one day of protest the police had jailed 959 children and had to bring in school buses to deal with the numbers. But the crusade did not stop. After three days over 2000 children had been arrested. The police used fire hoses and injured children in their attempts to stop the marchers. Their action showed how ridiculous the laws were and their brutal treatment shocked the nation.

These events combined to bring media and public attention to the civil rights campaign. Some whites responded with violence and hostility; others lent support to the struggle.

Activity Time

1 How might a journalist have written up these civil rights campaigns? Prepare a story she/he might have sent to the editor of a newspaper. Include some possible headlines, a summary of the stories, pictures, captions and some interviews with campaigners. You could also add a map showing the location of the different stories.

2 Which do you think was the most successful way of campaigning for civil rights? Discuss your ideas in groups.

FAMOUS CIVIL RIGHTS LEADERS

Martin Luther King and Malcolm X were probably the two most famous black civil rights leaders in America. Both men were popular and worked hard to bring about change for black people in America. They had different backgrounds and ideas about the way to achieve civil rights. Both men were assassinated for their beliefs.

Martin Luther King believed in non-violent protest. He was a Baptist minister who became a civil rights leader during the Montgomery bus boycott. He helped to set up the SCLC (the Southern Christian Leadership Conference) which campaigned peacefully for civil rights. Malcolm X argued that violence had to be met with violence and that violence was necessary to bring progress. He joined the Nation of Islam, a black Muslim organisation, and became its spokesperson. He encouraged black pride and black nationalism, which indirectly encouraged the separation of black and white people. Sources 4 and 5 demonstrate the views each men held.

Activity Time

As a group, write an editorial for a newspaper commenting on the different approaches used to fight for civil rights. Include examples from the 1960s, such as Martin Luther King and Malcolm X. Explain the advantages and disadvantages of each method. Decide which you think was the most effective in bringing about change.

SOURCE 4

I say to you today, my friends, so even though we face the difficulties of today and tomorrow, I still have a dream. It is a dream deeply rooted in the American dream. I have a dream that one day this nation will rise up and live out the true meaning of its creed: 'that all men are created equal.'

... I have a dream that my four little children will one day live in a nation where they will not be judged by the colour of their skin, but by the content of their character ... I have a dream that one day every valley shall be exalted, every hill and mountain shall be made low, the rough places will be made plain and the crooked places will be made straight ... From every mountainside, let freedom ring, and ... speed up that day when all of God's children, black men and white men, Jews and Gentiles, Protestants and Catholics, will be able to join hands and sing in the words of the old Negro spiritual, 'Free at last! Free at last! Thank God Almighty, we are free at last!'

Martin Luther King speaking at the March on Washington in 1963.

SOURCE 5

If you're interested in freedom, you need some judo, you need some karate – you need all the things that will help you fight for freedom. If we don't resort to the bullet, then immediately we have to take steps to use the ballot. Equality of opportunity, if the constitution at the present time [doesn't offer it], then change it. Either it offers it, or it doesn't offer it. If it offers it – good, then give it to us – if it doesn't offer it, then change it. You don't need a debate. You need some action! So what you and I have to do is get involved. You and I have to be right there breathing down their throats. Every time they look over their shoulders, we want them to see us ... It's going to be the ballot or the bullet ...

Malcolm X speaking at the Audubon Ballroom, Washington Heights, in Harlem, New York on Easter Sunday, 1964.

SOURCE 6

This picture of Martin Luther King and Malcolm X together was taken in 1964.

Question Time

1 Listen to or read the speeches of Martin Luther King and Malcolm X again. Copy and fill in this chart to compare them.

	Martin Luther King	Malcolm X
What are their aims?		
What sort of words do they use?		
How do they persuade people to follow them?		
How do they want to bring about change?		

2 Find out more about the background, education and actions of these two men. Include information from the Internet if you can.

3 What are
a the similarities
b differences
between these two civil rights leaders? Compare their background, their ideas and their style of speaking.

4 Look at Source 6. Use your knowledge to explain whether Martin Luther King and Malcolm X could work as closely as this picture suggests.

5 Why do you think that the photograph in Source 6 was taken?

AMERICA IN THE 1990s – FROM SLAVERY TO EQUALITY?

The lives and work of Martin Luther King and Malcolm X represented the start of steady progress towards equal civil rights in America. Black people are now famous in every walk of life including positions in the law, politics, films, sport and music. But problems still exist and many black Americans are still poor and disadvantaged.

Activity Time

Prepare for a debate on the question of whether black Americans have equality with white Americans in the twenty-first century. The facts opposite will give you some subject ideas but you will need to carry out more research. Here are some ideas you can research from books, TV, newspapers, magazines and the Internet:

Advertisements   Film   Music industry
Sports   Politics   Newspaper articles
The work of Human Rights organisations, such as Amnesty International

Half the group should find evidence to prove equality and the other half should find evidence against it. You will need key speakers, witnesses statements of evidence and a summary statement for each side.

From slavery to equality? What do these facts suggest?

- In 1990 the average income of a black family in America was less than half that of an average white family.
- Bill Clinton appointed five black people as members of his cabinet in 1993.
- In 1992 serious riots started in Los Angeles after four white policemen were acquitted of beating up a black man, Rodney King. A passer-by had filmed the attack, but the mainly white jury found the policemen not guilty. The riots caused thousands of dollars of worth of damage and over 20 people were killed.
- Many black people in TV, film, literature and music still feel the need to speak out for civil rights.
- Unemployment rates in the mainly black ghettos of America's large cities are as high as 65 per cent.
- In 1990 fewer than one per cent of partners in law firms were black people.
- The civil rights organisations such as NAACP have become less popular and influential.
- The Secretary of State in America is a black man, General Colin Powell.

Marion Jones, World and Olympic champion in many track and field events.

Will Smith, singer, TV and film star.

Maya Angelou, author of poetry and story books which sell worldwide.

Colin Powell, US Secretary of State. Before this he was Chairman of the Joint Chiefs of Staff, the highest military position in the US Department of Defense.

Unit 16: The franchise – why didn't women get the vote at the same time as men?

Imagine a country where only half of the citizens have the right to choose who rules them or how the country is governed. The other half have no such rights. In this country only men can vote in elections for Members of Parliament who will represent them. The other half – women – are not allowed. They are not allowed because most people believe that women do not have the right sort of intelligence or personality. They are emotional and weak. They need to be looked after and led. Important decisions about money, work, power, war, laws, education and health care cannot be made by them. They are not thought to be capable of thinking about these things.

During the nineteenth century many people in Britain thought that women were not able to think for themselves and take control of their own lives. Most women were dependent on their fathers, husbands and brothers. Married women were not allowed to own any property – this made it impossible for women to control their own lives or to show that they were responsible beings. Already, therefore, we have some idea about the answer to the big question 'Why didn't women get the vote at the same time as men?'

Not everyone believed that women were naturally weaker than men. In 1792, Mary Wollstonecraft demanded equal political rights for all men and women. Mary, the daughter of a handkerchief weaver, wrote a number of books in which she attacked the way girls were brought up to be kept in 'ignorance and slavish dependence' and encouraged to be 'docile and attentive to their looks to the exclusion of all else'. Most people were very shocked at what Mary had to say and she was nicknamed 'the hyena in petticoats'. In fact it was to be over a century before women got the vote.

Excluding one section of the population from citizenship rights has serious consequences. Without equal political rights, it can be impossible for them to change any other aspect of their lives, such as work, housing, marriage, education and health.

What does it mean?

The franchise
The right to vote in elections to choose Members of Parliament. This is also the meaning of **suffrage.**

THREE CAMPAIGNING WOMEN: WHAT WERE THEY FIGHTING FOR?

SOURCE 1

A portrait of Harriet Taylor.

Each of the three women described below wanted to change women's lives during the period 1800 to 1928. As you read the information, think about:

- What these three women were fighting for.
- What methods they used to achieve their aims.

HARRIET TAYLOR (1807–58)

Harriet Taylor was born in 1807, the daughter of a London surgeon. After marrying at the age of 18 she became influenced by radicals who believed that people were born equal, but that early-nineteenth-century society prevented most people from having equal rights.

John Stuart Mill

At the age of 23 Harriet met the author John Stuart Mill and they began to work together producing books and essays on a range of issues, including women's rights. According to Harriet, John Stuart Mill was the first man to treat her as an equal. Their relationship grew and Harriet eventually separated from her husband. For 16 years she lived alone and John Stuart Mill visited her at weekends. Many of their friends were so shocked by this behaviour that they refused to see Harriet or John Stuart Mill. In 1849, after the death of her husband, they were able to marry.

One of the books they wrote together was called *The Subjection of Women*. This argued that since there was no difference between men and women, there was no reason why they should not have equal rights. Throughout her writings Harriet cried out against the accepted position of women in society. She said that women were not treated equally to men and that this was humiliating. Harriet argued that marriage played an important role in keeping women powerless and unequal to men. She was saying this at a time when girls were expected to marry as soon as they could.

During Harriet's lifetime, the law did not allow married women to have their own property or keep their earnings. Instead, their husbands owned everything. Even his wife and children were seen as his property! Husbands could hit their wives – it was not against the law. Women could not have custody of their children after divorce.

What does it mean?

The Subjection of Women
A book written by John Stuart Mill and Harriet Taylor. It describes the state of women as being *subject to* (under the control of) men, both mentally and physically.

Most people thought these laws were right. They believed that women were not able to look after themselves and instead should be looked after by their husbands. Harriet did not agree! She criticised the law for making women dependent on men. She also said that new laws should be introduced to protect women from violent husbands.

JOSEPHINE BUTLER (1828–1906)

In 1863, the only daughter of Josephine Butler fell to her death in front of Josephine. To help herself cope with the sadness and grief, Josephine began to do charity work, helping prostitutes. Josephine's experience convinced her that women were forced into prostitution by poverty and to escape the workhouse.

Women were blamed for being prostitutes while men were not blamed for using prostitutes. Josephine pointed out that a double standard was being applied – one rule for men and another for women. This double standard was apparent in the Contagious Diseases Acts of 1866 and 1869. Sexually transmitted diseases like gonorrhea and syphilis could kill. Laws were passed that any woman suspected of being a prostitute could be forced to have a medical examination. This did not apply to men. Josephine campaigned against the treatment of prostitutes by making speeches all around the country. At this time it was very unusual for a woman to speak at a public meeting and even more unusual to speak about sex. While some people came to listen, others came to shout and throw things at her.

Josephine also wrote books calling for better rights for women. She was very committed to improving women's education. For most of the nineteenth century, women were not allowed to

Who was she?

The married life of Caroline Norton

Caroline's story shows how marriage placed a woman under the control of her husband. Caroline was a best-selling novelist from a middle class family. She married in 1827 and had three sons, but her husband was violent and often hit her. Sometimes she had to hide in the homes of family and friends. Under the law all Caroline's possessions, including money her father had left her and the money she had earned from her books, belonged to her husband. Furthermore, she could not divorce him unless she could prove that he was unfaithful to her - violence was not enough. Eventually, in 1836, her husband left her and took her children away from her. She had no right to see her children again. As a result Caroline campaigned to change the law. The first success was in 1839 when the Custody of Infants Act gave mothers legal custody of children under seven years old, as long as the woman had not committed adultery.

Question Time

❶ What reasons might Josephine Butler give for:
  • Campaigning against Contagious Diseases Acts?
  • Campaigning for equal rights to education?

❷ What do you learn from the lives of Harriet Taylor and Caroline Norton about attitudes to women in the nineteenth century?

❸ What do you learn from the life of Josephine Butler about attitudes to women in the nineteenth century?

go to university. In the 1870s women were allowed to take degrees at London University and Girton College for women was founded at the University of Cambridge.

EMMELINE PANKHURST (1858–1928)

Emmeline was born into a middle class Manchester family in 1858. As a teenager, she regularly went to women's suffrage meetings with her mother, a feminist who supported equal rights for women. In 1878 Emmeline met Richard Pankhurst, a socialist and a lawyer, who also supported equal rights for women. He was 24 years older than she was. The couple were married and by the age of 26 Emmeline had given birth to four children. Two of her daughters, Christabel and Sylvia, went on to become very important figures in the campaign for equal rights for women, including the vote for women.

Emmeline believed that only by having the vote could women change their living and working conditions. She was particularly shocked by the conditions in the workhouses, where families were split up, food was scarce and the work was very hard. For the poor and unemployed, the horror of the workhouse was great, for once inside it was almost impossible ever to find outside work again (see Source 2).

What was it?

Workhouse
House where beggars and the homeless were sent to live. Conditions were very bad, and the parish authorities were not encouraged to improve them.

SOURCE 2

I also found pregnant women in the workhouse, scrubbing floors, doing the hardest kind of work, almost until their babies came into the world. Many of them were unmarried women, very, very young, mere girls. After the child was born, the women could either stay in the workhouse and earn their living by scrubbing and other work, (in which case they were separated from their babies), *or they could leave – leave with a two-week-old baby in their arms, without hope, without home, without money, without anywhere to go.*

An extract from *My Own Story* by Emmeline Pankhurst, published in 1914. Girls who became pregnant before marriage were likely to be thrown out of home by their families.

WSPU

In 1903 Emmeline started the Women's Social and Political Union (WSPU). In particular, she wanted to get working class women involved in the struggle for the vote. The WSPU had its own journal, *The Suffragette*, which used articles and images to try and achieve votes for women. The WSPU organised petitions demanding that parliament discuss and pass a law allowing women to vote. It also tried to get letters and articles published in national newspapers.

By 1905, Emmeline and other Suffragettes began to believe that using peaceful tactics to try to win the vote was not working. So they decided to use different methods. In 1907 her daughter Christabel and another Suffragette, Annie Kenney, were arrested for assault during a political meeting. It was the first use of violence by Suffragettes. This change of tactics from peaceful protest to violent and direct action resulted in Emmeline being imprisoned many times. In one 18 month period, she went on hunger strike ten times.

When the First World War began in 1914, the WSPU stopped their campaign for suffrage in order to support the war effort. *The Suffragette* became *Britannia* and slogans such as 'We demand the right to vote' became 'We demand the right to serve'.

Emmeline died in 1928. In the same year, women got equal political rights with men for the first time.

What were they?

Hunger strikes

Women who used violence or broke the law to draw attention to their campaign were arrested and many were sent to prison. There many of them refused to eat – going on hunger strike and being force-fed – an agonising procedure.

Who were they?

Suffragettes

Women who campaigned for votes for women and used violence in their campaign.

WHO WAS THE ANGEL IN THE HOUSE?

Harriet, Josephine and Emmeline thought that women should have more rights in society. Not everyone thought this. Most people thought that women should not be involved in politics at all, and certainly not have the vote. Instead they thought women should be at home. This is because they believed that women and men were very different.

In a poem written by Coventry Patmore, called *The Angel in the House* women are celebrated as the 'angels' at home, full of love and kindness and caring for the family and for others. Men, meanwhile, are good at learning, doing things, defending others, fighting and taking responsibility. Men and women were not seen as equal: men were superior to women because they were stronger and more powerful. They were not just physically stronger, but also mentally stronger than women. Men could think better than women and that is why they should make decisions for everyone in society, including women.

The picture in Source 3 was one of three paintings that were displayed in a London exhibition to celebrate the ideal role of a woman. It shows her comforting her husband. The other two paintings, *Guide of Childhood* and *Comfort of Old Age*, show the woman looking after her son and her ageing father.

The artist Hicks wrote 'I presume no woman will make up her mind to remain single, it is unnatural for a woman to be single'. Many people went to see the exhibition and hung copies in their homes.

SOURCE 3

Woman's Mission: Companion of Manhood painted by George Elgar Hicks and exhibited in 1863.

Activity Time

Select information from 'Three campaigning women' to fill in the grid below. You will need at least one side of A4 for your grid.

	Harriet Taylor	Josephine Butler	Emmeline Pankhurst
Dates			
Aims: What was she struggling for?			
Methods: What did she do to achieve her aims?			

Use your grid to answer the following questions:

1 Look at the box about Aims.
 a In what ways were the aims of the three women similar?
 b In what ways were they different?
 c In what ways did the aims change towards the end of the nineteenth century?

2 Compare the methods of the three women. How did the methods change through the period?

3 Do we have to struggle for these aims today? Why/why not?

4 Carry out your own research to find out as much as you can about other important women of the nineteenth century. Organise your research around the following questions:
 a What was the background of the woman?
 b What did she want to achieve?
 c How did she try to achieve her aims?
 d What support/opposition did she have?
 e How successful was she?

Women that you could research include: Florence Nightingale, Mary Seacole, Mary Fildes, Charlotte Bronte, Mary Kingsley, Elizabeth Fry, Mary Shelley and Annie Besant. Find out a bit about all the women before you decide which one interests you most.

Question Time

Look carefully at Source 3 before you answer the questions.

1 The woman in the painting is comforting her husband because he has just found out about someone's death. Describe the clues in the painting that tell us this.

2 Look at the poses and the clothes of the man and the woman. How has the artist painted the woman to look weaker than the man?

3 Look at the titles of the three paintings. What was the message that the artist was trying to send about women?

In other paintings of the time, women were painted to look weak, pale, and in need of protection. Education, literature, laws and religion all helped to make people think about women in a certain way. The Church of England taught that women should sacrifice themselves for the needs of their family. Until 1870, when primary education was introduced for boys and girls, most girls were taught at home how to be good wives and mothers. Popular magazines for women were full of articles about how to look after a house and a family.

The painting in Source 3 shows a middle class family home. Although most working class people probably had the same beliefs about women, most working class women worked. Before the industrial revolution, they would be working at home or on the land, or as servants. But when many workers moved into the growing towns and cities, women and children had to find work outside the home in factories. Many young girls and boys worked as domestic servants and lived away from home. Some women took in work at home, such as making clothes. This was not as well paid as factory work, but it meant they could look after their family at the same time.

Activity Time

Copy the diagram below. The circle on the left represents the private life of a middle class home and family – traditionally women's roles. The circle on the right represents the public life of work and politics – traditionally men's roles.

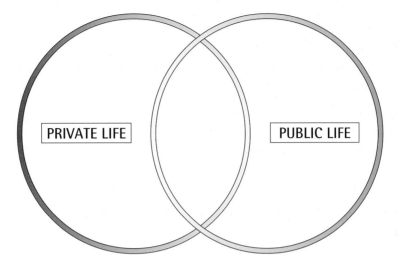

PRIVATE LIFE   PUBLIC LIFE

❶ Decide in which circle the following activities belong. You may want to put some activities in the middle area.
Earning money
Owning property
Sewing
Drawing
Playing music
Joining the army
Writing books and newspaper articles
Caring for children
Managing servants
Making laws
Spending money
Declaring war
Public speaking

❷ Look at your diagram. What beliefs were there in nineteenth-century Britain about the role of women? Think about how they were supposed to behave and what sort of activities they were they supposed to do.

❸ Look at your diagram. What beliefs were there in nineteenth-century Britain about the role of men? Think about how they were supposed to behave and what sort of activities were they supposed to do.

❹ In what ways did **a** Harriet Taylor, **b** Josephine Butler and **c** Emmeline Pankhurst challenge these beliefs? How were their beliefs different?

WHY DID SOME PEOPLE HAVE THE VOTE IN 1815 AND NOT OTHERS?

You should now have some good ideas about why it took so long for women to get the vote. In order to answer the question more fully, we need to think about the situation in 1815. Hardly anyone had the vote in 1815! Very few men could vote in 1815, let alone women.

THE POLITICAL SYSTEM IN 1815

Britain was ruled by Parliament, which was divided into the House of Lords and the House of Commons. The men who sat in the House of Lords were called 'Lords' while those who sat in the House of Commons were called Members of Parliament (MPs). Each MP represented an area of Britain called a 'constituency'. In 1815 these constituencies consisted of the counties of England, Wales and Scotland and 204 boroughs (towns). This system had remained almost unchanged since Tudor times. But since then new industrial towns and cities had grown up, mainly in the Midlands and the north of England, while the populations of other boroughs had become smaller. This meant that large numbers of people were not represented in Parliament at all. This was not democratic.

Men who wanted to become MPs had to own land or property worth a certain amount before they could stand at an election. In each *county* constituency men had to be sizeable landowners to be allowed to vote. In the *boroughs*, the rules as to who could vote in elections varied greatly from place to place. Often these elections were controlled by wealthy property owners who saw to it that their friends and relations were elected to Parliament.

Elections were important, popular and sometimes violent events. Two main political parties were well established by this time, the Tories and the Whigs. The party with a majority in the House of Commons formed the government. In many constituencies, there was only one candidate but in others voters had to choose a Whig or a Tory. Voting was not done in secret but in the open. Voters were often bribed or frightened into supporting a certain candidate.

The House of Lords was not elected. It was made up of members of aristocratic families who inherited their seats, and important members of the Church of England, such as bishops.

By 1815 this system no longer reflected the size of the population, and had become corrupt in other ways. To see this, you need to study the map on page 51 and the information boxes round it.

What does it mean?

Democratic
From ancient Greek meaning 'rule of the people' or 'people power'. In western Europe today a democracy is government by the people through their elected representatives.

Who were they?

Tories and **Whigs** were the two loose groups that formed in the House of Commons in Charles II's reign. The **Tories** were mostly landed gentry. The **Whigs** tended to have more supporters from the financiers, merchants and dissenters – people who did not belong to the Anglican Church.

Question Time

❶ Look at the map. In what ways was the distribution of MPs unfair?

❷ a What sort of person could stand at an election to be an MP?
b Why do you think boroughs like Sarum were called 'rotten'?

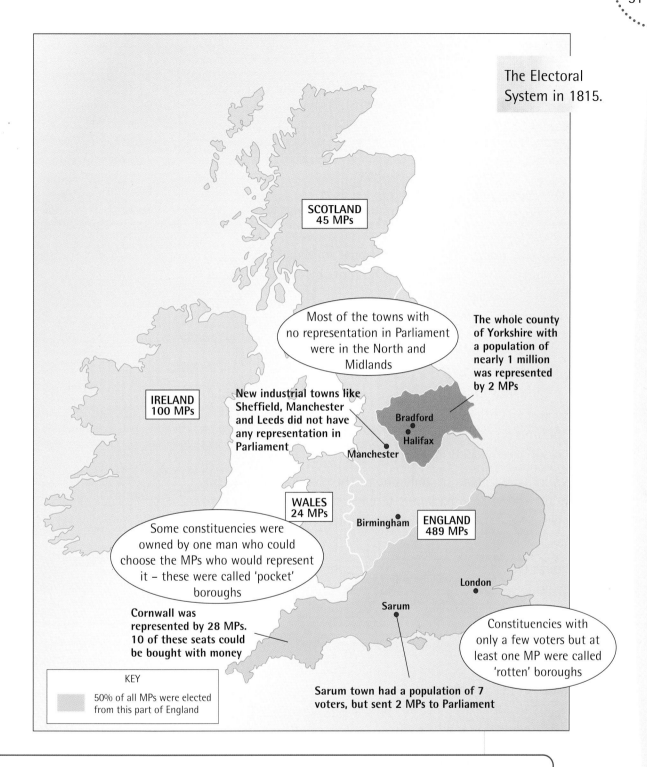

The Electoral System in 1815.

SCOTLAND
45 MPs

IRELAND
100 MPs

Most of the towns with no representation in Parliament were in the North and Midlands

The whole county of Yorkshire with a population of nearly 1 million was represented by 2 MPs

New industrial towns like Sheffield, Manchester and Leeds did not have any representation in Parliament

Bradford
Halifax
Manchester

WALES
24 MPs

Some constituencies were owned by one man who could choose the MPs who would represent it – these were called 'pocket' boroughs

Birmingham

ENGLAND
489 MPs

London

Cornwall was represented by 28 MPs. 10 of these seats could be bought with money

Sarum

Constituencies with only a few voters but at least one MP were called 'rotten' boroughs

KEY

50% of all MPs were elected from this part of England

Sarum town had a population of 7 voters, but sent 2 MPs to Parliament

c Find out why 'pocket boroughs' were given this name.

❸ Read the meaning of democracy. Use the information and the map to make a list of ways in which the political system in 1815 was undemocratic. In what ways was it democratic?

❹ Make a list of the ways in which Britain is democratic today, for example, voting, elections, constituencies.

Activity Time

1 Study the list of people below. It is 1815. Only one of these people is able to vote. Use the map and the information on pages 50-51 to work out which one this is. *Remember: women did not have the vote, so there are only men in this list.*

- A lawyer living and working in Leeds.
- An undergardener living and working on the small estate of a village parson.
- A skilled gunsmith renting his house in Manchester.
- A sheep farmer in Cornwall who rents his house and land from the local aristocrat.
- A soldier of ordinary rank who has fought against the French and is now unemployed.
- The manager of a woollen factory in Macclesfield. He owns a large house in the town.
- A farmer in Devon. He owns a large area of land, woodland and several cottages.
- An innkeeper in Oxford. He rents his inn.
- A shopkeeper in Brighton.

2 As you have found out, only one of the characters above has the right to vote in parliamentary elections in 1815. Write down the reason why this person has the vote, while all the others do not.

3 Choose two of the characters who might think that they should have the vote in 1815, but who do not. Write a short conversation between them to show why they think it is unfair that they cannot vote. Think about:
- Their jobs – do they have responsibility, do they employ others, have they experience of management, of working for others, of making decisions?
- Their wealth – do they own property?
- Their education – do they have a degree?

WHO WAS STRUGGLING FOR POLITICAL CHANGE BETWEEN 1815 AND 1848?

RIOTS AND UNREST

Unemployment and poverty

The years 1815-48 were a time of unrest and riots up and down the country. The wars against France and America had ended in 1815, and thousands of soldiers were coming home with no jobs to return to. The end of the wars meant that the demand for coal and iron dropped and many people employed in industry during the wars lost their jobs. 1815 was also a year of natural disaster. The harvest failed because of lack of rain, and this was at a time when the birth rate was rising. The introduction of the hated Corn Laws of 1815 made bread very expensive. This meant that the cost of bread rose when there were more mouths to feed. The working classes were suffering from low wages, heavy taxes and expensive bread all at the same time.

The new industrial towns

Those who moved to the new towns to look for jobs were faced with the terrible conditions of slum living and long hours of poorly-paid work in the factories. There were no laws to control conditions of safety, hours of work or rates of pay in the factories for anyone – men, women or children. And in many of these new towns, as we have seen, there were no elections to send MPs to Parliament, so that working class misery and discontent were rarely heard about in the House of Commons. With no representation, these people had no means of asking for changes in the law that would improve their lives.

Meanwhile the factory owners, industrialists, professional lawyers and developers were rapidly growing in numbers and wealth. These middle class people were also not represented in Parliament, and as they became richer and more powerful locally they wanted political power as well.

What were they?

The Corn Laws

These were first passed in 1815 to try and protect British agriculture, which was suffering from the effects of poor harvests and low prices at market. The laws prevented the import of most foreign produce, including wheat. They had the effect of making the prices of home-grown wheat, and so bread, very high.

Question Time

❶ Why was it important for the working class to have the vote?

❷ Why did some middle class people support the demand for more political change?

Radical ideas

Many people across the country were influenced by the events that had taken place in France since 1789 especially the French Revolution. Radicals were inspired by the political changes, even if they did not like the bloody way change had been brought about. They said the British political system was undemocratic and within the new industrial cities, like Manchester and Leeds, groups were formed to campaign for:

- universal male suffrage (all men in Britain allowed to vote)
- lower taxation
- help for poor people.

These radical people held open-air meetings and collected signatures for petitions to be presented to parliament. Leaders of some religious groups also encouraged people to think in new ways. They told people to think for themselves rather than accepting what they were told by their 'betters'. And as roads improved and railways developed, people began to travel more easily to attend meetings. News spread more quickly.

Who were they?

Radicals
People who wanted big changes in society.

What does it mean?

Revolution
Huge change which is often violent. Usually a government is removed by force and a new system is brought in.

THE FRENCH REVOLUTION – WOULD IT SPREAD TO BRITAIN?

This was what worried the government and the landed classes. They feared that so much hunger and unhappiness would drive people to demand big changes in the way the country was run. After all, the French Revolution had happened partly because of bad harvests, hunger and poverty! The king, all his family and many aristocrats had been executed. In 1815 any unrest in England made people remember the terrible events in France in the 1790s - would a similar revolution happen in Britain?

WHAT HAPPENED AT PETERLOO, MANCHESTER IN 1819?

On a summer's day in 1819, about 60,000 people made their way to St Peter's Field, outside Manchester, for a public meeting. It was the fourth big meeting that summer and, like the other three meetings, it was a peaceful gathering. People had come to listen to speakers talk about current problems and the need for change.

Manchester's local magistrates, the people responsible for law and order in the area, were worried that the meeting might end in a riot. They were not used to large public meetings and knew that, in other parts of the country, there had been riots after such meetings. They called for a large number of soldiers and ordered them to arrest the speakers and break up the crowd. It was this panic reaction that led to tragedy. The soldiers were not trained to deal with the public. Instead of making their way peacefully to the speaker's platform, the soldiers hacked their way through the crowd with their sabres (swords). Eleven people were killed and 400 seriously injured.

Respected journalists who were at the scene wrote about what happened and the news spread quickly. There was widespread horror in the country, but the government reacted by asking the Prince Regent publicly to congratulate the magistrates involved! Accounts of the massacre were denied and journalists who wrote about it were arrested and imprisoned.

What does it mean?

Peterloo

The event was called this as the Battle of Waterloo had taken place only a few years earlier, in 1815.

SOURCE 1

This drawing of Peterloo was made at the time. The woman on the platform dressed in white is Mary Fildes. During the meeting, the soldiers attacked Mary along with the other speakers. An eye-witness described what happened: 'Mrs Fildes, hanging suspended by a nail which had caught her white dress, was slashed across her exposed body by one of the brave cavalry'.

Factfile: Mary Fildes

Mary was one of the few women ever to speak in public at this time. She was leader of the 'Manchester Female Reform Group' and went on to become active in the Chartist Movement (see page 62). She believed in greater independence for women and that they should have control over their own lives. She also believed in birth control. She sold books about it, but people were so unused to discussing a subject like this that she was accused of spreading pornography!

But Mary was not asking for votes for women. She believed that women should support their husbands in their struggle for the vote rather than ask for it for themselves. This was a view Mary shared with most radicals at that time. For most radicals, universal male suffrage was the main aim.

Other women at Peterloo
These included 150 'Female Reformers' from Oldham. They carried banners with the slogans 'Universal Suffrage' and 'Let us die like men, not sold like slaves'. According to an eye-witness, onlookers shouted at them 'Go home to your families, and leave these matters to your husbands and sons, who better understand them'.

MARCHES, RISINGS AND REVOLUTIONARY PLOTS

Peterloo was not the only occasion of a mass meeting that ended in clashes with the authorities. In 1816, a huge political meeting took place in Spa Fields, Islington. Henry Hunt, one of the speakers who would later be at Peterloo, was speaking. A small group from the meeting left and broke into gunsmith's shops to arm themselves. They marched to attack the Tower of London, but failed and were arrested.

By 1817 the weavers in the cotton factories who still used hand looms were becoming increasingly afraid of being squeezed out of work by the introduction of mechanised (run by machines) power looms. They planned a peaceful march from Manchester to London to present a petition asking for help and reform. They were called 'Blanketeers' because of the blankets they carried to keep themselves warm on the march and to show that they were weavers. Magistrates in Manchester used soldiers to stop the marchers. This was violent and one man was killed.

A series of anti-government plots in Yorkshire, Derbyshire and Nottinghamshire were infiltrated by a government spy known as 'Oliver' and the ringleaders were arrested.

The government was more scared than ever when Peterloo happened – the climax to a series of demonstrations for change. In 1820 one of its spies uncovered a plot to blow up the government ministers while they were eating dinner. Five of the plotters were hung. Most of the crowd who gathered to watch the executions were sympathetic to the radicals. Their plot became known as the Cato Street Conspiracy.

In the weeks that followed armed crowds gathered in Huddersfield, Barnsley, Sheffield and Glasgow. A commentator who lived at the time said he had 'never known a period at which the people's hatred of the government was so general and so fierce'.

WHAT DID THE GOVERNMENT DO?

As well as spying on people, the government passed laws to stop political unrest and protest. The Six Acts were passed in 1819. They clamped down on radical newspapers and gave magistrates more powers to control and imprison people. The government refused to consider any political reform. It was another ten years before political reform was seriously considered in Parliament.

Question Time

❶ Thomas Paine was one of the most important radicals of the eighteenth and nineteenth centuries. Find out what his ideas were.

❷ Why did the events of 1815–1820 frighten the government?

❸ The Six Acts were passed soon after Peterloo. Why do you think they were passed?

WHY DID POLITICIANS START TO THINK ABOUT REFORM?

By 1830 there were some politicians in parliament who saw the need for political change. These politicians were from the Whig party and in 1830 a Whig called Earl Grey became Prime Minister. Whigs like Grey had been interested in political reform for a while, but it was only in 1830 that they became powerful enough to try and introduce reform.

Grey did not want to change the political system in the same way or for the same reasons as the radicals did. Unlike the radicals, Grey did not want to give more people the vote, instead he wanted to reform the political system to *protect* the existing power of the upper class. In 1831 Grey said: 'There is no one more against universal suffrage than I am. My aim is to put an end to such hopes...'

At first, Grey's idea might seem very strange! But Grey saw that the way 'to put an end to such hopes' (of universal suffrage) was to introduce just enough reform to please the middle classes and stop them supporting the radical working class demands for universal male suffrage. In this view he was influenced by a writer called Edmund Burke.

What did Edmund Burke say?

In his book, Burke put forward some very important ideas about power and change. He said that all living things have to change gradually as they grow in order to survive. If they cannot change and adapt to new circumstances, they will die. Burke went on to say that political systems are the same. Britain's political system had to change a bit to survive. If it failed to adapt to new circumstances, it might be destroyed by revolution, which is what had happened in France.

How did this influence Grey?

Many Whigs thought that Burke was giving very important advice. Grey told Parliament that Britain had changed since the eighteenth century and the political system would have to change, too. One important change was that the middle class had become bigger, richer and more influential and they wanted recognition through political power. Some of them were beginning to support the demands of the radicals for universal male suffrage, and this had to be stopped before it started a revolution!

What does it mean?

Reform
Change or improvement, usually changing the laws to make them fairer.

SOURCE 2

A portrait of Edmund Burke.

Activity Time

You are an adviser to Earl Grey. It is 1830.

1 What was Grey's main aim? Write it out.

2 Read the three pieces of advice set out below. Choose the advice that you think will help Grey achieve his aim.

a No change to the political system should be made. The government should continue to repress the radicals and their demands.

b Small changes to reform the political system should be made. The vote should be given to the middle class who own property, but not to the lower middle class or working class. This would encourage the middle class to support the upper class rather than support the working class and the radicals.

c Big changes should be made. The vote should be given to all adult men and the unfair system that keeps the upper class in power should be stamped out.

Now present your advice to Lord Grey. Explain your choice of **a**, **b** or **c** by referring to as many of the following as you can:

- French Revolution
- radicals, the working class and their demands
- events of 1815-20
- middle class and their demands
- ideas of Edmund Burke.

THE GREAT REFORM BILL IS PASSED

'The bill, the whole bill, and nothing but the bill!'
Grey decided to introduce some political reform in March 1831. Those MPs who represented rotten boroughs were against a bill that might get rid of their seats. The bill passed its first stage in the Commons by only one vote. During the next stage Grey was defeated and resigned as Prime Minister. A general election had to be called. Grey and the Whigs were returned to power and got the bill through the Commons, only to see it promptly thrown out by the House of Lords.

Immediately there was widespread excitement, with riots and demonstrations across the country. A newspaper appeared with black edges and muffled bells were tolled as signs of mourning for the loss of the bill. Grey resigned again and a Tory government, led by the Duke of Wellington (who was so unpopular that he had to fix iron shutters to the windows of his house in London) tried to introduce a less far reaching version. This infuriated the reformers, who cried out for 'the whole bill', and forced the Duke to back down. Eventually, Grey had to persuade the King to intervene and use his influence with the House of Lords to pass the bill. The whole process took over a year of bitter struggle.

Who was he?

The Duke of Wellington was famous for his victories in the wars against Napoleon and the French, ending in the battle of Waterloo in 1815. He was a bitter opponent of the Great Reform Bill, saying '... no nobleman, nor any gentleman ... will govern the country six weeks after the Reform Parliament shall meet, and the race of gentlemen will not last long afterwards'.

SOURCE 3

George Cruikshank, a well-known cartoonist of the time, published this drawing in 1832. The words on the tree trunk say 'Rotten Borough System', and the nests above are all named after well-known rotten boroughs. Cruikshank is showing those who were for the Great Reform Bill (trying to cut the tree down) and those who were against (trying to prop it up).

Question Time

❶ Why do you think that Cruikshank chose a rotten tree to represent the political system of Britain in 1832?

❷ Do you think Cruikshank was for or against political reform? Use details from the cartoon to explain your ideas.

❸ Do you think the cartoon was published before or after the Great Reform Bill was passed?

WHAT DID THE GREAT REFORM BILL OF 1832 CHANGE?

Political System before 1832	Political System after 1832
CHANGES TO THE FRANCHISE (the qualification to vote)	
Who could vote in boroughs varied greatly from place to place	Who could vote in the boroughs became the same everywhere – householders with property worth a certain amount, which included most of the middle classes
13 per cent of the adult male population could vote	18 per cent of the adult male population could vote
CHANGES TO THE CONSTITUENCIES (how votes and MPs were distributed)	
Many towns and cities in the Midlands and north had no MPs	65 MPs given to some of these areas
Many rotten boroughs	56 rotten boroughs abolished 30 other rotten boroughs now elected only 1 MP instead of 2 41 new boroughs created
Nearly 200 pocket boroughs	130 pocket boroughs abolished

WHAT DID THE GREAT REFORM BILL NOT CHANGE?

- The franchise in the county constituencies remained the same, so the influence of the landowners was left untouched.
- During elections people still voted in the open. So they could still be bribed or forced to vote for a candidate by landlords.
- Men still had to be wealthy property owners before they could become MPs.

Activity Time

❶ Here are some results of the Great Reform Bill:
- Places like Birmingham, Leeds, Sheffield, Bradford and Swansea were now represented in Parliament.
- In the boroughs, the wealthier middle classes now had the vote and some could afford to stand as MPs.
- In the counties the landlords' influence remained unchanged.
- The increase in the electorate was very small.
- Elections were still open to corruption.
- The working class could still not vote.
- Many constituencies were still very unequal in size – one in Liverpool had 11,000 voters, while 35 constituencies had only 300 people.

See how many other results you can think of, using all the information in this section. Divide them up into the results that brought improvements to the political system, and non-results where nothing changed.

CHARTISM: A WORKING CLASS MOVEMENT

The working class and the radicals who had campaigned for political reform were disappointed with the Great Reform Act of 1832. The act had given the vote to middle class men but not to working class men. Without the vote, the poorer British people could not persuade Parliament to help them.

After 1832 many working class and radical men and women set up local groups, started newspapers, held meetings and collected signatures for petitions to be presented to Parliament. These petitions demanded that the political system be changed and made more democratic. The demands for change were written as a 'Charter' and the people who supported the Charter were called 'Chartists'.

SIX POINT CHARTER

Universal male suffrage

Secret ballot

Annual elections

Payment of MPs

No property qualification for MPs

All constituencies to have equal numbers of voters

Activity Time

Each point of the Charter was meant to make Britain more democratic.

❶ First you must think about the meaning of 'democratic'. Look back to the meaning of 'democratic' on page 50.

❷ Work in pairs or small groups, and copy out the six points of the Charter onto a large sheet of paper. Discuss each point in turn and write next to it:

a What it means.

b How it would make Britain more democratic.

For example: Payment of MPs is more democratic because anyone, whether rich or poor, can try to be elected as a MP. In the 1840s you had to be rich to be an MP. You had to own property by law, and you had to have money of your own to live, as there would be no time to work while sitting in Parliament. This was not democratic.

WHAT HAPPENED TO THE CHARTISTS?

In total, the Chartists presented three petitions to Parliament in 1839, 1842 and 1848. All the petitions were rejected by Parliament. All but a few MPs were horrified at the idea of giving the vote to men without property. The failure of the last petition in 1848 marked the end of Chartism as a large, popular movement.

WHY DID CHARTISM FAIL IN 1848?

The Chartists were not well united as a movement. There were many different groups across the country with different leaders who had different ideas about what they wanted and how to achieve it. Some argued that presenting petitions and other peaceful demonstrations was enough. Others said this was a waste of time and believed in violent action. An armed uprising was planned in North Yorkshire, one of the most radical areas of Chartists, but nothing came of it.

The government was much better prepared to deal with riots and risings from the Chartists than it had been between 1815 and 1820. The building of the railways meant that soldiers could be sent more quickly around the country to put down trouble. The new telegraph system meant that information about possible uprisings could be passed on quickly. The government was far less likely to be taken by surprise!

Sources 4 and 5 give more clues about why Chartism as a movement died in 1848. However, Chartism was not a complete failure. During this period more and more working class people became aware of the importance of gaining the vote in order to change their lives. Many became active in other movements, such as the trade unions to protect workers' rights and reform groups to change political rights. By 1928 all but six of the demands of the Chartists had been achieved. Find out which one of the demands of the Charter was never achieved.

SOURCE 4

Poor creatures, their threats of attack are miserable. With half a cartridge, and half a pike, with no money, no discipline, no skilful leaders, they would attack men with leaders, money and discipline, who are well-armed and have 60 rounds of bullets each.

General Napier, in charge of law and order, wrote this about some Nottingham Chartists in 1839.

SOURCE 5

The number of working class people who supported the Charter increased in times of economic depression. The 1830s and early 1840s was a time of great suffering among the poor. This was also a time when Chartism was very popular among the working class. In the middle of the 1840s there was less unemployment, hunger and poverty and Chartism was less popular at this time. A sudden drop in living standards in 1847 revived Chartism until things improved in the 1850s.

A modern historian writing about why Chartism ended in 1848.

WHY DIDN'T THE CHARTISTS CAMPAIGN FOR VOTES FOR WOMEN?

Look back to the six points of the Charter on page 62.
The Charter supported universal *male* suffrage not universal suffrage.
The lack of support for female suffrage was not because there were no women Chartists. Women were very active within the Chartist movement and, according to a newspaper report on the women

Chartists of Hyde, they were the 'better men' or, in other words, more militant than the men!

Most Chartists, men and women, did not support universal suffrage because they did not believe in it. They believed in votes for all men, but not votes for women. The role of women was to support men in their campaign for the vote, and a clause asking for votes for women in an early draft of the Charter was removed because it might make it harder to achieve universal male suffrage.

Two Chartists who did believe in votes for women

Elizabeth Pease and Anne Knight were two of the few people who did believe in votes for women, as well as for men. Both were middle class women and supported the anti-slavery movement, as well as universal suffrage. Elizabeth Pease complained that most of her friends and family thought she was being very 'unladylike and ungenteel' in supporting votes for women! Anne Knight was also frustrated by the behaviour of those around her. She called on the Chartists to campaign for 'true universal suffrage' and was angry at the lack of support she received from male and female Chartists (see Source 6). She also criticised male Chartists for excluding women from positions of power in the movement.

SOURCE 6

FELLOW COUNTRYWOMEN! We call on you to join us and help our fathers, husbands, and brothers, to free themselves...we have been told that the place for woman is in her home and that politics should be left to men. We deny this. Is it not true that the interests of our fathers, husbands, and brothers, ought to be ours? Our husbands are over-worked, our houses half-furnished, our families ill-fed, and our children uneducated. The fear of want hangs over our heads... We are powerless because we are poor.

Written in a leaflet to the Women Chartists of Newcastle-upon-Tyne by Anne Knight and published in the *Northern Star* newspaper on 9 February 1849. She was trying to persuade the Newcastle Women Chartists to support the vote for all men and women.

Question Time

1 Read Source 6. The Women Chartists of Newcastle-upon-Tyne did not support votes for women. According to the source, what did they think should be the role of women? How did Anne Knight try to persuade them to change their minds?

2 Anne Knight wrote political and feminist slogans which she printed onto labels and stuck on envelopes. Why might this be a good strategy?

3 What did Anne Knight mean by 'true universal suffrage'?

4 Elizabeth Pease's friends said it was 'unladylike' to campaign for votes for women. How is this backed up by Source 6?

5 On pages 43 to 48 you found out about attitudes to women in the nineteenth century. How do nineteenth century ideas and attitudes help to explain why Chartists did not demand 'true universal suffrage'?

WHY DID MORE PEOPLE GET THE VOTE IN THE SECOND HALF OF THE NINETEENTH CENTURY?

In 1867 the Second Reform Act was passed. This Act:

- Gave the vote to all male householders in the boroughs. This meant that almost all men in the town constituencies now had the right to vote. A large number of these men were working class.
- The property qualification in the counties was changed – some tenants could now vote.
- How MPs were distributed in the constituencies was changed again. MPs were taken away from constituencies with fewer people and given to constituencies with more people.

Result
- The number of electors was increased from 18 per cent of the adult male population to 36 per cent of the adult male population.
- In the towns and cities the working class was now the biggest group of voters, and this meant that the system in the boroughs was now more democratic than in the counties.

WHY WAS THE 1867 REFORM ACT PASSED?

Historians need to explain why things happened. It is also important to think about why something happened when it did and not earlier or later.

Look at the statements below. Some of them help to explain why the Second Reform Act was passed in 1867 and not in the 1850s. Pick out the ones that you think provide the most sensible reasons for the passing of the Act at this time.

- **1864** a group called the 'National Reform Union' was set up to put pressure on the government to reform the political system into a more democratic one. Many members had been Chartists before 1848. Some politicians were worried about the Union – would it lead to political unrest similar to the unrest between 1815 and 1820?

- **1854** The Crimean War started against Russia. This kept the government busy and people became interested in who was winning the war rather than in political change.

- **1846** The Corn Laws were repealed. This meant that they no longer were in force. These laws had caused hardship for many people by keeping food prices high (see page 53).

- In the **1850s** reform was talked about in Parliament.

- Other countries in Europe, for example Italy, were changing their political systems and making them more democratic. An Italian reformer called Garibaldi visited England in **1864** and got a warm welcome from radicals.

- During the **1850s** living standards rose in Britain. Most people had more food and money than they had had in the 1840s.

- **1866** There were demonstrations for political reform in various parts of the country. In July a demonstration in Hyde Park turned into a riot. Although there was not as much trouble as there had been in 1832, some politicians were afraid of revolution.

By 1867, as Source 1 shows, the question of whether women should be given the vote was being debated in Parliament. A small group of MPs, including John Stuart Mill (husband of Harriet Taylor, see page 43), supported women's suffrage, but the vast majority did not.

SOURCE 1

There were certain things which women could do better than men, and others which they could not do as well. In all that required rough, rude, practical force, stability of character, and intellect, man was superior: whereas in all those relations of life that demanded mildness, softness of character and amiability, women far excelled.

An MP debating the Second Reform Act, recorded in Hansard on 20 May 1867.

Question Time

❶ Which statements help to explain why political reform happened in the 1860s?

❷ Which statements help to explain why political reform did not happen in the 1850s?

❸ Read Source 1. Does this source support what you have learned so far about attitudes to women?

❹ Are you surprised that the question of women's suffrage was being debated in Parliament at this time? Give reasons for your answer.

AND MORE REFORM – WHY?

However, after 1867 further reform was needed. there was still a big difference between who could vote in the countryside and in the towns. In 1884 the Third Reform Act was passed. This Act gave the vote to all male householders in the counties, as well as the boroughs. It also gave each constituency one MP and made the constituencies more equal in terms of population.

The 1870s and 80s were years that saw great social reforms. Laws were passed to do with:

- education
- public health
- housing for the poor
- factory conditions
- trades unions
- the reform of the army.

The Secret Ballot Act 1872

This Act made a big difference to the political system. People now had to vote in secret at elections. This meant they would no longer be bullied or bribed into voting for a particular candidate, as no one could see how they voted. The Act virtually removed altogether the control of landlords or the rich over elections, and corruption was much reduced. In 1883 the Corrupt Practices Act went a stage further and made it possible to punish corruption in politics.

By 1900, therefore, 65 per cent of adult males could vote in secret at elections. Those men who could not vote were those without their own households, for example, domestic servants living in other people's homes. The table above shows the increases in the percentage of adult men who could vote between 1832 and 1884.

Date	Percentage of adult men (over 21) allowed to vote
1831	13
1832	18
1867	36
1884	65

Question Time

❶ In the nineteenth century, the working class were the largest group in the population. Why do you think many upper class people did not want working class men to get the vote?

❷ Look back to the demands of the Charter on page 62. How many of their demands had been achieved by 1900? Which demands had not been achieved?

❸ Look at the table above. Do you think political change between 1800 and 1900 was fast or slow? Explain your answer.

❹ In pairs discuss why political change might have been fast or slow between 1800 and 1900.

WHAT FREEDOMS WERE WOMEN OBTAINING?

Think back to the section on 'the angel in the house' model of Victorian women (see page 47). In pairs write down everything each of you remembers about this 'ideal woman'.

Towards the end of the nineteenth century there were signs that the role of women was changing in important ways. In 1870 a system of primary education for boys and girls was established, and in 1880 it was made compulsory. Women were now needed as teachers. By 1900, 75 per cent of all teachers were women. There were other changes which opened up opportunities for women, such as the invention of the typewriter in 1870, which led to women taking on clerical and secretarial work, and the opening of more shops in the growing towns and cities. Nursing had become another occupation for many women by 1900. However, all these women had to give up their jobs when they married.

WOMEN'S FIRST STEPS TOWARDS EQUALITY WITH MEN

Activity Time

❶ You are going to find out how the law was changed to give more rights to women. Each of the statements below describes a change in the existing laws. None of the statements is complete, and you must complete each one by researching each law.

- 1857 – the Marriage and Divorce Act was passed:
  (i) It gave a married woman the right to own property if her husband left her.
  (ii) It said women could divorce their husbands if they could prove cruelty, incest or sodomy, as well as adultery.
  (iii) What did men have to prove?
  (iv) What did this law say about a mother's right to her own child?

- 1870 – an act was passed that said women could keep their own money and property acquired after they married. What was the name of this act?
- 1873 – mothers who were divorced could have custody of their children until they were how old?
- 1882 – the second Married Women's Property Act said what about women's ownership of property?
- 1888 – women ratepayers could vote in what sort of elections?
- A law was passed to say that men could no longer force their wives to live with them at home. When was it passed?

SOURCE 1

I longed ... to be of some use in the world, but as we were girls with a little money and born into a particular social position, it was not thought necessary that we should do anything but amuse ourselves until the time and the opportunity of marriage came along. 'Better any marriage at all than none,' a foolish old aunt used to say.

Charlotte Despard writing about her feelings as a young woman in the 1850s.

SOURCE 2

To remain single was thought a disgrace and at thirty a woman was called an old maid. After their parents died, what could they do, where could they go ...? The only paid occupation open to a gentlewoman was to become a governess under despised conditions and with a miserable salary ...

Louisa Garret Anderson describing attitudes in the 1860s.

SOURCE 3

A girl is not necessarily a better woman because she knows the heights of all the mountains in Europe ... but she is decidedly better fitted for the duties she will be called upon to perform if she knows how to wash and tend a child, cook simple food and thoroughly clean a house.

Written by a school inspector in 1874.

SOURCE 4

The Queen is most anxious to enlist everyone who can speak or write to join in checking this mad, wicked folly of 'Women's Rights' with all its attendant horrors on which her poor feeble sex is bent, forgetting every sense of womanly feeling and propriety. Lady Amberley ought to get a good whipping.'

Queen Victoria on hearing that Lady Amberley had spoken at a suffrage meeting.

Think about what else you can work out about the lives of women from the information about laws and changes in the law. For example: *For most of the nineteenth century married women could not leave home if they wanted to.*

❷ These laws showed that there had been changes in how people thought about women. But how much had ideas about women changed? Use the sources to find out how much attitudes to women had changed by 1900. As you read think about:

What evidence is there that people still believed in the 'angel in the house'? What evidence is there that people did not believe in the 'angel in the house'?

WHO WAS CAMPAIGNING FOR VOTES FOR WOMEN?

The position of women under the law was changing, but very slowly. The fact that women could not change the law themselves as MPs in Parliament, or put pressure on male MPs to do so through voting, was a big barrier to change. As you have found out, a few women, like Mary Wollstonecraft, had been campaigning for the vote for women at the beginning of the century. By the 1870s the campaign for votes for women had become a mass movement and had even won a few supporters in Parliament. However, most MPs and many other people still opposed women's suffrage in 1900.

SOURCE 1

Convicts and lunatics poster by Emily Harding Andrews for the Artists Suffrage League, 1908.

SOURCE 2

That the improved status a vote would give these women would be a large factor in raising their wages there cannot be the smallest doubt. In the language of the girls themselves about it. 'They don't dare put on a man same as they do on us; not they! 'Of course not,' said a male trade unionist, 'you see men have the vote.'

Written by Isabella Ford in 1901, explaining why it was important for industrial women workers to get the vote.

SOURCE 3

At the debate on women's suffrage, Mrs Maconochie spoke against the extension of the franchise to women. Mrs Maconochie was opposed to the suffrage because there were too many women to make it safe. There were 1,300,000 more women than men in the country.

Reported in the *East Grinstead Observer* on 3 June 1911.

SOURCE 4

SOME REASONS WHY WORKING WOMEN WANT THE VOTE

Because as long as women cannot vote for Members of Parliament they are not asked what they want, and they are treated like children who do not know what is good or what is bad for them.

Because laws are made which specifically affect women's work and the work of their children.

Because the way to help women is to give them the means of helping themselves.

From a pamphlet published by the National Union of Women's Suffrage Societies (NUWSS) in 1913.

Question Time

1 Study the sources.
a What arguments were used in favour of giving the vote to women?
b What arguments were used against giving the vote to women? Make a chart listing the arguments in note form from each source under the two headings 'For' and 'Against'.

2 In pairs, choose one of the following people, and decide whether you think they would be in favour of women's suffrage or against it. Then hold a conversation with another pair, explaining the views of your character, while listening to the views of their character.
• Queen Victoria
• a governess in a gentleman's home
• a nurse in one of the London hospitals
• the owner of a woollen mill in Leeds with a large workforce of men and women
• a captain in the army
• a farmer in Norfolk

WHAT METHODS DID THE CAMPAIGNERS USE?

Those who favoured votes for women did not agree on the methods that should be used. Some believed that peaceful methods should be used. Some believed in direct action, such as picketing MPs and deliberately breaking the law. Some believed that direct action was not enough and used militant action, including violence, to try and achieve the vote.

Since the 1860s women and men across Britain had been campaigning for political equality for women. They gave talks, wrote pamphlets, newspaper articles and collected signatures for petitions that were presented to parliament. Asking for votes for women was unpopular and great courage was needed. For example, it was still very unusual for women to speak at public meetings. Speakers were shouted at and had things thrown at them.

Suffragists

In 1897 Millicent Fawcett became leader of the National Union of Women's Suffrage Societies (NUWSS) which united local suffrage groups from all over Britain. Their methods were peaceful. They produced a journal called *The Common Cause*, made speeches and presented petitions to Parliament.

From 1907 they had the support of the Artists Suffrage League which designed symbols and banners for the group. They adopted red, white and green as their colours, wearing the colours on badges, hats and on their banners. By 1914 the NUWSS was the largest suffrage organisation.

Suffragettes

In 1903 Emmeline Pankhurst founded the Women's Social and Political Union with the motto 'Deeds not Words'. Like the NUWSS, the WSPU also used artists to support their campaign and adopted purple, white and green as their colours. Newspapers did not often report on Suffragette meetings and often refused to publish articles and letters that supported votes for women. In 1905, therefore, the Suffragettes decided to try and get greater publicity by using violence.

> ## SOURCE 5
>
> *The Suffragette is the militant lady who attempts by forcible means to interview Cabinet Ministers and Members of Parliament, and for whose safety large bodies of police are called out. They prefer a short rest in one of His Majesty's 'homes of seclusion' to the quiet domesticity of their own fireside, but as a rule they only try the experiment once.*
>
> *The Suffragist is a much quieter lady. She does not believe in the tactics of her sister, the warlike Suffragette, but is content to urge her claims for a vote simply by her own persuasive speaking.*
>
> From the *South London Press*, March 1908.

SOURCE 6

This image appeared on the cover of the NUWSS pamphlet published in 1914.

NATIONAL UNION OF WOMEN'S SUFFRAGE SOCIETIES

6 46 17 16
38 60 23 20 25
34 56 39
22 UNIVERSITY WOMEN'S SOCIETIES
MANCHESTER LONDON SCOTTISH OXFORD BERKS. BUCKS. SURREY. SUSSEX. HANTS. NORTH EAST RIDING WEST RIDING
NORTH WESTERN 25 MIDLANDS EAST NORTH EASTERN
26 WEST LANCS. W.CHESHIRE. N.T WALES.
WEST MIDLANDS
WEST of ENGLAND NORTH EASTERN COUNTIES
18 EASTERN COUNTIES KENT
SOUTH WALES 12
22 SOUTH WESTERN

N.U.W.S.S.

FOUNDED 1867

THE NUWSS CONSISTS OF 449 SOCIETIES UNITED INTO 16 FEDERATIONS THE LONDON SOCIETY & UNIVERSITY WOMEN'S SOCIETIES.

In 1906, the Liberal Party won a large majority at the general election. It seemed at first as though this government might give votes to women, and the militant campaign was called off for a brief period. When this did not happen, the militant campaign continued. Windows of important buildings were smashed, reservoir water was dyed purple, pillar boxes were set on fire and the property of important people was burnt. Some Suffragettes chained themselves to railings of public buildings and made false emergency calls.

The government responded by arresting and imprisoning Suffragettes who used violence in their campaign. Suffragettes in prison claimed to be political prisoners and demanded to be treated differently. Their most famous form of protest was the hunger strike. At first hunger strikers were released. The government did not want them to die and become martyrs.

Hunger strikes and force-feeding

Many imprisoned suffragettes went on hunger strike, hoping to be released. But the government did not want to release so many suffragettes and in 1909 responded to the hunger strikers by force-feeding them. This was a painful and humiliating experience carried out against the will of the prisoners. The women were treated violently and with little regard for their health. In 1910 Emmeline Pankhurst, who endured ten hunger strikes, again called off militant action by Suffragettes. This was in response to the government's proposal to consider giving votes to women. However, when the bill failed to be read in Parliament, the militant campaign began again. Suffragettes smashed windows across central London. Many were imprisoned and went on a hunger strikes.

Question Time

❶ What can you learn from Source 6 about the suffrage movement in England and Wales?

❷ Why do you think the artist who designed this image has used an oak tree and an acorn?

❸ What message was the WSPU sending out with their motto 'Deeds not Words'?

❹ Force-feeding of hunger strikers won support for the Suffragettes. Why do you think this was the case?

Cat and Mouse Act

This time the government changed its tactics. The 'Cat and Mouse Act' was rushed through by the government in 1913 to deal with the problem of the women's hunger strikes in prison. The prisoners who became too weak to stay in prison were released, but once they had recovered their strength they could be re-arrested without any further cause and taken back into prison.

Propaganda

Although the two main suffrage groups had different methods, both used propaganda as part of their tactics. The poster in Source 7 'Forcible Feeding in Prison' was produced in 1910 on the front cover of the WSPU journal *Votes for Women*. It shows what the Suffragettes thought of force feeding.

What does it mean?

Propaganda
Information, true or false, put out to spread a particular opinion or gain support for a cause.

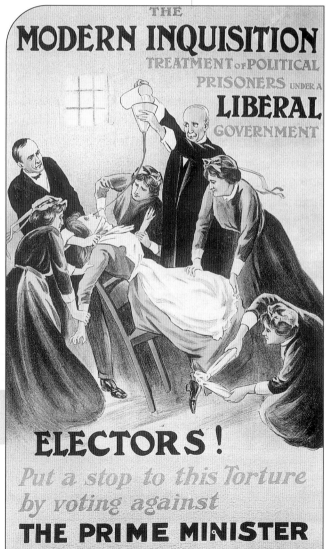

SOURCE 7

A 1910 front cover of the WSPU journal, *Votes for Women*.

Question Time

1. Look at Source 7. What messages are being sent by the source about the Liberal government?

2. Source 7 was drawn by 'A. Patriot'. Why do you think the artist chose to use this name?

3. Why do you think the government rushed through the Cat and Mouse Act in 1913?

4. Why do you think the Act of 1913 became known as the 'Cat and Mouse Act'?

Activity Time

Draw a timeline from 1895-1914. Give it the title: 'How people campaigned for votes for women'. Make two columns called 'Methods of the NUWSS' and 'Methods of the WSPU'. Fill in the columns with as much information as you can. Then add a third column to show if/when methods changed, how they changed, and explain why.

	Methods of the NUWSS	Methods of the WSPU	Change of Methods
1895			
1900			
1905			
1910			
1914			

WHY DID WOMEN GAIN THE VOTE IN 1918 AND NOT BEFORE?

By the summer of 1914 there were signs that the government's opposition to votes for women was weakening. It seemed likely that women's suffrage would be debated in the House of Commons again. However, in 1914 the First World War began, and the WSPU agreed to stop its militant activities, after the release of Suffragettes from prison, and throw their energies into war work.

Women and the war

During the war the contribution of women was crucial. Outside the home, women were needed to do the work traditionally done by the men who were away at the war, such as work on the railways, and on the land as farm workers. They also undertook war work, like making weapons in the munitions factories and nursing. Inside the home, women's work was vital, as feeding their families and caring for children became more difficult with wartime food shortages. Women were raising the next generation at a time when the existing generation of young men was being slaughtered on the battlefields. Most members of the WSPU and NUWSS joined with millions of other women to support the war effort.

The importance of the role of women can be seen in the amount of propaganda directed at them. Happy, smiling women were shown in films, newspapers and posters contributing to the war effort and helping to make Britain a country worth fighting for. See Source 4, for example.

Vera Brittain

Women, like Vera Brittain, have recalled the way that the war dramatically changed their lives. Vera was from a middle class family and had been chaperoned everywhere before the war. During the war she worked as a nurse in the Voluntary Aid Detachment (VAD), travelling alone and mixing with people from different social groups. When her father asked her to come home, she no longer wanted that restricted life (see Source 1).

SOURCE 2

During the war men and women were so thrown into daily contact that ideas about the sexes changed. Chaperons (companions) disappeared, and so did the delicate ignorance in which many girls were kept. Many girls used language that would have shocked their mothers; many started to wear cosmetics; smoking became widespread and women bought drinks in public houses. Young girls were gripped by 'khaki fever'. By the end of the war the illegitimacy rate had increased by 30 per cent.

Louise Black remembers the war years.

SOURCE 1

Nothing – beyond sheer necessity – would induce me to stop doing what I am doing now, and I should never respect myself again if I allowed a few slight hardships to make me give up what is the finest work any girl can do now. I do not agree that my place is at home doing nothing, for I consider that the place now of anyone who is young and capable is where the work that is needed is to be done.

From *Testament of Youth*, by Vera Brittain, written in 1933 recalling the war years.

SOURCE 3

A lotion distributed to the women counteracted the effect of TNT poisoning. The pale lemon colour and deep gold of the workers skin soon returned to their normal appearance. However, toxic poisoning could cause death ... There was also the danger of explosions. Women nevertheless sought munitions work, partly because the pay was higher, partly because the alternatives available were worse and partly because there was a strong feeling that it was the right thing to be doing for the war effort.

From a book by Sheila Rowbotham, written in 1999, describing the dangers for women working in the munitions industry.

SOURCE 4

A poster urging women to enrol as munitions workers.

Question Time

❶ Why do you think so much propaganda was directed at women? Give as many reasons as you can.

❷ From the text and the sources find different ways that women contributed to the war. Show your findings on a poster that has the title 'How women helped to win the war!'

❸ Jane Cox, a munitions worker, had this to say about how the war changed women: 'It taught women to stand on their own feet. It was the turning point for women'. Find evidence from this section that supports what Jane said.

❹ During the First World War women were praised for behaviour that was criticised before 1914. Why do you think there was this change in attitudes?

ON HER THEIR LIVES DEPEND

WOMEN MUNITION WORKERS

Enrol at once

CLARKE & SHERWELL, LTD., PRINTERS, LONDON

MINISTRY OF MUNITIONS

78

VOTES FOR WOMEN!

Before the war ended the government had found time to introduce a Parliamentary Reform Bill, and the House of Commons voted for it by 341 to 62. This Act came into force in February 1918 and it gave the vote to:

- all men over the age of 21

- women over the age of 30 who
  - were householders, or the wives of householders
  - paid rent of £5 or over
  - were graduates (there were not many at this time).

The part played by women during the war had convinced most people who had opposed women's suffrage up to that time that women should have the vote. Ten years later, when it was seen that giving some women the vote had not had the terrible consequences that some anti-suffrage MPs had feared, the Equal Franchise Act of 1928 was passed. This Act gave women the vote on the same terms as men – all women over the age of 21 had the vote. It was over 130 years since Mary Wollstonecraft had first voiced her demands for equal political rights for men and women.

SOURCE 5

I have seen great days, but this is the greatest. I remember when we started 21 years ago ... I never believed that equal votes would come in my lifetime. But when an impossible dream comes true, we must go on to another. The true unity of men and women is one such dream.'

Charlotte Despard, from a speech she made in 1919, when she was 83.

SOURCE 6

A cartoon from *Punch* in 1928.

AT LAST!

Question Time

① The Act of 1918 changed the voting system for men, and introduced votes for women for the first time.

a What differences were there between men and women's suffrage in 1918?

b Why do you think there were these differences?

② How did the First World War help to change attitudes towards women?

WHY DIDN'T WOMEN GET THE VOTE AT THE SAME TIME AS MEN?

Activity Time

You now need to use all your learning from this unit to answer the big question: Why didn't women get the vote at the same time as men?

You will need to
- Select information from the Unit that answers the question.
- Organise your ideas in a way that answers the question.
- Use evidence to support your arguments and ideas about why women's suffrage took so long.

Think about the following areas:
- Nineteenth century beliefs about what sort of person should vote.
- Nineteenth century beliefs about women.
- When, why and how beliefs about voting changed.
- When, why and how beliefs about women changed.

Now you can begin to plan your essay.

Unit 17: Divided Ireland – why has it been so hard to achieve peace in Ireland?

At the end of the twentieth century, the island of Ireland was two separate parts: Northern Ireland, part of the United Kingdom, and the Republic of Ireland, a separate and independent country. The whole of Ireland was once one country, which, largely by force, gradually became part of the United Kingdom. The division into north and south happened in 1922 and was accompanied by much bitterness, hatred, violence and death, known as 'The Troubles'.

The twentieth century 'Troubles' in Northern Ireland were a result of deep divisions amongst the Irish people. The population was divided by:

- **Religion** Protestants and Catholics lived in separate communities.
- **Politics** Most Protestants were Unionists who wanted Northern Ireland to stay part of the United Kingdom. Most Catholics were Nationalists, who wanted Northern Ireland to become part of the Republic of Ireland.
- **History** Both Catholics and Protestants held fiercely to traditions that went back hundreds of years.

Irish people, when they met strangers, could tell immediately whether they were Catholics or Protestants. They could tell by their accents, their jobs and by where they lived.

This map shows how Ireland was divided in 1922.

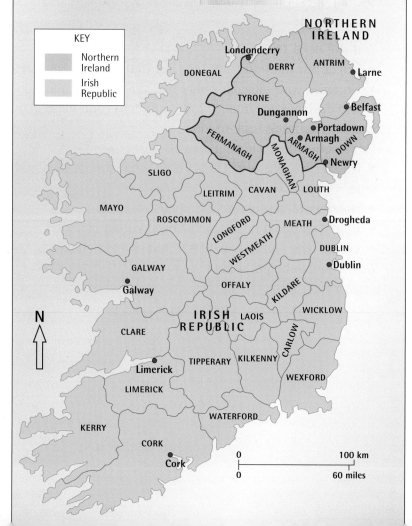

KEY

Northern Ireland

Irish Republic

NORTHERN IRELAND

Londonderry
DONEGAL
DERRY
ANTRIM
Larne
TYRONE
Dungannon
Belfast
FERMANAGH
Portadown
Armagh
ARMAGH
DOWN
MONAGHAN
Newry
SLIGO
LEITRIM
CAVAN
LOUTH
MAYO
ROSCOMMON
LONGFORD
MEATH
Drogheda
WESTMEATH
DUBLIN
GALWAY
OFFALY
Dublin
Galway
KILDARE
WICKLOW
IRISH REPUBLIC
LAOIS
CLARE
CARLOW
TIPPERARY
KILKENNY
Limerick
WEXFORD
LIMERICK
WATERFORD
KERRY
CORK
Cork

N

0   100 km

0   60 miles

In Northern Ireland in the 1970s and 80s, people began expressing their feelings and their loyalties by painting huge murals on the sides of buildings. Here are two of these wall paintings, one by Protestants and one by Catholics.

SOURCE 1

Wall paintings in Northern Ireland, by Protestants (right) and by Catholics (below).

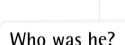

Who was he?

Cuchulainn

In ancient Irish folk stories, Cuchulainn, the son of a Celtic god called Lugh, was renowned for his great strength and heroic deeds. He defended Ulster against Medh, Queen of Connacht, and singlehandedly defeated her invading army. Stories tell of his bravery being so great that he defended the whole of Ireland from attack by evil forces, within and without.

Question Time

1 Look carefully at the two wall paintings (Source 1) Which one was painted by Unionists and which by Nationalists? What historical clues can you pick up that helped you make up your mind?

2 Read the story of the Irish hero Cuchulainn. Cuchulainn has appeared on both Nationalist and Unionist wall paintings. How could he be a hero to both sides?

WHY IS THE PAST SO IMPORTANT TO SOME PEOPLE IN IRELAND?

One of the problems with history is that you can look at it in many ways. It's rather like watching a football match: we're all at the match, but looking at it from different parts of the ground and so see things differently. One person may define an armed man as a terrorist, another as a freedom fighter. It all depends on where you're standing. Nowhere is this more true than in Ireland. To begin to understand we're going to look at Ireland in the seventeenth century.

WHAT WERE THE FLASH POINTS IN SEVENTEENTH CENTURY IRELAND?

The Plantation of Ulster 1607

In 1607, advisers of James I had what they thought was a brilliant idea to maintain control over the warlike Irish. When Elizabeth was queen, her troops had fiercely put down a rebellion against English authority by the Catholic Earls of Tyrone and Tyrconnel, and England had eventually gained control of the whole of Ireland. This was important to Elizabeth and her government, as an unruly, rebellious, Catholic Ireland close to Protestant England might be a temptation to England's enemies, particularly the Catholic Spanish and their Armada.

The two Earls fled to Europe, and James and his advisers decided that the only way to prevent further Irish rebellions, which might be encouraged by England's enemies, was to send Protestants to live there. In this way, the country would become controlled, peaceful, prosperous and Protestant. That was the theory, anyway! The English government seized the lands of the Earls of Tyrone and Tyrconnel, sacked the Irish landlords and put Protestants in their place. These new, 'planted' Protestant landlords arranged for more Protestants to go over from Scotland and England to live and to farm. But the land they were farming was land that had been seized from Irish Catholics. The Irish Catholics deeply resented this Ulster 'Plantation' and vowed to take revenge.

The massacre at Portadown, 1641

In 1640, Protestants dominated the English Parliament. Charles I, whom many people believed was a secret Catholic, had been forced to give in to many of Parliament's demands. The Catholics in Ireland were afraid that the English Protestant Parliament would pass anti-Catholic laws. Matters came to a head in 1641 in Portadown, when

> ## What is it?
>
> **Ulster**
> The most northerly of the four original ancient provinces of Ireland, made up of nine counties.

the Catholics rebelled and massacred around 3000 Protestant settlers there and in the surrounding countryside. Charles asked Parliament for money to raise an army. He said he wanted to use it to put down the Irish rebels. But Parliament was afraid that Charles would use this army against his enemies in England and not against the Catholic Irish. An MP, John Pym, demanded that Parliament control any army sent to Ireland.

Cromwell in Ireland

Oliver Cromwell and many Protestants believed that Charles I was a secret Catholic and that he and his openly Catholic wife, Henrietta Maria, were behind the massacre of Protestants at Portadown in 1641. They became even more certain when, after Charles' execution, the Irish Catholics and Irish Royalists joined together in a rebellion against Parliamentary rule. Cromwell and Parliament were determined to teach the Irish Catholics a lesson. A Parliamentary army had defeated the Catholic forces before Cromwell arrived in Ireland. But Cromwell was determined to have his revenge.

The massacre at Drogheda, 1649

Cromwell began killing Catholics. The worst of these massacres happened at Drogheda, north of Dublin. There, he laid siege to the town, which was defended by English Protestants opposed to Cromwell as well as Irish Catholics. They were no match for Cromwell's 12,000-strong army and siege weapons. These weapons blasted two holes in the town walls and Cromwell, on the second attempt, led his men on foot through them. The Parliamentary forces quickly overran the town. Cromwell ordered 'any that are in arms' to be killed. Dismayed and alarmed, his soldiers let many of their prisoners escape. The next day, in cold blood, Cromwell's troops massacred 3500 people – soldiers, clergy, women and children.

SOURCE 1

This picture of Catholics murdering Protestant settlers was drawn in 1641. It was probably a propaganda picture, designed to convince English people that Irish Catholics were planning to massacre all the Protestants in Ireland.

Driuinge Men Women & children by hund: reds vpon Briges & casting them into Riuers, who drowned not were killed with poles & shot with muskets.

Question Time

❶ Draw up a data capture sheet, with the headings 'Where?' 'When?' 'Who was killed?' 'Who did the killing?' 'Why?' Fill in one sheet for Portadown and another sheet Drogheda.

❷ Think back to the wall paintings and remember how twentieth-century Protestants and Catholics used the past to support their own view.

a Under the data capture sheet for Portadown, write an answer to 'What might twentieth-century Nationalists say about this event?'

b Under the data capture sheet for Drogheda, write an answer to 'What might twentieth-century Unionists say about this event?

FAST FORWARD!

We are now going to look at Ireland in the twentieth century.
But quite a lot happened between 1649 and 1900!

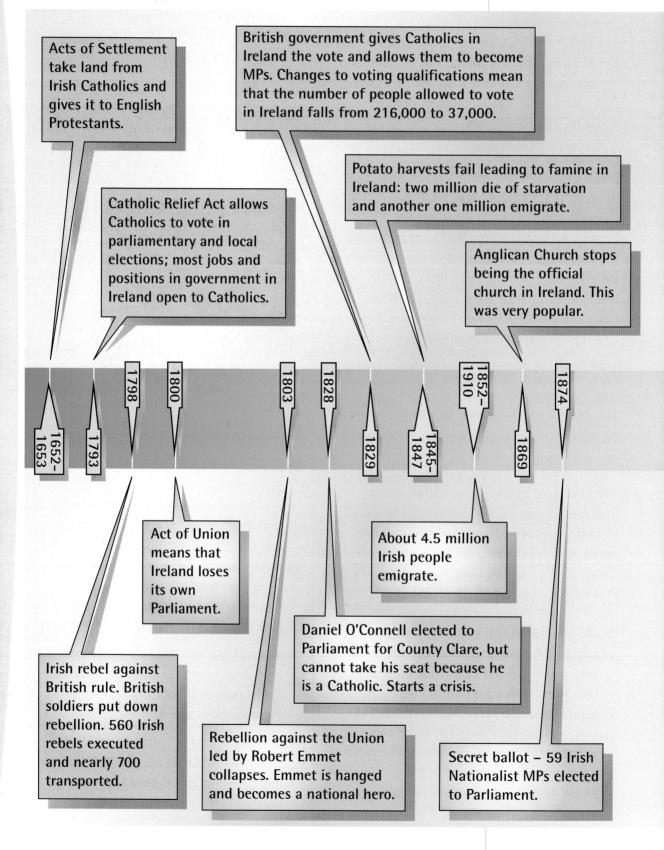

Acts of Settlement take land from Irish Catholics and gives it to English Protestants.

British government gives Catholics in Ireland the vote and allows them to become MPs. Changes to voting qualifications mean that the number of people allowed to vote in Ireland falls from 216,000 to 37,000.

Potato harvests fail leading to famine in Ireland: two million die of starvation and another one million emigrate.

Catholic Relief Act allows Catholics to vote in parliamentary and local elections; most jobs and positions in government in Ireland open to Catholics.

Anglican Church stops being the official church in Ireland. This was very popular.

1798   1800   1803   1828   1852–1910   1874

1652–1653   1793   1829   1845–1847   1869

Act of Union means that Ireland loses its own Parliament.

About 4.5 million Irish people emigrate.

Daniel O'Connell elected to Parliament for County Clare, but cannot take his seat because he is a Catholic. Starts a crisis.

Irish rebel against British rule. British soldiers put down rebellion. 560 Irish rebels executed and nearly 700 transported.

Rebellion against the Union led by Robert Emmet collapses. Emmet is hanged and becomes a national hero.

Secret ballot – 59 Irish Nationalist MPs elected to Parliament.

Charles Stewart Parnell elected to Parliament and becomes the 'uncrowned King of Ireland'. He is the leader of the Land League Campaign, fighting for fairer rents and a more secure living for the peasants. He is also the leader of the campaign to obstruct Parliament business in order to promote the idea that Ireland should rule itself. This idea was called 'Home Rule'.

Parnell does a deal with the British government: he agrees to support them in return for more protection for Irish tenants.

Chief Secretary for Ireland, appointed by the government, and his deputy murdered in Phoenix Park, Dublin.

General Elections end with Irish Nationalist MPs holding balance of power.

Third Home Rule Bill introduced.

Third Reform Act increases Irish voters by four times.

First Home Rule Bill fails in the House of Commons.

1875

1879–1882

1881

1882

1884

1885

1886

1893

1903

1910

1912

Irish Land Act gives some protection to tenants.

Nationalist MPs from Ireland hold the balance between the parties in the House of Commons. The government cannot work without their support.

British government helps Irish tenants buy their land.

Agricultural depression in Ireland and 'Land War' breaks out in the form of a massive protest against the fact that tenant farmers (who worked, but did not own the land) were being turned off their farms.

Prime Minister Gladstone announces that he supports Home Rule. This would end the Act of Union and set up an independent Parliament for the whole of Ireland in Dublin.

Second Home Rule Bill gets through Commons, but is defeated in the Lords.

WHY WAS IRELAND PARTITIONED?

'Partition' means 'split in two' and that is just what happened to Ireland in 1922. Like any event in history, there is no simple answer to why this happened nor any answers to why it happened in the way it did. We can look at the sequence of events leading up to partition and then try to work out how the reactions of Irish Nationalists, Irish Unionists and the British Government determined the next step. Remember, Irish Nationalists were Republicans, usually Catholic, who wanted a free and independent Ireland. Irish Unionists were Irish people, usually Protestants, who wanted to keep the Union with Britain.

WHAT WERE THE EVENTS LEADING UP TO THE DECISION TO PARTITION IRELAND?

- The Home Rule Act was due to become law in September 1914.
- The First World War breaks out in August 1914 and the government suspends the Home Rule Act until the war ends. Hundreds of thousands of Catholic and Protestant Irishmen join the British army to fight Germany.
- Two extreme Nationalist groups, Sinn Fein and the Irish Republican Brotherhood, form the Irish Volunteers who rebel against the British.
- On Easter Monday 1916 the Irish Volunteers take control of 14 key points in Dublin and fire on British troops. In five days of street fighting, 60 Volunteers, 150 British troops and 300 ordinary people were killed.
- In the 1918 General Election, Sinn Fein wins 73 of the 105 Irish seats. Led by Eamon De Valera, Sinn Fein MPs refuse to take their seats and set up their own parliament, the Dail Eireann, in Dublin. This parliament demands independence for Ireland.
- The Irish Volunteers reform as the Irish Republican Army (the IRA).
- 1919-22, Ireland is immersed in war between the IRA and demobbed British soldiers, called the 'Black and Tans', and hundreds are killed.
- In December 1921, the British Government agreed to the Anglo-Irish treaty which divided Ireland between British Ulster in the north and the independent Irish Free State in the south.

What does it mean?

Demobbed is short for *demobilised*, meaning the discharge of an individual serviceman from the army, navy or air force.

Question Time

❶ Read through these events carefully. For each event, work out what the Unionist reaction and the Nationalist reaction would have been (Remember, the Unionists wanted to stay united with Britain and the Nationalists wanted independence. They were now calling themselves Republicans.)

❷ In August 1916, Roger Casement was hanged in London as a traitor. Irish Republicans said he was a hero. Find out why!

WHY DID DAVID LLOYD GEORGE DECIDE THAT PARTITION WAS THE ONLY SOLUTION?

The Dail Eireann

In the General Election of 1918, Sinn Fein (who wanted a free and independent Ireland) won 73 of the 105 Irish seats and, as you read, refused to take up their seats in the House of Commons. Instead, they set up an alternative parliament – the Dail Eireann – in Dublin. But 26 Unionists (who wanted Ireland to stay in the United Kingdom) were also elected to the House of Commons and 23 of these represented Ulster constituencies. These men did take up their seats in the House of Commons. So you can see immediately that the people who were most likely to argue in the British Parliament for an independent Ireland simply weren't there.

Lloyd George suggests two parliaments

The Irish Dail wanted the whole island of Ireland to become a republic. It began by simply not co-operating with the British administration of Ireland. By the end of 1919, Prime Minister David Lloyd George thought he had the answer to the problem. He put forward a Government of Ireland Bill which proposed two parliaments for Ireland, with the suggestion that they could later be joined together. One parliament was to be in Dublin the other in Belfast. These proposals gave the Dublin parliament very few powers and so were of little interest to Sinn Fein. The Unionists in the House of Commons were prepared to accept the bill, but with misgivings. This was because the proposal was that six counties, Antrim, Armagh, Derry, Down, Fermanagh and Tyrone should make up the new Ulster, with a Parliament in Belfast. But the historic Ulster had contained nine counties; these six, plus Monaghan, Cavan and Donegal. Many Unionists were unhappy that these three counties would be 'given' to southern Ireland.

The IRA

Meanwhile, the IRA abandoned the Dail's policy of non co-operation in favour of more direct tactics. By 1920, there was full-scale war in Ireland between the IRA and the British. At first, the main British force was the Royal Irish Constabulary, but recently demobbed soldiers, the 'Black and Tans', quickly reinforced them. These men had just finished fighting in the First World War, and were hardened soldiers. They wore khaki uniforms and black police helmets and belts, which is why they were nicknamed 'Black and Tans'. The war was terrible, with atrocities committed by both sides. However, the treatment of the Irish by the Black and Tans, who specialised in burning whole towns and villages so leaving hundreds of families homeless, drove more and more people to support the IRA.

88

SOURCE 1

This row of houses in Balbriggan was burnt by the Black and Tans in 1921.

SOURCE 2

These burnt out railway wagons were the result of an attack by the Dublin brigade of the IRA in July 1920.

SOURCE 3

A solid Protestant Ulster will be a prop in Ireland to the Empire, without which the whole naval strength of England would be jeopardised. A Protestant and loyal Ulster would be an invaluable jumping off point for the British Navy and Army if it were found necessary to use them in case of serious trouble in Ireland or elsewhere. This is sufficient justification for supporting the six-county policy.

A Protestant man living in Ulster explains why he wants to keep Ulster independent from Dublin. He wrote this in a leaflet issued in April 1920.

SOURCE 4

Politically, we shall continue to deny the right, and to combat the exercise, of any foreign authority in Ireland. In particular, we shall refuse to admit that our country may be carved up and partitioned by such an authority.

A Sinn Fein leader explains why he is opposed to the partition of Ireland. Eamon De Valera, in an interview, 23 July 1923.

Question Time

❶ Why did David Lloyd George decide to partition Ireland? Use the information in this section and Sources 1-4 in your answer.

❷ Look at the map below and the text on page 90. Why do you think they drew the partition line where they did?

❸ Working in groups, write four headings on a large sheet of paper: 1 Why Lloyd George had to do something 2 Why Lloyd George couldn't ignore the Nationalists' claim to independence 3 Why Lloyd George couldn't ignore the Unionists' claim to union with Britain 4 Our views – did he have a choice? Sort the information in this section, including the sources, under these headings. Compare what you have done with other groups in your class.

❹ Now try to reach a conclusion to the question 'Did partition stand a chance?'

This map shows the proportion of Catholics and Protestants in the counties and large towns of Ulster in 1926. This is the year in which a population survey was undertaken, and is the closest survey to 1922, the year of partition.

KEY
- Boundary of Ulster
- Boundary of Northern Ireland
- County boundary
- ● County town
- △ Protestants
- ▲ Catholics
- △ Other religion

Percentage of population **Total NORTHERN IRELAND**

Percentage of population **Total ULSTER**

HOW WAS THE ANGLO-IRISH TREATY DECIDED?

The growing number of atrocities led to demands from the British public for a truce. In June 1921, King George V visited the parliament in Belfast and appealed to all Irish people to forgive and forget, and begin a new era of peace. On 11 July 1921 the fighting between the IRA and the British army stopped. Eamon De Valera, who was the president of the Dail Eireann, met British Prime Minister David Lloyd George to talk about a settlement. Lloyd George wanted the whole of Ireland to have Home Rule, but as a dominion, which meant that Britain still held overall control of things like Ireland's foreign policy. De Valera wanted a completely independent Ireland. After a lot of arguing, a treaty was finally signed on 6 December 1921 only after the British had said that if the Irish didn't agree to their terms, the fighting would begin again. So what were these terms? Ireland was to become a Free State (later called Eire), but six of the original nine counties of Ulster (later called Northern Ireland) would remain part of the UK. Not surprisingly, the Irish Dail was not at all keen on this arrangement. They wanted the whole of Ireland to be free and independent. But finally, on 7 January 1922, the Dail accepted the Treaty by 64 votes to 57.

DID ULSTER AND THE IRISH FREE STATE DEVELOP DIFFERENTLY AFTER 1922?

Yes, they did. Both parts of Ireland faced a range of economic, political and social problems that their governments tackled in different ways. These were complicated by religious differences between and within the Irish Free State and the new Ulster.

WHAT HAPPENED IN THE IRISH FREE STATE?

- An economic slump in the 1920s meant hard times for the people of Eire. The government did not, for example, have the money to improve conditions in the slums of Dublin.
- De Valera became Prime Minister of the Irish Free State in 1932, and changed the country's name to Eire. But the Irish Constitution still laid claim to the whole of Ireland.
- Thousands of Irish people emigrated every year because living conditions in Ireland were so poor. By the end of the 1920s, nearly half the people born in Ireland were living overseas.
- Gaelic became the official language was used for all business in government, the police and the law courts.

- The Catholic Church became the official church. This meant that contraception and divorce were forbidden. The Catholic Church controlled education.
- Eire remained neutral in the Second World War (1939–45).

WHAT HAPPENED IN ULSTER?

- The six counties of Ulster that formed Northern Ireland made up the most prosperous part of Ireland because they had more industry. Since they were united with Britain, they stayed reasonably prosperous in the economic slumps of the 1920s and 1930s.
- Troops from Northern Ireland fought alongside the troops from the rest of Britain in the Second World War.
- The link with Britain benefited the people in Northern Ireland in many ways. For example, in the 1940s and 1950s, the welfare state set up by the British government to help everybody with pensions, education and medical treatment extended to Northern Ireland. Contraception and abortion became legal in Northern Ireland at the same time as in the rest of Britain.
- The assembly (parliament) of Northern Ireland that met in Stormont Castle was dominated by Protestants. Because of this the police force, the Royal Ulster Constabulary (RUC), was also dominated by Protestants. Catholics did not have the same civil rights as Protestants. They were, for example, discriminated against in housing and in jobs.

Activity Time

Working in pairs with a large outline map of Ireland show how the new Ulster and the Irish Free State developed differently. You can use pictograms, information boxes – whatever will make the map informative and lively.

What does it mean?

Discrimination against Catholics
- In County Fermanagh there were 75 school bus drivers and only 7 of these were Catholic.
- The Belfast shipyard employed 10,000 workers. Only 400 were Catholics.
- Fermanagh County Council built 1589 council houses between 1945 and 1969, and 1021 of them went to Protestants.
- In Londonderry, the heads of all City Council departments were Protestant.

WHY WERE THERE VIOLENT PROTESTS IN NORTHERN IRELAND IN 1968–9?

The Protestant Unionists in Northern Ireland could have governed in the interests of both Protestants and Catholics. They chose not to, and as a result, the divisions between Catholics and Protestants became deeper and deeper. Northern Ireland gradually became a place of suspicion, mistrust and fear.

CIVIL RIGHTS FOR ALL

Civil rights are those freedoms that people living in a democratic society believe they should be entitled to have as a right. These include the right to vote, the right to free speech, the right to freedom of religion, the right to be free from discrimination. The people of Northern Ireland, particularly the Catholics, grew increasingly angry that Protestants and Catholics did not have equal civil rights.

In 1967, Catholics in Northern Ireland set up the Northern Ireland Civil Rights Association (NICRA) Their aims were:

- Equal voting rights for Catholics and Protestants.
- An end to the system that enabled Protestants to dominate local councils.
- An end to discrimination against Catholics by local councils.
- Fair distribution of council houses between Catholics and Protestants.
- An end to the Special Powers Act, which gave the RUC almost unlimited powers in an emergency.

LONDONDERRY, 5 OCTOBER 1968

Civil rights supporters arranged a march through the Protestant area of Londonderry on 5 October 1968. Marching is a traditional Irish way for Protestants and Catholics separately to celebrate important dates in their history. Marching was becoming, too, a way for people throughout Western Europe and the USA to demonstrate their feelings on a range of subjects. But many Protestants felt threatened by the civil rights movement; they could not believe that the Catholic demands were genuinely peaceful, particularly when some of the civil rights demonstrators were IRA supporters. The Northern Irish Government in Stormont, dominated by Protestants, banned the march. The civil rights supporters took no notice of the ban and started marching. Eamon McCann, who took part in the march, tells what happened next in Source 1.

> ## SOURCE 1
>
> *Our route was blocked by a cordon of police and tenders drawn up across the road about three hundred yards from the starting point. We marched into the police cordon, but failed to force a way through. Gerry Fitt's head was bloodied by the first baton blow of the day. We noticed that another police cordon had moved in from the rear and cut us off from behind. There were no exits from Duke Street in the stretch between the two cordons which moved simultaneously on the crowd. Men, women and children were clubbed to the ground. People were fleeing down the street from the front cordon and up the street from the rear cordon, crashing into one another, stumbling over one another, huddling in doorways, some screaming. A water cannon – the first we had ever seen – appeared. About a hundred had to go to hospital for treatment.*
>
> **Eamon McCann records his experiences in his book *War and an Irish Town*.**

SOURCE 2

Police begin a baton charge in Duke Street, Londonderry, on 5 October 1968.

SOURCE 3

Street fighting broke out again in Londonderry tonight (Sunday) and 20 more people were taken to hospital bringing the total injured since yesterday afternoon (Saturday) to 96.

About 800 people surged up a street leading to one of the city gates but were forced back by baton charges by police in steel helmets. The crowds regrouped and running battles broke out.

A petrol bomb, thrown at a passing police Land Rover, missed the vehicle and burned out in the street. Water cannons were brought in to put out other small fires.

Several speakers addressed the crowd but, as it had done before the march started, the people involved ignored appeals from the police to disperse. In the crowd were many placards nailed on to poles and sticks. Poles were smashed and thrown at the police.

Part of a report in *The Times* newspaper, 7 October 1968.

Question Time

❶ Which gives you the better idea of what happened in Duke Street, Londonderry, on 5 October 1968 – the extract from Eamon McCann's book (Source 1) or the photograph (Source 2)?

❷ Which source do you think is the more reliable, Eamon McCann's book or the photograph? Why?

❸ Now read Source 3, an extract from a newspaper. In what ways does this disagree with what is written in Source 1? Why do you think there is this disagreement?

❹ Does Source 2, the photograph, support what is written in Source 1 or Source 3? Explain your answer.

❺ Use the information in this section to explain why what started as a peaceful march ended so violently.

ONE STEP FORWARD?

The Prime Minister of Northern Ireland in 1968, Terence O'Neill, tried to introduce the sort of reforms the civil rights movement wanted. But all the time he had to face the suspicion, fear and opposition of his own party, the Protestant Unionists. The Londonderry march gave him just the lever he wanted. After high-level talks with the British Prime Minister, Harold Wilson, and the Home Secretary, James Callaghan, he announced five reforms:

- Local councils were to allocate their houses fairly, on a basis that took no account of religion.
- An Ombudsman, a sort of referee who would hear grievances from both sides, was appointed.
- The Londonderry Borough Council was replaced by a Development Commission.
- All local government was to be reformed by 1971.
- Parts of the Special Powers Act, which gave the RUC such enormous powers, were to be withdrawn when this could be done 'without undue hazard'.

Catholics were encouraged by these reforms, though many Protestants were outraged and afraid. They could see their dominant position slipping away and were afraid of Catholic reprisals. Civil rights workers tried to appeal to both Catholics and Protestants, but in vain. Catholics flocked to join the civil rights movement, with a few Protestants joining them. Protestant resistance to change hardened, as did their hostility to Catholics.

THE BATTLE OF BURNTOLLET BRIDGE, 4 JANUARY 1969

Londonderry people formed the Derry Citizens' Action Committee and vowed they would work for full civil rights. Londonderry became the centre of discontent and demands. In January 1969, the People's Democracy, a movement started by students from Queen's University, Belfast, organised a three-day march from Belfast to Londonderry to demand full civil rights for everyone in Ulster. The march began peacefully, but trouble was brewing elsewhere. On 3 January 1969, Ian Paisley held a religious meeting in the Londonderry Guildhall. He was an extreme Protestant minister and leader, and he urged Protestants to hold to their faith and defend Protestantism against the 'evils' of Catholicism. Windows were smashed and fighting broke out. On 4 January, when the civil rights marchers (most of whom were Catholic) arrived at a little place called Burntollet, where they had to cross a narrow bridge, the Protestants were waiting for them.

SOURCE 4

And then we came to Burntollet Bridge, and from lanes at each side of the road a curtain of bricks and boulders and bottles brought the march to a halt. From the lanes burst hordes of screaming people wielding planks of wood, bottles, laths, iron bars, crowbars, cudgels studded with nails, and they waded into the march beating hell out of everybody ... What had been a march was a shambles. The first few rows had managed to put a spurt on when the attack came, had got through the ambush, and were safely up the road. The rest of us were all over the place. The attackers were beating marchers into the ditches, and across the ditches into the river. I saw a young fellow getting a thrashing from four or five Paisleyites, with a policeman looking on.

Bernadette Devlin, who took part in the march when she was a student, describes what happened next. She wrote about the Battle of Burntollet Bridge in her book *The Price of my Soul* which was published in 1969. She was also elected to the British Parliament in 1969.

The violence continued throughout the spring and summer of 1969.

SOURCE 5

The Battle of the Bogside, August 1969. After the annual Protestant Apprentice Boys march in Londonderry, the police (the RUC) fought for control of Bogside, a Catholic part of the city. The residents declared their part of the city 'Free Derry' and flew a republican flag. The police were forced to withdraw.

Northern Ireland was sliding into civil war. The British Government decided it could no longer trust the RUC to keep control fairly and impartially. On 14 August 1969, it sent British troops onto the streets of Belfast and Londonderry to bring an end to the violence.

SOURCE 6

The Downing Street Declaration

1 *The United Kingdom Government reaffirm that Northern Ireland should not cease to be a part of the United Kingdom without the consent of the people of Northern Ireland.*

2 *The United Kingdom Government have ultimate responsibility for the protection of those who live in Northern Ireland when a breakdown of law and order has occurred. In this spirit, the United Kingdom Government responded to the request of the Northern Ireland Government for military assistance in Londonderry and Belfast in order to restore law and order. They emphasise again that troops will be withdrawn when law and order has been restored.*

3 *The United Kingdom Government have welcomed the decisions of the Northern Ireland Government relating to local government ... the allocation of houses ... machinery to consider citizen's grievances ... as demonstrating the determination of the Northern Ireland Government that there shall be full equality of treatment for all citizens.*

This is how the British Prime Minister announced that the British Government would send troops into Northern Ireland. It is called the 'Downing Street Declaration'.

Question Time

1 Why did so few Protestants join the civil rights movement in Ulster?

2 'Bernadette Devlin took part in the civil rights march and so her account of what happened at Burntollet Bridge cannot be trusted.' Explain whether or not you agree with this statement.

3 Read the Downing Street Declaration (Source 6).
How would Catholics be **a** encouraged and **b** worried by what was said?
How would Protestants be **a** encouraged and **b** worried by what was said?

4 Did the British Government have any choice but to send in the troops? Explain your answer.

WERE HUMAN RIGHTS ABUSED IN NORTHERN IRELAND?

In 1948, the United Nations agreed a Declaration of Human Rights which was to be followed by all member nations.

SOURCE 7

1 *When children are born, they are born free and each should be treated in the same way.*

2 *Everyone can claim the following rights, despite: a different sex, a different skin colour, speaking a different language, thinking different things, believing in another religion, owning more or less, being born in another social group, coming from another country.*

3 *You have the right to live, and to live in freedom and safety.*

4 *Nobody has the right to treat you as his/her slave and you should not make anyone your slave.*

5 *Nobody has the right to torture you.*

6 *The law is the same for everyone; it should be applied in the same way to all.*

...

9 *Nobody has the right to put you in prison, or to keep you there, or to send you away from your country unjustly, or without good reason.*

10 *If you go on trial, the trial should be held in public. The people who try you should not let themselves be influenced by others.*

11 *You should be considered innocent until it can be proved that you are guilty. If you are accused of a crime, you should have the right to defend yourself.*

12 *You have the right to ask to be protected if someone tries to harm your good name, enter your house, open your letters, or bother you without good reason.*

13 *You have the right to come and go as you wish within your country. You have the right to leave your country and return to it.*

...

18 *You have the right to profess your religion freely, to change it, and to practice it either on your own or with other people.*

19 *You have the right to think what you want, to say what you like, and nobody should forbid you from doing so. You should be able to share your ideas also, with people from any other country.*

20 *You have the right to organise peaceful meetings or to take part in meetings in a peaceful way. It is wrong to force someone to belong to a group.*

21 *You have the right to take part in your country's political affairs either by belonging to the government yourself or by choosing politicians who have the same ideas as you. Governments should be voted for regularly and voting should be secret. Every adult should have a vote and all votes should be equal.*

A simplified, plain language version of the United Nations Declaration of Human Rights.

British soldiers
patrolling the streets
of Londonderry
in 1970.

Question Time

❶ Read the Declaration of Human
Rights in Source 7. Use the
information in this section to work
out which Human Right was being
infringed by which action in
Northern Ireland in the 1960s. Write
a sentence about each one.

❷ Write a caption for Source 8 that a
Protestant Unionist might have

written. Now write one that a
Catholic Nationalist might have
written.

❸ Look back at your answer to Question
2, above. Given these attitudes, do
you think the people of Northern
Ireland could ever live together
peacefully?

WHY HAS IT BEEN SO HARD TO ACHIEVE PEACE IN IRELAND?

KEY EVENTS 1969–98

1971 Internment (imprisonment of suspected terrorists) introduced to try to reduce terrorist activity.

1972 Increased terrorist activity leads the British Government to suspend the Northern Ireland Parliament and run Northern Ireland directly from London. Violence increases.

1973 The British Government holds a referendum in Northern Ireland over whether the people living there want to be part of the Irish Republic. The majority voted 'No'.

1974 15-member power sharing organisation, made up of Protestants and Catholics, is formed in Northern Ireland. Protestant extremists organise a general strike in protest. Power-sharing collapses.

1982 Elections for a Northern Ireland Assembly take place.

1985 British Government invites the government of the Irish Republic to advise them on what should happen in Northern Ireland's affairs. This is opposed by many Protestants.

1986 Northern Ireland Assembly is abolished. Direct rule continues.

1993 Downing Street Declaration about the future of Northern Ireland is signed by British and Irish Prime Ministers.

1994 IRA ceasefire; British Government holds talks with the IRA.

1996 IRA ends ceasefire by exploding a massive bomb in the heart of London's dockland.

1998 Talks between Catholics and Protestants and the British Government result in the Good Friday Agreement.

Referendums held in Northern Ireland and the Irish Republic approve the Good Friday Agreement.

Omagh bomb blast kills 29 people.

1999 Peace process stumbles over the problem of decommissioning (Protestants and Catholics giving up their weapons).

Behind the violence and hatred of these years, there was a quiet desire, often unrecognised by the world's media, for peace amongst the people of Northern Ireland. In the 20 years between the arrival of British troops and the signing of the Good Friday Agreement in 1998, there were several peace moves. They came from different sources. Some were the result of:

- Government initiatives in Britain, the Republic of Ireland and the USA.
- The actions of churches (e.g. the Corrymeala Community in working with Catholics and Protestants).
- The actions of individuals (e.g. Gordon Wilson who publicly forgave the IRA for killing his daughter).

Question Time

❶ Ireland today! Collect information about Ireland today from newspapers, TV, radio and the Internet. Is there peace? Are there still problems between different groups? Is there still violence on the streets? Make a fact file called 'Ireland today'.

❷ Work out how your group would best like to present their findings. This could be by way of a wall display, drama, a TV interview or via a web site.
Present your findings to the whole class.

❸ Work through this unit and extract the information you would need to answer the question 'Why has it been so hard to achieve peace in Northern Ireland in the twentieth century? Now write an answer to the question, remembering to back up your ideas with facts.

Unit 18: Hot war, cold war – why did the major twentieth-century conflicts affect so many people?

INTRODUCTION

In this unit you are going to find out about some of the major wars and conflicts of the twentieth century. We shall look at why and how some of them were fought, and this will help you to research other conflicts. Three of these wars (the First World War, the Second World War and the Cold War) involved most people in the world. The First and Second World Wars were 'hot' wars, when war was openly declared. During the Cold War, however, war was never openly declared and the two main 'enemies', the USA and the USSR, never openly fought each other.

According to the writer William Golding, the twentieth century was 'the most violent century in history'. During the two world wars, more than 50 million people died. To give you an idea of how many people this is, the population of Britain today is only about 10 million more than this. People all over the world were affected in many different ways – some of these ways were new to the twentieth century, for example, the organisation of women into war work, the evacuation of children, bombing attacks on civilians within their homes and the development of bombs powerful enough to destroy the whole world.

People were made poorer by wars and conflicts. Many lost their homes and had to escape to other countries and continents. Starvation and famine in many parts of the world have been caused by and made worse by war. Sometimes this was because of the disruption caused by war to farming and to food supplies. Sometimes this was because governments spent vast amounts of money on attacking other countries and defending their own, instead of spending it on people.

At the end of the unit, you will write about why twentieth-century conflicts affected so many people all over the world.

Activity Time

Before you start the work in this unit you need to:

❶ Write a definition of 'war'. Do this in no more than three sentences. Thinking about the following questions will help you:
- How does a country know that it is at war?
- What happens when a war starts?
- What is the difference between a fight and a war?
- How are people's lives affected by war?
- How does a war end?

❷ Collect images of war from newspapers, magazines, books and the Internet. Find images of war like the ones in this unit, to show the many different ways that war affects people.

WHAT HAPPENED IN TWENTIETH-CENTURY WARFARE?

In this section, you will begin to think about the main features of twentieth-century warfare:

- how wars were fought in the twentieth century
- how people were affected.

This means thinking about warfare on land, sea and in the air. What changes happened during the century? What different types of fighting existed? How were ordinary people affected by warfare? How did ordinary life change? In what different ways and why have countries been involved in wars?

SOURCE 1

The bombing of London during the Second World War, December 1940.

SOURCE 2

A woman war worker in a munitions factory during the Second World War.

SOURCE 3

The war in Sierra Leone brought us to Liberia. The war was very serious; there was gunfire everywhere. I fled with nothing. I was running and carrying one of the children, but my other child was shot. He was six years old. So many people died in our village, no one is left there now. Everyone fled for their lives.

Fatima Kemokai fled her home in Sierra Leone in 1997 as a result of the civil war. The war has been going on for nine years and more than one million people have lost their homes. 4000 civilians have been executed or mutilated since 1998. Fatima is now living as a refugee in Liberia.

SOURCE 4

Between 1981 and 1990, women held demonstrations against the siting of US cruise missiles at Greenham Common in Berkshire, UK.

SOURCE 5

TAKE ACTION: The UK is one of the three top arms exporters in the world ... Write to Stephen Byers, Secretary of State for Trade and Industry and ask him to take action now!

Oxfam 'Cut Conflict' campaign, June 2000.

SOURCE 6

Kosovan refugees at a camp in Macedonia in April 1999.

SOURCE 7

Nigeria is contributing to the war effort ... Her extensive tin mines are helping to send more and still more weapons to the battle areas. This tin is vitally important for making engine bearings for army lorries and for the railway engines. Nigeria is also an important producer of cotton, used for making tropical uniforms for desert warfare, and of hides and skins necessary for army boots and belts and flying kit for Royal Air Force pilots. Rubber production is rising rapidly.

Taken from a booklet distributed in Nigeria during the Second World War to promote the war effort there. Nigeria was a British colony at the time.

SOURCE 8

The battlefield is fearful. One is overcome by a peculiar sour, heavy and penetrating smell of corpses. Men that were killed last October lie half in swamp and half in the beet-fields. The legs of an Englishman stick out into a trench, the corpse being built into the parapet: a soldier hangs his rifle on them.

Letter home from a German soldier fighting in France during the First World War, dated 27 April 1915.

SOURCE 9

During the Second World War, India was a supply base for the soldiers of the Commonwealth, the Chinese and US forces as well as its own troops. It provided an estimated £287 million in materials plus a further £130 million for US forces alone. Donations were made to the value of £23 million by 1943, and a further £11 million was given in interest-free loans.

This extract describes the contribution made by India to the war effort during the Second World War.

SOURCE 10

Money spent on the Second World War by USSR, USA and UK:

USSR spent £48 billion

USA spent £85 billion

UK spent £28 billion.

SOURCE 11

Estimate of the number of people killed from five countries in the Second World War:

Country	Approximate number killed	Approximate number in military forces
Britain	*0.5 million*	*4.5 million*
USSR	*20.0 million*	*12.0 million*
USA	*0.4 million*	*11.0 million*
Germany	*4.2 million*	*12.0 million*
Japan	*1.2 million*	*4.0 million*

SOURCE 12

Japanese paratroopers marching at the Annual Defence Force Day Parade in Tokyo, 19 October 1990.

Activity Time

1 Look at Sources 1-12. Make a card for each source and on it write in note form (and draw if you want):

a A brief description.

b What you can learn about twentieth-century war.

For example, for Source 12:

• big armies, marching, wearing uniform

• twentieth-century war: well organised, cost money, fighting by trained specialists, uniform gives strong identity, many involved, prepared for war.

2 Now fill in cards for all the other sources. Look at the other images of twentieth-century war that you have found and make similar cards for as many as you can.

3 Sort the cards into different categories. First of all think about what categories you could make. For example, all the cards and images to do with 'civilians' could go together. You decide! Some images may be used in more than one category.

4 What have you learned from these categories about war in the twentieth century? Make a list of statements – here are some to start you off:

• Twentieth-century warfare affected civilians – they worked in factories/hospitals/auxiliary services/were bombed where they lived.

• Big armies were used in twentieth-century warfare.

5 Look back to the definition of war that you wrote before doing this activity. Do you want to change it or add to it? What have you thought about since that was not included in your earlier definition?

6 Think of wars and conflicts you have studied that happened before 1900, for example, the Crusades, and the English Civil War. Fewer people were affected by these wars. Discuss some of the differences between the fighting during one of these wars and the fighting during a twentieth-century war. Think about:

• organisation of soldiers and armies

• methods of fighting and types of weapons

• how people, including civilians, were affected.

KILLING MACHINES: FOCUS ON WAR AND TECHNOLOGY

You will now have some ideas about what happened in twentieth-century warfare. There were big changes in how wars were fought. In this section we will focus on how developments in technology changed warfare over the last hundred years.

THE FIRST WORLD WAR

The First World War (1914-18) was a very different kind of war from any that had gone before, partly because of technological change. Areas of important technological change included weapons, vehicles and medicine. Together these had a big impact on how many people died while fighting. During the First World War, nine million people died – far more than in any previous war. Artillery, which could fire large amounts of big explosives, and machine guns which fired very rapidly, were used to attack the enemy.

Faced with these weapons, it was safer to be below ground and out of the 'firing line'. Soldiers built trenches on the battlefields and it was from these that most of the fighting took place. This also meant that the war was mostly static. Soldiers dug down into their trenches and stayed there to fight for long periods of time.

Medicine

Developments in medicine meant that soldiers were healthier and fewer died from their wounds than in any previous war. Combined with the use of more lethal weapons, this meant that the First World War was the first war where more people died from fighting than from disease.

THE SECOND WORLD WAR

Aeroplanes and tanks were used for the first time in the First World War, but they had only recently been invented and it was not until the Second World War that they significantly changed the way war was fought. By 1939, when the Second World War started, aircraft could fly long distances, firing machine guns and dropping bombs. They were used to bomb civilian targets and strategic targets such as factories, shipping ports, bridges and roads, as well as

SOURCE 13

A Lancaster bomber in flight during the Second World War.

enemy troops and warships. Source 1 shows a British Lancaster bomber used to drop explosives on German targets. Up to 1000 Lancaster bombers would fly out together on bombing raids. This changed the way that people were affected by war. The use of aircraft and longer range missiles meant that more civilians than soldiers were killed.

Tanks and armoured cars

Tanks and fast armoured vehicles were also significant weapons of the Second World War. They could drive over rough ground and through machine gun fire. They were often used to drive through and break up enemy lines of defence. They were also used to carry vital supplies to their own armies. This meant that fighting in far away places could happen more than had been possible in the First World War. It also meant that very fast attacks could be made by armoured divisions, such as the 'blitzkrieg' (lightening war) invasions of France and the USSR by Germany. Unlike the 'static' warfare of the trenches, these were years of 'mobile' warfare.

Radar

During the Second World War other new technologies were developed to help win the war. The development of RADAR (Radio Detecting and Ranging) in Britain was stimulated by the need to have a warning system if enemy planes were approaching, particularly at night. It also helped to hunt for submarines in the sea and was used in aeroplanes to find and attack targets more accurately.

SOURCE 14

This tank is a German Sturmgeschutz III. Tanks like this continue to be used today. For example, during the Gulf War of 1991 tanks were used to attack the enemy, to transport supplies and as ambulances.

Penicillin, the first antibiotic, was also developed in Britain during the war and helped many wounded soldiers to recover.

Atomic bombs

However, the most significant development in the technology of warfare between 1939 and 1945 was completion of the atomic bomb – the first weapon to use nuclear power. Later in this unit you will find out about the devastation caused by the dropping of atom bombs on two Japanese cities in 1945. Although no atom bombs have been dropped in war since 1945, the threat of nuclear weapons has played an important part in warfare and international relations from that date onwards. The first atomic bombs had to be carried by aeroplanes that risked being shot down or crashing. By the 1960s inter-continental ballistic missiles were developed that could carry nuclear warheads to any target in the world and at great speed. This meant that countries had the ability to destroy each other from a long way away without any soldiers being involved.

NUCLEAR WEAPONS AND THE COLD WAR

Since the 1960s nuclear weapons have been powerful enough to destroy the whole world, making a 'nuclear winter' which would turn the world into a huge radioactive desert. No people would survive. Nuclear weapons changed the way people thought about war. For instance, if a country had nuclear weapons, it no longer had to have a large number of soldiers. Powerful countries built up stockpiles of nuclear weapons as deterrents to nuclear attacks from their enemies. 'Kill us and we'll kill you' was the message being sent. This policy became known as 'Mutually Assured Destruction' or MAD. Countries became very reluctant to declare war on a country that had nuclear weapons. This strange situation happened during the 'Cold War' which you will learn more about later in this unit.

Activity Time

1. Draw a chart like the one below. Using the information in this section, fill in the bottom row with information on the weapons and technology used in each war. An example has been started for you.

2. Use your chart to explain why the weapons and technology of the Second World War made it a 'mobile' war.

War	First World War	Second World War	Cold War
Type of war	Static war	Mobile War	Nuclear war
Weapons and Technology	Machine guns used that could fire rapidly		

3. Research one technological development used during twentieth century warfare that you are interested in. For example: submarines, aeroplanes, radar, satellite, atomic bombs, antibiotics, etc. Structure your research around the following questions:
   - Why was the technology invented?
   - Who invented it, and where?
   - What impact did it have on the way wars were fought?

DOES THE ADVANCE OF TECHNOLOGY ALWAYS MAKE A DIFFERENCE IN WARFARE?

Although nuclear weapons were developed during the twentieth century, all the wars and conflicts during this period, except for the Second World War, were fought using more conventional weapons like guns, bombers and tanks. Read the extract in Source 15 about the civil war in Rwanda of 1994 and think about what you learn about the importance of technology in warfare.

What is it?

Civil war in Rwanda

Rwanda is a country in central East Africa that used to be a colony of Belgium. It has two main ethnic groups, the Hutus and the Tutsi. Civil war broke out between them in 1994, and after the massacres nearly two million Rwandans fled the country and became refugees.

SOURCE 15

Decimation means the killing of every tenth person in a population, and in the spring and early summer of 1994 a program of massacres decimated the Republic of Rwanda. Although the killing was low-tech – performed largely by machete – it was carried out at dazzling speed: of an original population of about seven and a half million, at least eight hundred thousand people were killed in just a hundred days. Rwandans often speak of a million deaths, and they may be right. The dead of Rwanda accumulated at nearly three times the rate of Jewish dead during the Holocaust. It was the most efficient mass killing since the atomic bombings of Hiroshima and Nagasaki.

From *We wish to inform you that tomorrow we will be killed with our families* by Philip Gourevitch, 1999.

Question Time

❶ Why does Philip Gourevitch say that the killing in Rwanda was 'low-tech'?

❷ Why does he say the killing in Rwanda was 'the most efficient mass killing since the atomic bombing of Hiroshima and Nagasaki'?

❸ What does this tell us about killing, technology and people?

THE SECOND WORLD WAR: TOTAL AND GLOBAL WAR IN THE TWENTIETH CENTURY

During the twentieth century, global and total war occurred for the first time with both the First World War and the Second World War. These wars affected far more people than other wars had done, in fact nearly everyone and everywhere was affected in some way.

Factfile: Second World War

- During the Second World War, more than 40 million people were killed.

- Over half of the people killed were civilians.

- Over 20 million of the people killed were Russian.

- Ten per cent of the people of Poland were killed during the war. Half of those killed were Jewish.

- During the war, over 11 million people had to leave their homes to escape war/death. They were called 'Displaced Persons' or refugees.

- By 1948 the total number of 'Displaced Persons' or refugees had reached 46 million because of the continuing effect of the war.

- Some European countries, like France, were occupied by German soldiers during the war. The soldiers lived in every town and village in occupied France. French people had to obey them.

- Switzerland, Sweden and Spain were European countries who stayed 'neutral' during the Second World War.

Second World War in Britain

- The Emergency Powers Act of 1940 gave the British Government total power over the British people.

- Unmarried women in Britain aged between 19 and 40 years old were conscripted to work for the war effort from 1941 to 1945.

- Food and clothes were rationed in Britain.

- Everyone in Britain had to carry identity cards.

- War work in Britain was directed – for example, people could be sent to work anywhere.

- During the war, London and other British cities were bombed extensively. This became known as the 'blitz', and about 60,000 people were killed.

- Children in Britain were evacuated out of cities at risk from the blitz. They were separated from their families and sent to safe places, usually in rural areas.

Question Time

1 The Factfile states that 'over 40 million people were killed'. Some historians think that 50 million were killed. Why do you think we cannot be certain how many people died?

2 Which statement in the Factfile helps to explain why so many civilians were killed during the war?

3 The British Government acquired much more power over people during wartime. Which statements describe what the government did with this power?

4 The British Government used propaganda as well as laws to maximise the war effort. Most of this propaganda was directed at women. Why do you think this was the case?

5 The Second World War was a **global** war because most countries were involved. Why do you think the Second World War has been called a **total** war?

6 What information have you collected about the Second World War that helps to answer the big question: 'Hot war, cold war – why did the major twentieth-century conflicts affect so many people?'

A STORY OF SEPARATION

For many people, war means separation from loved ones, sometimes forever. As you have found out, about 46 million people became 'Displaced Persons' or refugees during and immediately after the Second World War. Being 'displaced' was not a twentieth century development – some people became refugees when William the Conqueror took control of England. However, the number of people displaced by war and conflict increased significantly during the twentieth century. Some of these refugees never returned home, but

SOURCE 16

Now I remember very well preparing to come over to England. I didn't fully understand about Hitler, but I just understood we had to get out ... I was able to choose my clothes and my toys and my mother helped me as best she could ... I was six and a half. The entire family saw me off at the railway station, and I do remember there was a deathly silence on the platform, and all the parents were seeing off these children. And we had labels round our necks with our names.

My foster mother ... made it absolutely clear to me, in words, not just by implication, that I was the child of servants, and that I was lucky to be alive. I was definitely a good deed as far as my foster mother was concerned ... she would boast about it at the church ...'This is my little Czech refugee'. I detested being a refugee. But as far as my own age group were concerned, they were quite ... I mean they were neutral, they treated me like another friend ... I can't say I was ever treated badly at school.

An account from *Voices of the Holocaust*, an audio collection of memories made in 1993.

were forced to settle in other countries with very different cultures. In 1922, for example, 1.5 million Greeks and Turks were forced to move from their homes to another country due to political and religious conflict.

The extract in Source 16 describes some of the memories of a very young Czechoslovakian Jewish girl sent to safety in Britain by her parents just before the Second World War began. They had intended to follow her but were not allowed to leave. Most of the young Jewish refugees who reached Britain never saw their parents again.

Question Time

❶ Read Source 16. Why do you think the mother sent her child away from home?

❷ What did being a refugee mean to this child?

❸ To which statements in the Factfile on page 110 does this story link? Try to explain your links between the statements and the story.

❹ Which of the statements in the Factfile are to do with separation? Make a list of all the ways that families and friends could be separated from each other during the Second World War.

DO THE CAUSES OF TWENTIETH-CENTURY WARS HAVE ANYTHING IN COMMON?

In this section, you will find out the causes of some of the major wars of the twentieth century. There were many different types of conflict:

- civil war
- religious war
- war of conquest
- wars fought for independence.

Below is a list of meanings for the terms above. Match the correct meaning to each term.

- war to gain more land
- war between people of different faiths
- war for freedom from rule by another country
- war within a country between two or more groups.

These different types of war start for different reasons. All wars have more than one cause. Historians use sources of information to identify different causes. They organise different causes into different categories. They look for links between causes and similarities between the causes of different conflicts. Why do you think historians are very interested in the causes of war?

There is not room here to look at the causes of all the different conflicts of the twentieth century, but after you have studied the causes of the First World War, the India-Pakistan War and the Cold War in the following pages you should know how to start examining the causes of other conflicts.

Over nine million people died during the First World War between Britain, France, Russia and the USA on one side and Germany, Austria-Hungary and Italy on the other. When the war broke out, many young men were caught up in a wave of patriotism and rushed to join the army and have some excitement. Men and women from other parts of the British Empire also played a part and fought for Britain. They were soon cruelly disillusioned by the horror of trench warfare and there was great rejoicing when the war ended in November 1918. At the time some called it 'the war to end all wars' – but they were wrong. Why did the First World War happen?

SOURCE 1

A photograph from the First World War showing 'No Man's Land' at the Western Front. Why do you think this area between the German and Allied trenches, often quite a short distance, was called 'No Man's Land'?

CAUSES OF FIRST WORLD WAR

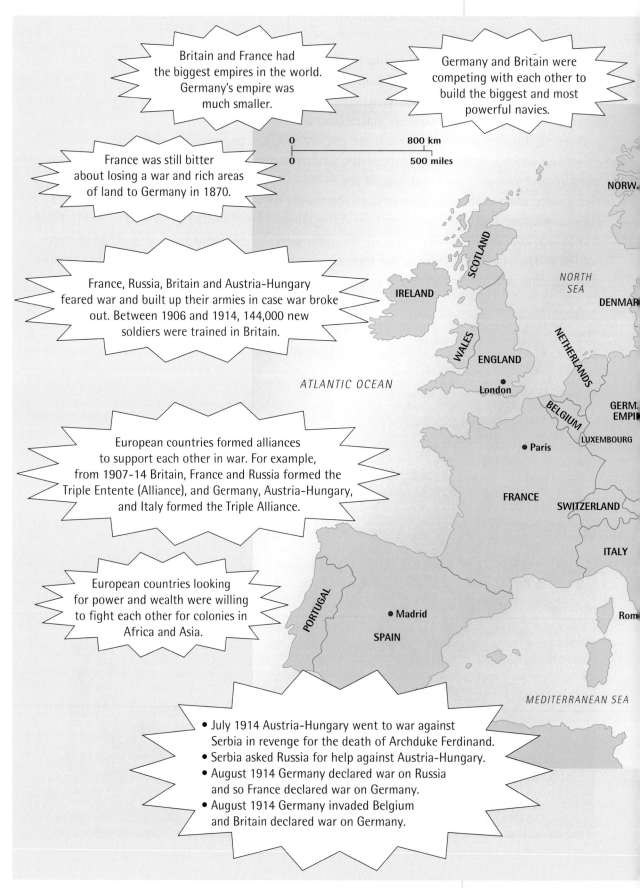

Britain and France had the biggest empires in the world. Germany's empire was much smaller.

Germany and Britain were competing with each other to build the biggest and most powerful navies.

France was still bitter about losing a war and rich areas of land to Germany in 1870.

France, Russia, Britain and Austria-Hungary feared war and built up their armies in case war broke out. Between 1906 and 1914, 144,000 new soldiers were trained in Britain.

European countries formed alliances to support each other in war. For example, from 1907-14 Britain, France and Russia formed the Triple Entente (Alliance), and Germany, Austria-Hungary, and Italy formed the Triple Alliance.

European countries looking for power and wealth were willing to fight each other for colonies in Africa and Asia.

- July 1914 Austria-Hungary went to war against Serbia in revenge for the death of Archduke Ferdinand.
- Serbia asked Russia for help against Austria-Hungary.
- August 1914 Germany declared war on Russia and so France declared war on Germany.
- August 1914 Germany invaded Belgium and Britain declared war on Germany.

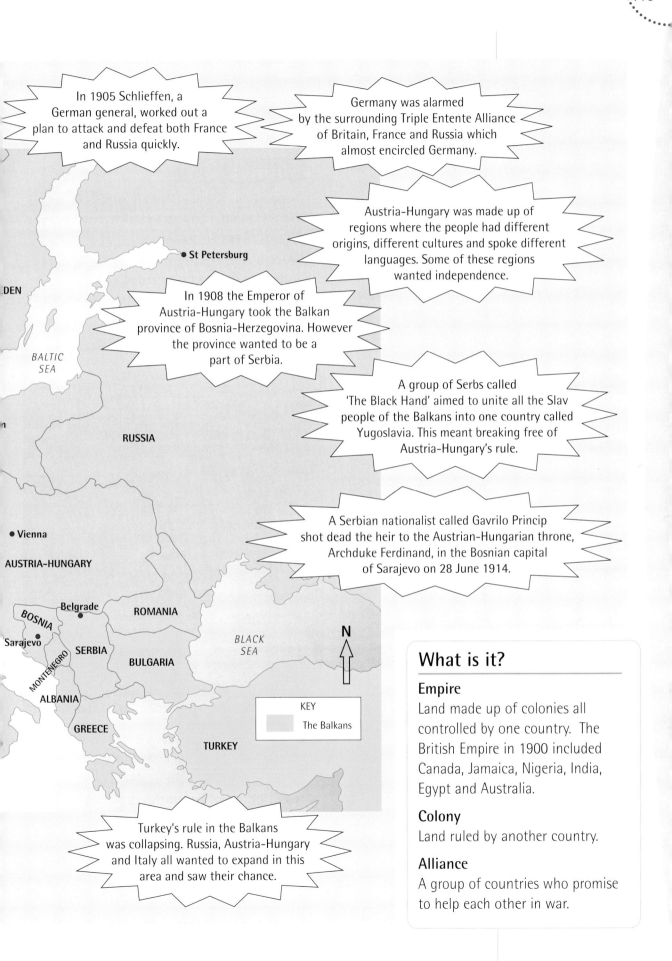

In 1905 Schlieffen, a German general, worked out a plan to attack and defeat both France and Russia quickly.

Germany was alarmed by the surrounding Triple Entente Alliance of Britain, France and Russia which almost encircled Germany.

Austria-Hungary was made up of regions where the people had different origins, different cultures and spoke different languages. Some of these regions wanted independence.

In 1908 the Emperor of Austria-Hungary took the Balkan province of Bosnia-Herzegovina. However the province wanted to be a part of Serbia.

A group of Serbs called 'The Black Hand' aimed to unite all the Slav people of the Balkans into one country called Yugoslavia. This meant breaking free of Austria-Hungary's rule.

A Serbian nationalist called Gavrilo Princip shot dead the heir to the Austrian-Hungarian throne, Archduke Ferdinand, in the Bosnian capital of Sarajevo on 28 June 1914.

Turkey's rule in the Balkans was collapsing. Russia, Austria-Hungary and Italy all wanted to expand in this area and saw their chance.

St Petersburg

BALTIC SEA

DEN

RUSSIA

Vienna

AUSTRIA-HUNGARY

BOSNIA

Belgrade

ROMANIA

Sarajevo

SERBIA

MONTENEGRO

BULGARIA

BLACK SEA

ALBANIA

GREECE

TURKEY

N

KEY

The Balkans

What is it?

Empire
Land made up of colonies all controlled by one country. The British Empire in 1900 included Canada, Jamaica, Nigeria, India, Egypt and Australia.

Colony
Land ruled by another country.

Alliance
A group of countries who promise to help each other in war.

Activity Time

❶ Working in small groups, share out the causes shown on pages 114–115 and copy them onto separate cards. Decide whether your card is mainly about:
- freedom
- power
- revenge.

Write your decision on the card.

❷ Take it in turns to explain how your card is a major cause of the war. You must try to convince the other groups. They can ask questions and give reasons to support your argument or not.

❸ Not all causes are the same. Historians categorise causes in order to look for patterns and links. You have already used the categories of freedom, power and revenge. These three categories are all about *motivations* – the reasons *why* countries went to war. Another way is to look for patterns over time. Working as a group, organise your causes into:
- tensions – long-standing problems between countries
- trends – ways in which the world was changing
- triggers – what made the war start in 1914?

This Activity can be used as an exercise to learn about the causes of other conflicts.

❹ The conflict of 1914–18 was a *world* war. Look at the causes again and find those that help to explain why it was a *world* war.

❺ How does this poster from the other side of the world help to explain why it was a world war?

SOURCE 2

A painting of Naik Darwan Sing Negi leading a bayonet charge against German soldiers in November 1914. He was the first Indian soldier to be awarded the Victoria Cross, a medal awarded for acts of bravery.

❻ How does what you have learnt in this section help to answer the big question: **Why did the major twentieth-century conflicts affect so many people?**

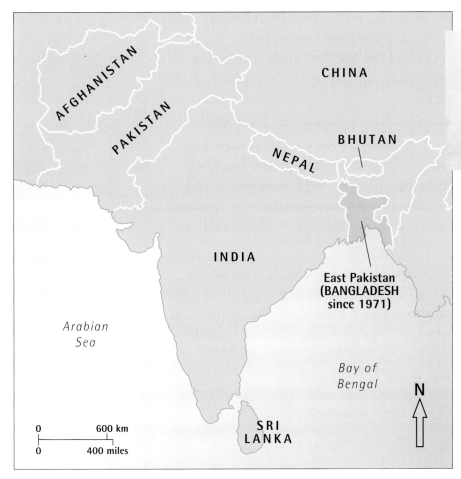

This map shows how British India was partitioned into Pakistan, India and East Pakistan (Bangladesh).

INDIA–PAKISTAN WAR

Now we are going to look at the causes of another major conflict in the twentieth century in order to compare them with the causes of the First World War.

In 1971 India and Pakistan went to war against each other. This war led to the creation of Bangladesh.

In 1946 India and Pakistan were both part of British India, where there were more Hindus than Muslims. By 1946 it seemed that India would soon be independent and Indian politicians discussed what sort of government they would have. Some Muslims wanted a country of their own where they would not be in the minority. They were worried that a mainly Hindu government would not be fair to Muslims.

In 1947 when British India became independent, the separate countries of India and Pakistan were established. Pakistan was made up of two areas, Pakistan and East Pakistan (see map). It was hoped that this would solve the problems between the Muslims and the Hindus, since the majority of Hindus lived in India and nearly all

Who were they?

Muslims believe in one God, Allah, and that the greatest prophet of all ancient prophets was Muhammad, the founder in 600 AD of their religion, Islam.

Hindus worship God in many different forms, and believe that they are born again many times. Hinduism is India's main religion, and its scriptures are thousands of years old.

Muslims lived in Pakistan. However, in the Punjab and Bengal, where both Muslims and Hindus lived, many thousands of people found themselves on the wrong side of the frontiers. Their attempts to move led to outbreaks of terrible fighting and riots in which up to a million people were killed.

Although peace was established, the problems remained. The majority of people in East Pakistan, although Muslims, were also Bengali, with a different language and culture to the people of Pakistan. In 1971 East Pakistan declared itself independent from Pakistan and called itself Bangladesh. The Pakistani army was sent in to try and crush the independence movement and started to massacre civilians.

Millions of refugees fled to neighbouring parts of India where many Bengalis, with whom they had family and cultural links, also lived. India was overwhelmed by the support needed by the refugees, and there was huge popular backing for the Bengalis. The Indian government, led by Prime Minister Indira Gandhi, responded by declaring war on Pakistan and sending troops to help Bangladesh. The Indians soon defeated the Pakistanis and the independence of Bangladesh was made official.

Activity Time

1 You are going to do the same cause sorting exercise as you did on page 116 for the First World War. First you must decide what to put on your cards. Select information from the description you have just read on why the war started between India and Pakistan. You should have no more than six cards.

2 Decide whether each card is about:
- freedom
- power
- revenge
- fear.

Compare the causes of this war to those of the First World War. What similarities do you notice? What differences are there?

SOME TWENTIETH CENTURY CONFLICTS

Use history textbooks and other resources to find out why other twentieth-century wars and conflicts started. Here are some of the main ones:

Russian Civil War (1918-21)

British, French and American troops fought with the Whites, who were made up of all Russians who opposed the communist revolutionaries. These were known as the Reds, led by Lenin and Trotsky, who had taken control in the Revolution.

Civil War in China (1927–49)

The intermittent struggle between the American-backed anti-communist Chiang Kai-shek and communist troops led by Mao Zedong was finally won by Mao, and communist rule was established.

First Arab-Israeli Conflict (1948–9)

This started as soon as the state of Israel was created in Palestine. All neighbouring Arab countries as well as the Palestinians opposed its creation. Israel was attacked by Egypt, Syria, Jordan, Iraq and the Lebanon. The Israelis defeated all of them and made even more of Palestine part of Israel. These countries also fought the Six Day War (1967) and the Yom Kippur War (1973).

Korean War (1950–3)

At the end of the Second World War, North Korea had surrendered to Soviet troops and South Korea to American troops. Two separate governments were set up; both claimed to control the whole of Korea. War broke out between the communist North Korea, supported by the Soviets and the Chinese, and South Korea, supported by the Americans and United Nations troops. In 1953 a truce was agreed and Korea was divided into the communist North and the capitalist South.

Vietnam War (1964–73)

The guerrilla warfare between communist North and anti-communist South Vietnam was supported by China and the USA. Communist China supported the North and the USA, which was determined to stop the spread of communism, supported the South.

Falklands War (1982)

Britain had occupied the Falkland Islands in the South Atlantic since 1833, but Argentina claimed the islands were theirs, attacked and occupied them. A British naval expedition was sent to re-occupy the islands.

Morocco and the Western Sahara (1975–88)

The Western Sahara, a country south of Morocco, rich in minerals gained independence from Spain in 1975 and was immediately occupied by Morocco. The Western Saharans fought back with the help of Algeria. A ceasefire was negotiated in 1988, but Morocco still occupies the country and many Western Saharans live in refugee camps.

Gulf War (1990–1)

Saddam Hussein, dictator of Iraq, invaded the neighbouring small, but rich, oil-producing country of Kuwait. Various countries, including Britain and America, went to war to protect Kuwait and its oil supplies so vital to the western world. Iraq surrendered after an intense bombing campaign.

Activity Time

Draw a table like the one below with the title **Twentieth-century wars**.
Make the boxes big enough for all the information you will want to
include. You could do this as a whole class activity, displaying the table
where everyone can see it and contribute to it. The purpose of the table
is to create an overview, make comparisons and see change over time.

Twentieth-century wars

WAR	CAUSES: Why did the war happen?	NATURE: How was the war fought?	IMPACT: How were people and places affected in the short term?	EFFECTS: How were people and places affected in the long term?
First World War (1914-18)	Rivalry over the size of empires	Trench warfare	9 million died	
Second World War (1939-45)		Mobile: fast and far reaching		Many refugees in Europe
Cold War				
???				

You will add to your table as you do your research and continue your work through the unit. You should be able to fill in the table for the First and Second World Wars and for the India-Pakistan War, and then decide which conflict or conflicts you or your group are going to research. Start by finding out the causes and use the cause-sorting exercise outlined on pages 116 and 118 to help you.

WHY DID THE END OF THE SECOND WORLD WAR HAVE THE EFFECT OF STARTING ANOTHER, DIFFERENT WORLD CONFLICT?

We have looked at the causes of some of the 'hot wars' of the twentieth century, and we are now going to look at the how the Cold War developed after the end of the Second World War. You have read about the development of nuclear weapons on page 108 and we shall now examine in more detail the causes and consequences of the rivalry between the 'Great Powers' and the arms race.

SOURCE 1

Hiroshima after the bomb was dropped on 6 August 1945.

MASS KILLING IN HIROSHIMA

On 6 August 1945 an American B-29 bomber, the *Enola Gay*, dropped an atomic bomb on the Japanese city of Hiroshima. 120,000 people were killed and 78,000 injured, half of them very severely. Three days later a second bomb was dropped on the city of Nagasaki killing around 74,000. Both bombs were dropped without warning.

On 15 August 1945, Japan surrendered to the Allies and the Second World War ended.

SOURCE 2

A watch that belonged to Kengo Futagawa, who was badly burned by the fire from the explosion, and died two weeks later. The watch stopped when the atomic bomb detonated above Hiroshima.

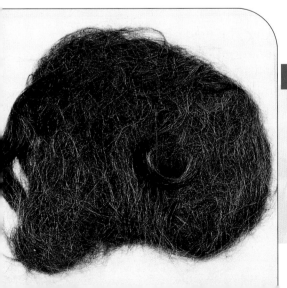

SOURCE 3

One of the effects of the radiation was that people lost their hair. This piece belonged to Hiroko Yamashita, who was eighteen at the time.

Question Time

1. What do Sources 1 to 3 on page 121 tell you about the impact of the atomic bombs on Hiroshima and Nagasaki?

2. The artefacts (Source 2 and Source 3) are being kept in a museum. Why would people today want to remember what happened to Hiroshima and Nagasaki in August 1945?

HIROSHIMA: A CONTROVERSIAL DECISION

The rights and wrongs of the decision by the US Government to drop a nuclear bomb on Hiroshima and Nagasaki continues to be a matter of debate. The big question for many is: Did the use of atomic bombs kill fewer people than would have died fighting to bring the war to an end?

SOURCE 4

In all it had been estimated that it would require until the late fall (autumn) of 1946 to bring Japan to her knees. All of us realised that the fighting would be fierce and the losses heavy. General Marshall told me that it might cost half a million American lives to force the enemy's surrender on his home ground ... I regarded the bomb as a military weapon and never had any doubt that it should be used. In deciding to use this bomb I wanted to make sure that it would be used in a manner prescribed by the laws of war. That meant I wanted it dropped on a military target.

This is what President Truman of the USA (1945–53) said about the decision in his memoirs.

SOURCE 5

The Japanese were on the verge of surrender. In mid July they sent out peace feelers...General Groves...was desperate to see the fruits of his – and the project's – labours before the end of war. The military equipment was available and had been developed at a cost of $2000 million. It would have been difficult to justify not using it...Both bombs were atomic bombs. The Nagasaki bomb produced a greater blast. Some of the leaders of the Manhattan project were keen for both types of bomb to be tested. Nagasaki was, in short, an experiment.

From the magazine *Sanity* produced by CND (Campaign for Nuclear Disarmament) in 1984 about Hiroshima and Nagasaki. The atom bombs were developed by the Manhattan Project; General Groves was the director.

SOURCE 6

A British cartoon from the London newspaper
Evening Standard, 1960.

JAPAN WAS SEEKING PEACE **BEFORE** THE FIRST ATOM BOMB WAS DROPPED ON HIROSHIMA, ACCORDING TO DOCUMENTS JUST LEAKED TO THE U.S. PRESS.

VICKY

" DON'T YOU SEE, THEY <u>HAD</u> TO FIND OUT IF IT WORKED..."

Question Time

❶ Study Source 4 carefully. According to Truman, did the atomic bombs save lives? Give a reason for your answer.

❷ Do you think there are any reasons why we should be careful about using Source 4 to answer the question 'Did the use of atomic bombs kill fewer people than would have died fighting to bring the war to an end?'

❸ Read Source 5. What information does CND use to support their argument that atomic bombs should not have been dropped on Hiroshima and Nagasaki?

❹ *Sanity* is the magazine of the Campaign for Nuclear Disarmament. Does this mean we cannot trust what it says?

❺ Do you think the artist who drew the cartoon in Source 6 was for or against the use of the atomic bomb? Does the cartoon agree or disagree with Source 5 that the atom bombs were an experiment?

HIROSHIMA AS A MESSAGE TO THE USSR

Some people think that the atomic bomb was dropped to show the USSR how powerful the USA was. The USA and the USSR had fought on the same side against Germany but by 1945 the American President, Truman and the Soviet leader, Stalin, were already starting to be suspicious of each other. This was to lead to a 'war' that was to last for 40 years.

Who was he?

Joseph Stalin
Dictator of Soviet Russia (USSR) from 1924–53.

HIROSHIMA AS THE START OF THE ARMS RACE

Stalin was determined that the Americans would not be the only people to know how to make nuclear bombs – he ordered scientists in the USSR to develop their own atom bomb. In 1949 the USSR tested its first atom bomb in Siberia. In 1952 the USA tested the even more deadly hydrogen bomb. The Soviets followed suit in 1953. From then on each side built up vast stockpiles of nuclear weapons. Each side raced to get ahead of the other.

HIROSHIMA AND PEACE

Hiroshima and Nagasaki became symbols to promote peace movements, representing the catastrophic effects of nuclear weapons. From 1945 onwards, the world knew that it had the power to destroy itself. A flame of peace was started from the fires of Nagasaki after the bomb. It is still alight in Japan today.

WHAT WAS THE COLD WAR? HOW DID IT START?

The surrender of Japan ended the Second World War. But as soon as the Second World War ended, another war began. This was called the Cold War and it lasted until 1989. It was between the USA and the USSR, two countries that had been on the same side during the Second World War. It was called the Cold War because neither the USA nor the USSR directly attacked each other at any time during the 45 years they were at 'war'. In this section you will find out how they did 'fight' each other and why the 'war' started.

Throughout the Cold War, the three Great Powers were USA, USSR and communist China. They were called 'Great Powers' because of their great military and economic strength. They all used this strength, or threatened to use this strength, in the affairs of other countries.

The USA and the USSR had different ideas and beliefs about the best way for people to live. They had very different ideas about how countries should be run and how governments should be elected. Both called themselves 'democratic', but both had opposite ideas about what 'democracy' meant. We call these sets of beliefs 'ideologies', and once the common enemy – Germany – had been defeated in 1945, the differences between these ideologies became dangerously apparent. The USA was a capitalist country while the USSR was communist. Read the two different interpretations of democracy below.

We are democratic! We believe that all people should be equal and free. Our whole political system is based on these ideals. People are free to vote for their rulers of their choice. There are at least two political parties and governments can only be in power for a limited period. People are also free to own property, voice their opinions and move around as they want.

We are democratic! We believe that all people should be equal and free. We believe that they cannot be free until they are equal. Otherwise freedom is just for the rich. Under our system there is no private ownership of property. Instead the state owns everything and it uses its resources to look after people. It gives them jobs, health care, housing and education. People can vote for the one political party that will truly take care of their interests.

SOURCE 7

A Soviet cartoon about the political system of the USA entitled 'The land of the free'.

Activity Time

❶ Sort these statements into 'capitalist' and 'communist' and write them into the correct column of the table.

- Governments are chosen from one political party.
- People can be told what jobs to do and where to live.
- Private property is protected by the law.
- People can move around as they want.
- Unemployment is very low.
- Unemployment can be very high.
- Governments are elected by people who have a choice of political parties to vote for.
- All property is owned by the state.

COMMUNIST	CAPITALIST

Being free and being equal are important ideas in both systems.

- Which system puts equality above freedom?
- Which system puts freedom above equality?

Add these as statements to your table.

❷ What clue is there to show that the cartoon in Source 7 is about the USA?

❸ What is the message of the cartoon?

❹ What is the tone of the title: sincere/kind/humorous/sarcastic/nasty/ironic?

❺ **'My way is better than yours!'** In pairs, take up the ideas and beliefs of a 'communist' and a 'capitalist'. You could prepare some notes by answering the questions below and discussing them in your pairs. Then try to convince your partner that your system is better.

- How do people get jobs?
- How do people find houses to live in?
- Are there very rich and very poor people in your country?
- How fair is your system of government?
- Are people free?
- Are people equal?

WHY DID THE COLD WAR START WHEN IT DID?

The ideological differences between the USA and the USSR were a source of tension that had existed since Russia became the communist USSR in 1922. But there were other reasons for the increase in tension between the USA and the USSR at the end of the Second World War.

PROBLEMS OF PEACE

At the end of a war there are new problems that need to be solved. How should the losers be treated? Should they be allowed to be independent and try to grow powerful again, or should they be weakened and controlled? How were countries to rebuild after the devastation of war? Who should pay for the damage done by the war? What was to happen to all the homeless refugees? What should happen to land conquered during the war? Should it all be given back to the original rulers, or had new movements for nationalism and independence started? What should be done to stop other wars from starting?

These were the questions that faced the world in 1945. There were no easy answers. In attempting to solve these problems, the relationship between the USA and the USSR deteriorated very quickly. Between 1945 and 1947 the two countries became more and more suspicious of each other. As you read the information here, try to work out why this happened.

At the end of the war, the USSR occupied the east part of Germany while Britain, France and the USA occupied the west part. The Soviets also occupied the countries of eastern Europe.

This map shows the spread of Soviet influence in eastern Europe.

Land taken by USSR at the end of Second World War

Soviet-controlled communist countries

Non-Soviet-controlled communist country

250 miles
400 km

Timeline: USA and USSR 1945–49

1945
• **February** Peace talks at Yalta between the USA, Britain, France and the USSR and in
• **July** at Potsdam. USSR determined to control eastern Europe.
• USSR supports communist government in Yugoslavia.

1946
• **March** 'Iron Curtain' speech made by Winston Churchill.
• USSR sets up communist governments in Albania and Bulgaria.

1947
• USSR sets up communist governments in Poland and Romania.
• Civil War in Greece, trouble in Turkey as Soviet-supported communists try to take over the government.
• Truman Doctrine – USA makes it clear that it will help people everywhere to keep their political freedom in the face of communist aggression.
• Marshall Plan – USA gives massive financial help to non-communist countries in western Europe (16 in all). This is to help make western countries strong enough to defend themselves against the spread of communism – a policy called **containment**.

1948
• Communists seize power in Czechoslovakia from a democratically elected government.
• USSR cuts off Berlin from the West. Berlin Airlift 1948-9.

1949
• Western powers merge their three zones in Germany into the German Federal Republic. The Soviet zone becomes the German Democratic Republic.
• USSR backs communist take over of government in Hungary.

127

THE SOVIET POINT OF VIEW

The USSR had suffered terribly during the war. Nearly 20 million Russian people had died defending eastern Europe against Germany. The USSR wanted to make sure that this would not happen again. The country had been invaded twice by Germany in the last 30 years, and Stalin wanted to set up a barrier in eastern Europe between the West and the USSR. He kept six million soldiers in eastern Europe, to prevent an invasion by capitalist countries.

Question Time

❶ Use the map and the timeline on page 127 to show how the relationship between the USSR and the USA became increasingly tense between 1945 and 1949.
a How did the influence of the USSR in Europe increase between 1945 and 1947?
b How did Soviet land increase between 1945 and 1949?
c How did the USA feel about these changes?

❷ Look at the cartoon in Source 8.
a Who is Joe?
b Why does the notice say NO ADMITTANCE?
c What messages are being sent about eastern Europe and western Europe?

❸ Use the map, timeline and cartoon to explain what was meant by 'Iron Curtain'.

❹ Use the map and the timeline to write the USA's side of the story. Think about:
a The reasons to fear and dislike the USSR.
b Why the USA feared Soviet influence in Europe.

SOURCE 8

This cartoon was published in the British newspaper the *Daily Mail*. It refers to a speech made by the British Prime Minister, Winston Churchill in March 1946 in Fulton, Missouri, USA. In his speech he said, '...from Stettin in the Baltic to Trieste in the Adriatic an iron curtain has descended across the continent'.

PEEP UNDER THE IRON CURTAIN

❺ Look at your table **Twentieth-century wars** on page 120. You should now have ideas and information to add to the Causes column for the Cold War.

❻ Think back to what you have learned about the trends, tensions and triggers that caused the First World War. Write a few sentences explaining why political and ideological difference was <u>not</u> the trigger that started the Cold War after 1945.

FORTY YEARS OF COLD WAR?

In this section you will find information about four incidents of the Cold War. Before you begin to find out about what happened, read the statements below. These statements all describe characteristics of the Cold War. They describe how the Cold War was fought or, in other words, the nature of the Cold War.

Characteristics of the Cold War:
- support of other countries with money and weapons
- use of military force to threaten other countries
- use of nuclear weapons to threaten other countries
- political control and influence over other countries
- use of spies and secret surveillance
- mistrust of the 'other side'
- competion to appear the most powerful to the rest of the world
- no formal declaration of war between the USA and the USSR.

1 BERLIN AIRLIFT 1948–9

For ten months in 1948–9, planes carrying coal, cocoa, sausages, frogs legs, hot water bottles, manhole covers, ping pong balls and many other items used for life in a twentieth-century city, flew to the German city of Berlin. This was the only way all these things could reach Berlin. How did this extraordinary situation come about?

After the surrender of Germany, the country was divided up between France, the USA, Britain and the USSR. The city of Berlin was also divided: most of the city was under the control of the capitalist western powers, but westerners could only reach the city by passing through East Germany, because Berlin lay in the Soviet sector of Germany (see map). By 1948, the French, British and American sectors had joined together while the Soviet section remained separate and isolated. Furthermore, while the Soviet section of East Germany had become communist, the rest of Germany remained capitalist. With the help of aid as a result of the

This map shows the air corridor routes for planes flying goods from West Germany into West Berlin.

Key	
	Soviet zone
	American zone
	French zone
	British zone
	Gatow airport
	Tegel airport
	Templehof airport
	Air corridors to West Berlin

0 — 190 Miles
0 — 300 km

Hamburg ○
Hanover ○
GERMANY
Frankfurt ○
Berlin

West Berlin — East Berlin

N

Marshall Plan, capitalist West Germany made a good economic recovery after the war, while communist East Germany remained poor.

Stalin, the leader of USSR was very suspicious of these developments. In June 1948, Stalin cut off all road, rail and canal links with West Germany. Berlin was isolated in Soviet territory, and the capitalist zones could no longer be reached via East Germany. The USA, Britain and France were determined to keep control of their zones in Berlin. They decided that supplies of food and other items would have to be flown in for West Berliners to survive. Between June 1948 and May 1949, two million tonnes of supplies were airlifted in.

Finally in May 1949, the USSR gave up the blockade and road, rail and canal links with West Germany were reopened. The Berlin Airlift had been a success.

The Berlin Wall

But ten years later, the Soviet leader, Khrushchev, made it clear that he wanted Berlin to be wholly controlled by East Germany. When talks with the American President, John F Kennedy, failed, Khrushchev ordered the building of the 'Berlin Wall' in August 1961, and within two weeks East and West Berlin were divided by a heavily fortified and guarded wall. Anyone trying to escape from East Berlin to the West was shot.

Question Time

1 Why do you think Stalin cut off all links between communist East Germany and capitalist West Germany?

2 The USSR did not try to shoot down any planes during the Berlin blockade. What does this tell you about the Cold War?

3 Look back to the list of characteristics of the Cold War. Which ones are relevant to the Berlin Airlift?

2 HUNGARY 1956: A HOLE IN THE IRON CURTAIN?

In 1956, there was an uprising in Hungary against Soviet rule. Many of those who rebelled were young students and teenagers. Since 1945 the standard of living of Hungarians had fallen. Communism meant that Hungarians did not have the same freedom as people in capitalist countries.

At school, all information was tightly controlled. History teachers, for example, were only allowed to teach the communist version of the past. Political parties had been crushed and the newspapers, the media and industry were under government control. Soviet troops were stationed on the borders.

At first, the demonstrators were successful, and a new, less extreme government was established. However, Khrushchev, leader of the

USSR since 1955, feared that the rebellion might spread to other communist countries under Soviet control, and was not prepared to tolerate any further reforms. Many of the demonstrators hoped for and expected help from the USA, but no help arrived. Khrushchev reacted with force; 6000 tanks were sent in and in the next ten days of street fighting, 30,000 Hungarians and 7000 Soviet troops were killed. 200,000 Hungarians fled abroad.

Question Time

1 Look at the map on page 127. Explain why the break away of Hungary from Soviet control would make a 'hole' in the Iron Curtain.

2 Why were the Soviets so keen to repair the curtain?

3 Look back to the list of the characteristics of the Cold War. Which ones are relevant to Hungary in 1956?

4 Some children as young as ten died fighting against the USSR in Hungary. Are there any causes for which you would risk your life?

3 COMMUNISTS IN THE USA'S BACK YARD! THE CUBAN MISSILE CRISIS, 1962

The Cuban Missile Crisis of 1962 caused fear and panic throughout the world and especially in the USA. For a few weeks in October 1962 it actually seemed possible that nuclear war was going to break out between the USA and the USSR.

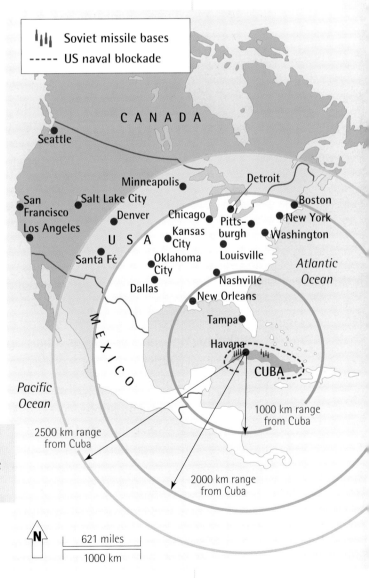

This map shows the major towns and cities in the USA which were in range of nuclear missiles based in Cuba.

'COUNTDOWN TO THE END OF THE WORLD?'

1959		Fidel Castro, a communist, takes over power in Cuba. He replaces Batista, a capitalist, who flees to the USA.
1961	April	Batista tries to regain power in Cuba with help of the USA.
		A small, American-backed force lands at the Bay of Pigs hoping for an uprising against Castro. No uprising happened and the invading force is easily defeated, to the great embarrassment of the USA and President Kennedy.
		Castro, meanwhile, fearing another invasion, asks Khrushchev to help him.
		Khrushchev agrees to supply weapons to Cuba.
1962	16 October	USA spy planes, U2s, take surveillance photographs of Cuba. The photographs show launch pads for long-range nuclear missiles being built in Cuba. Long-range missiles could fire at least 2500 kms – enough to hit the USA from Cuba. As yet there are no missiles to be seen.
		John F Kennedy, President of USA, orders U2 spy planes to photograph all ships travelling towards Cuba. Some photographs show long-range missiles on Soviet ships.
	22 October	Kennedy orders a naval blockade of Cuba to stop Soviet ships getting through. 156 rockets are set to fire at the USSR. US B52 bombers armed with nuclear weapons fly patrols around Cuba. Kennedy says that if the blockade is forced it will be war, but the Soviet ships carry on towards Cuba.
	24 October	At the last minute Soviet ships stop when they reach the American blockade.
	26 October	Kennedy receives a message from Khrushchev saying he will not put any long range missiles on Cuba if Kennedy ends the naval blockade.
		Kennedy agrees to Khrushchev's proposal. But he adds that the missile launch pads must be removed by 29 October or the USA will invade Cuba.
	28 October	Khrushchev agrees to Kennedy's proposal. All missile bases are removed from Cuba. In return, the USA naval blockade is lifted.

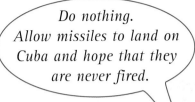

Do nothing. Allow missiles to land on Cuba and hope that they are never fired.

Attack the Soviet ships travelling towards Cuba.

Attack Cuba with nuclear weapons and destroy the missile launch sites.

Try to stop missiles reaching Cuba by imposing a naval blockade.

Activity Time

1 In pairs, take up the characters of
- President John F Kennedy
- a British journalist.

Using the four choices above as your starting point, the journalist interviews Kennedy about the crisis. The world is watching and holding its breath – what will Kennedy do? Prepare yourselves by making notes of the advantages and disadvantages of the four options.

2 Use the map on page 131 and the timeline to write a short account that answers the question: Why was there an international crisis over Cuba in 1962?

3 In his memoirs, Kennedy's brother Robert said that during the Cuban crisis:
'There was a feeling that the noose was tightening. The President's mind went to other parts of the world. We were deciding really for all of mankind.'
Explain why Kennedy felt he was deciding for 'all of mankind'.

4 What does Kennedy's final decision tell you about the characteristics of Cold War?

5 Look back to the list of the characteristics of the Cold War. Which ones are relevant to the Cuban Missile Crisis?

4 THE 'GREAT POWERS' AND AFGHANISTAN

On Christmas Day 1979, the USSR sent troops into Afghanistan. A new communist government had been elected there which was supported by the USSR. In return it allowed the Soviets to build military bases inside its borders. But this government was being threatened by Islamic (Muslim) rebels and thought that these rebels might, with help from the large Muslim population over the border in the USSR, try to set up a Muslim state. The USSR feared that the Soviet Muslims would break away to join the Afghan rebels.

Soviet troops were sent in to Afghanistan to support the communist government and protect Soviet military bases.

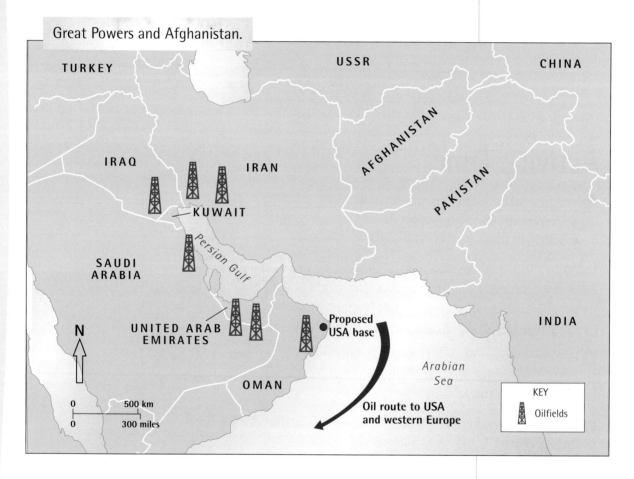

Great Powers and Afghanistan.

Question Time

❶ Look at the map above.

a Why would the USSR be interested in who was in control in Afghanistan?

b Why would the USA also be interested in who rules Afghanistan?

The USA also had good reasons to be interested. Soviet troops were getting too close to the life blood of the west – oil. The big oil-producing countries were Iran, Iraq and Saudi Arabia. What did the USA do? The USA stopped selling food to the USSR, sent soldiers to the area and supported the Afghan rebels by giving them weapons. They, and other countries, withdrew athletes from the Moscow Olympics in protest at the behaviour of the USSR in Afghanistan and the threat to world peace. Soviet troops finally left Afghanistan in February 1989.

Activity Time

Whose side was China on in the war in Aghanistan?

❶ In groups of three you must take on the role of advisers to Deng Xiaoping, leader of China. Deng wants the three of you to give him advice. You must decide before you meet with him what you will say. Study the information below and then discuss what advice you will give him about which 'side' to join.

Factfile: China

- China had a different type of communism to the USSR. The two countries were rivals and suspicious of each other.
- China and the USSR both wanted to increase their influence in other countries.
- China was furious at the American support for Chinese anti-communists based in Taiwan, a big island off the coast of China where the government defeated by Mao Zedong had fled in 1949.
- China had supplied arms to East Pakistan (later Bangladesh), an Islamic country that supported the Afghan rebels.
- China and the USSR had been arguing over exactly where their borders were.
- China and the USA had supported different sides in civil wars in Korea, Vietnam and Cambodia.

❷ China supported the Afghan rebels against the Afghan Government and the USSR. Why do you think China made this decision?

❸ What do you learn about the Cold War from China's decision?

USE OF PROPAGANDA

Propaganda was also an important 'weapon' in the Cold War. The cartoons below are examples of propaganda from the Cold War. Look at each cartoon and decide whether it is anti-Soviet or anti-American propaganda. Make a sketch of one of the cartoons and then annotate it to show how you decided it was anti-Soviet or anti-American. Finally, look at your table 'Twentieth-Century Wars' on page 120. You should now have ideas and information to add to the Nature and Impact columns of the Cold War.

look at your table 'Twentieth-Century Wars' on page 120.

SOURCE 9

'Who's next to be liberated from freedom?'

" WHO'S NEXT TO BE LIBERATED FROM FREEDOM, COMRADE ?"

SOURCE 10

A cartoon from 1950 showing arms reaching from The White House, residence of the President of the USA.

HOW DID THE COLD WAR END?

DÉTENTE

The word *détente* means 'relaxing', and it refers to the relaxing of the arms race.

By the end of the 1960s the vast amount of money being spent on the arms race by the USSR meant that there was not enough money being spent on the development of industry and agriculture at home. The USA was pouring money and men into the Vietnam War and the President, Richard Nixon was looking for a way out. For both Great Powers some agreement to limit the arms race would be welcome. The next ten years saw the development of talks and links between the Great Powers of the USA and USSR.

'STAR WARS'

By 1980 negotiations were breaking down. The USSR had invaded Afghanistan and the new President of the USA, Ronald Reagan, was violently anti-communist. He started the programme of 'Star Wars' – the anti-missile system in space. Both the USA and the USSR built up even more deadly and accurate nuclear weapons, such as Cruise, a pilot-less aeroplane with a nuclear warhead. To many people, nuclear war seemed very close.

The situation improved when Mikhail Gorbachev became leader of the USSR in 1985. He realised that the USSR was nearly bankrupt, and he persuaded President Reagan to start talking about arms limitation. The USA also needed to cut back on arms spending, and by 1987 they had reached an agreement to end the arms race.

POLICIES OF MIKHAIL GORBACHEV

Gorbachev had two main policies:

- *Perestroika* – improving the economy to raise the standard of living.
- *Glasnost* – greater openness with the west, including the USA.

The first step towards trying to improve the economy was to limit spending on the arms race. The cost of the Cold War had been huge, and money spent on building up weapons and supporting communism around the world was creating widespread poverty in the USSR. In contrast to this hardship a corrupt elite of politicians and military chiefs had a very high standard of living.

Gorbachev met not only Ronald Reagan, but also the leaders of all the most powerful capitalist countries to talk about how to end the Cold War. The communist governments of eastern Europe were no longer supported by the USSR and were losing control. Gorbachev's policies encouraged other eastern European people to challenge and overthrow their repressive governments.

THE WALL COMES DOWN!

Source 1 shows one of the extraordinary scenes in Berlin in November 1989. The account in Source 2 describes what happened in Romania in 1989 when the communist dictator Ceausescu was overthrown by the people.

SOURCE 1

In November 1989 this extraordinary scene took place in Berlin. 'We are one people!' shouted the many West and East Berliners who were reunited for the first time in 28 years when they breached the Berlin Wall.

SOURCE 2

Power of the people: Romania

The Ceausescu regime was widely condemned for corruption and for economic mismanagement, which left the vast majority of Romanians with insufficient food and power. On 21 December Ceausescu addressed a large rally in central Bucharest. His speech, to his evident astonishment, was interrupted by heckling, leading to scuffles between members of the crowd and Securitate men. In the morning of 22 December, he made a final attempt to address the hostile crowd, but was shouted down with cries of 'Death! Death!' Shortly after he finished speaking, demonstrators broke into the building. Apparently under orders from their commanders, troops made no efforts to intervene. Ceausescu

and his wife, accompanied by bodyguards, were airlifted by helicopter from the roof, even as the demonstrators emerged on to it. Both the US and the Soviet governments declared open support for the revolution against Ceausescu.

Nicholae and Elena Ceausescu were captured on 22 December. They were placed on trial, facing a range of charges including genocide, corruption and the destruction of the national economy. They were both condemned to death and executed by firing squad. Televised excerpts of the trial, and pictures of their corpses, were broadcast on Romanian television the following day.

From Keesing's *Contemporary Archives,* December 1989.

Question Time

❶ According to Source 2, Ceausescu was astonished to be interrupted. What does this tell us about his rule before December 1989?

❷ The army did not help Ceausescu. Why would losing their support be so terrible? Why do you think the army commanders did not support him?

❸ What did the USA and the USSR do about events in Romania in December 1989?

Timeline: The Cold War

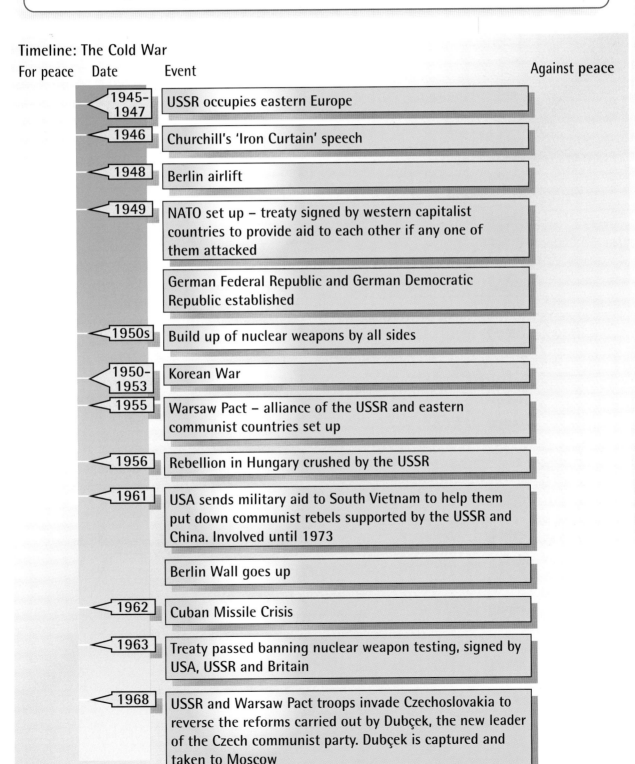

For peace	Date	Event	Against peace
	1945–1947	USSR occupies eastern Europe	
	1946	Churchill's 'Iron Curtain' speech	
	1948	Berlin airlift	
	1949	NATO set up – treaty signed by western capitalist countries to provide aid to each other if any one of them attacked	
		German Federal Republic and German Democratic Republic established	
	1950s	Build up of nuclear weapons by all sides	
	1950–1953	Korean War	
	1955	Warsaw Pact – alliance of the USSR and eastern communist countries set up	
	1956	Rebellion in Hungary crushed by the USSR	
	1961	USA sends military aid to South Vietnam to help them put down communist rebels supported by the USSR and China. Involved until 1973	
		Berlin Wall goes up	
	1962	Cuban Missile Crisis	
	1963	Treaty passed banning nuclear weapon testing, signed by USA, USSR and Britain	
	1968	USSR and Warsaw Pact troops invade Czechoslovakia to reverse the reforms carried out by Dubçek, the new leader of the Czech communist party. Dubçek is captured and taken to Moscow	

Timeline: The Cold War

For peace	Date	Event	Against peace
	Late 1960s	The beginning of Détente	
	1972	SALT 1 (Strategic Arms Limitation Talks) USSR and USA agree to limit the building and stockpiling of nuclear weapons	
	1975	Helsinki Agreement – USA, USSR, Canada and most European countries accept European frontiers drawn up after the Second World War. Soviet dominance recognised in eastern Europe. All countries agree to recognise human rights, including freedom to leave a country	
		American and Soviet astronauts meet in space	
	1979	USSR invades Afghanistan	
	1980	USA gives support to right-wing rebels against the communist government in Nicaragua	
	1981	Reagan elected president of the USA, and doubles amount of money spent on defence	
	1984	'Star Wars'. Reagan starts programme of anti-missile system in space	
	1985	Gorbachev becomes leader of the USSR	
	1986	Gorbachev introduces policy of *Glasnost*, meaning greater openness with the west	
	1987	Treaty signed between USA and USSR agreeing to withdraw missiles from Europe	
	1989	Berlin Wall comes down	
		Soviet troops leave Afghanistan	
		Eastern European countries end Soviet domination of governments	

Activity Time

1 Since 1949 some events made the Cold War seem worse and others made peace seem more likely. Copy the timeline and then decide which events might have been 'For peace' and which were 'Against peace'. Write your reasons in the two columns. You may find some events could work for as well as against peace.

2 Look back over this section on the Cold War. Make a note of all the different ways in which people were affected by the 'war'.

3 Look at your table **Twentieth-century wars** on page 120. You should now be able to add much more information to the Impact and Effect columns of the Cold War.

WHAT DO LOCAL PEOPLE REMEMBER ABOUT THE MAIN CONFLICTS?

As we have seen in this unit there are different ways in which areas of the world have been affected by war. Using Britain as an example, we can see that:

- Some areas have been bombed.
- Some areas have taken in people displaced from other parts of the world.
- Some industrial areas and ports have been particularly important in supporting the war effort with supplies.
- All areas will have sent servicemen and women to support the First and Second World War effort.
- Perhaps it is not surprising that nearly all cities, towns and villages remember at least one of the world wars through a permanent memorial.

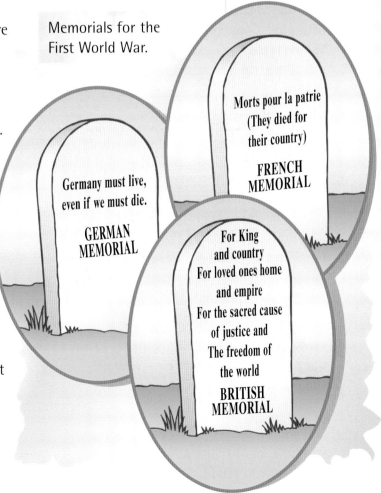

Memorials for the First World War.

Germany must live, even if we must die.

GERMAN MEMORIAL

Morts pour la patrie (They died for their country)

FRENCH MEMORIAL

For King and country
For loved ones home and empire
For the sacred cause of justice and
The freedom of the world

BRITISH MEMORIAL

Activity Time

1 Look at the three national memorials on page 141. They are all from the First World War. Think back to the reasons mentioned in this unit why the war was fought. What reason(s) do these memorials give for the deaths of 1914–18?

2 Find your local war memorial(s). You could include plaques inside chapels and churches, so you may find a large number. Record the war that the memorial commemorates and the words on the memorial. Your school may even have a war memorial.

3 What do you learn about feelings and attitudes to war from each memorial? For example:
- Do they try and explain why people died?
- How do they do this?
- Why do you think the memorial was put up?

4 Look through all the images in this book and create a photomontage with the title 'What war means to me'. You may wish to include images from your own home or community. For example, quotes from family members, personal photographs, photographs of local war relics, memorials, vacant sites, etc.

5 Write an essay that answers the question: Hot war, cold war – why did the major twentieth-century conflicts affect so many people?

You will need to think about everything you have learned and select from it to answer the question. Here are some of the different ways you could organise your information:

- Organising around wars
Use the three headings:
TOTAL   GLOBAL   COLD
Under each heading write down why that type of war affected so many people.

- Organising over time
You could work through each war chronologically. Prepare yourself by doing a timeline of wars in the twentieth century. You will need to keep your timeline simple – write on it the key points about each war and its affect on people.

- Organising around people
Use a spidergram like the one opposite that has a person in the middle. Write down all the different ways a twentieth-century person could be affected by war. Remember to think of people across the world and throughout the century. Remember that people can be affected indirectly by war, such as suffering from famine as a result of war, as well as directly.
You may want to organise your information in other ways.

Factfile

The Commonwealth War Graves Commission

This organisation will help you find out about any of the servicemen and women listed on memorials to either the First of Second World War. The Commission's website can give you information about who died, where they died and how their deaths are remembered in memorials. You can also trace all the casualties from a particular home town or from a particular regiment. Choose one of the names on your local memorial and use the Commission's website to find out more about this person.

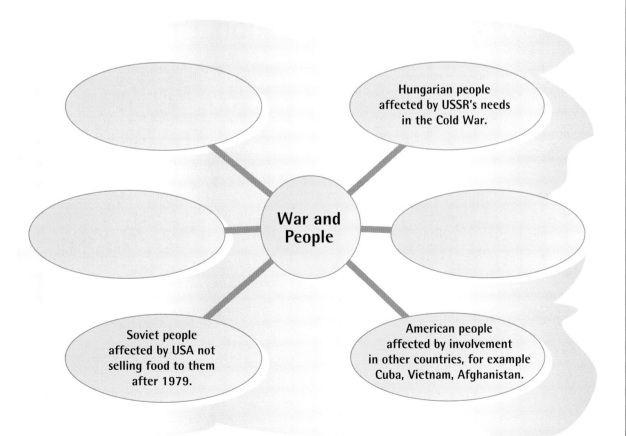

Unit 19: How and why did the Holocaust happen?

RIGHTS AND RESPONSIBILITIES?

The Holocaust is the word used for the deliberate murder of over six million Jews in Europe between 1933 and 1945. Adolf Hitler's Nazi Party exterminated other people as well as Jews, including gypsies, homosexuals and the mentally ill, but wanted to make the whole of the Jewish people extinct. The story is a disturbing one. In this unit we will examine some difficult issues and ask why the Holocaust happened at all. The Jewish people had no rights to protect them from persecution and murder at the hands of the Nazi Party in Europe. Do you understand what basic rights you have in society today? This is the starting point for our investigation.

THE UNIVERSAL DECLARATION OF HUMAN RIGHTS – THE EXAMPLE FOR THE MODERN WORLD

In 1948 the United Nations drew up a list of civil and political rights. This Universal Declaration of Human Rights consists of rules for governments and countries to follow and offers basic protection to individuals. The Declaration includes the rights to:
- life
- liberty
- education
- equality in the law
- freedom of movement
- freedom of religion
- freedom of information
- a nationality.

Question Time

❶ On a copy of your school mission statement or student charter underline the key words that represent your rights.

❷ Work in pairs to make a spider diagram of your rights in school and next to it draw another spider diagram of your responsibilities. These may include attending school or completing homework.

❸ How do the responsibilities match up to the rights? Link them up with arrows.

❹ In school can you have rights without taking up responsibilities?

❺ What other basic rights do we have that are not to do with school? Add more examples of rights and responsibilities that affect other aspects of our lives.

You should be able to find the Declaration on the Internet, and there is a summary of the main points on page 97. We take most of its ideas for granted but groups like Amnesty International exist to monitor the actions of governments and organisations all over the world and check if they are taking notice of human rights.

Does your school have a mission statement which outlines its main aims? What rights do you have? Along with rights we have responsibilities which involve us in society. What responsibilities do you have at school?

THE PROTECTION OF RIGHTS

The European Court of Human Rights can pass judgements against governments or organisations that may have abused people's rights. Our society is democratic and believes that everyone should have an equal say. We are therefore protected by our laws, our Parliament and our police force. We have committees and courts to try to make sure that people in control do not abuse their power.

In school there are rules and people there to protect you against violence, bullying, theft and other injustices. What else might you need protection from at school? How are you protected in any way?

THE DENIAL OF PEOPLE'S RIGHTS

On the news each evening we are shown places somewhere in the world where people's rights are being ignored. Sometimes situations are complicated where there is an argument or even war over land and power. How do some countries, governments and groups deny people their basic rights? One example is when a government uses the power of an army to make people agree with it and do as they are told. Governments and political parties also make great use of the media to control people's ideas. Often this means that they do not have freedom of information. Taking away people's rights can also mean denying them their responsibilities so that they cannot be involved in society.

Question Time

❶ Find an example from the recent news which shows human rights being ignored. If you get stuck look on the Internet under 'Human Rights' or ask an adult.

❷ How many different ways can you think of that might be used to deny people their rights? Add this list to your diagrams of rights and responsibilities. Share your ideas with the rest of your group.

❸ What is wrong with taking away people's responsibilities?

❹ Which basic right would you hate to lose the most? Discuss your answer with a partner.

HOW DID NAZI PERSECUTION OF THE JEWS DEVELOP?

ANTI-JEWISH ATTITUDES IN NAZI GERMANY

Although there were many Jewish people living throughout Germany in the 1930s, they were not considered to be of German nationality and did not have rights as German citizens. Jewish people were integrated in German towns and cities and many of them had developed successful businesses and grown wealthy. This caused resentment and added dislike of a group already considered to be outsiders. The Nazi Party, led by Adolf Hitler, came to power in 1933. The Nazi Government believed that the Aryan race should dominate the world and said that the Jews were a threat to German unity and strength. They blamed the Jewish people for Germany's economic and political problems.

> ### What does it mean?
>
> **Aryan race**
> Hitler claimed that the people of the world could be divided into superior and inferior races. The most superior of all was the Aryan race, made up of most Germans and some other northern Europeans. He considered the Jews to be the most inferior, and that Germany should be 'purified' until all Germans were Aryans.

GERMANY'S PROBLEMS – WORLD DEPRESSION IN THE 1920s AND 30s

The period after the First World War brought debt and depression across Europe and the USSR. The USA experienced boom years in the 1920s but then suffered a financial crisis in 1929, followed by years of economic depression. This crisis, the Wall Street Crash, affected Europe, and the world-wide problems were exaggerated in Germany which was suffering from the terms of the 1919 Treaty of Versailles. This treaty at the end of the First World War forced Germany to accept blame for the war. Germany had to pay massive reparations (compensation in money for having started the war), hand over certain lands and cut back all military forces. These terms not only dented the national pride but also created huge debts. Money lost its value and unemployment reached 40 per cent by 1932. The Jewish people, including many wealthy businessmen, became scapegoats for these problems. Soon after gaining power, the Nazi Party started introducing laws to restrict the freedom of Jews living in Germany. Persecution by the government had begun.

ANTI-SEMITISM – AN OLD IDEA

Hitler and the Nazi Party were by no means the first to think of the Jews as different and treat them with hostility as outsiders. You will be able to find examples of anti-Semitism in many European countries dating back to the Middle Ages.

Jewish people stood out as different in areas across Europe. They had a different religion and different customs when most of the population had become Christian. Some Christians blamed the Jewish people for the execution of Jesus Christ and argued that Jews should be punished forever.

What does it mean?

Anti-Semitism
Against, or dislike of the Jews

Rumours spread about Jewish traditions and in the larger cities Jews were often forced to live together in their own areas, called ghettos. Some Jews became money lenders because they were banned from other work. This increased resentment and suspicion from people who owed them money or were jealous of their success. Jews were also barred from some universities. Often Jewish people had to mark themselves, with a yellow badge, or a distinctive hat. The aim of this was to identify the Jewish people as different and to degrade them. In some cases Jewish people were made scapegoats. They were blamed for causing the Black Death in parts of Europe, and chased out of countries by some rulers. As Jews moved away from religious persecution in eastern Europe in the nineteenth century and made new homes in new countries, they became a focus for attention once more.

This map shows where acts of anti-Semitism took place in Europe before the twentieth century.

KEY

- Principal ghettos
- Close-knit communities of Jews
- Russian Jews forced to live in the Pale of Settlement
- Muslim North Africa. Jews lived in a special quarter, the Mellah
- ★ Church Councils where Jews must wear a special badge on their clothes

North Sea

Baltic Sea

RUSSIA

THE PALE OF SETTLEMENT

Oxford 1222 ★

Frankfurt 1460–1864

Posen ●

Mainz ●

Prague 1473 ●

Breslau 1266 ●

Kazimierz 1494 ●

Vienna 1570 ●

Buda 1279 ★

Mantua 1612 ●

Verona 1605 ●

Venice 1571 ●

Ferrara 1624 ●

Tarascon 1378 ●

Turin 1400 ●

Florence 1571 ●

Rome 1556–1870 ★

Adriatic Sea

Black Sea

BYZANTIUM

Pera (a suburb of Constantinople) ●

PORTUGAL

SPAIN

Madrid 1480 ●

Barcelona 1350 ●

Valencia 1390 ●

Murcia 1412 ●

Naples 1215 ●

Palermo 1312 ●

Patras ●

Coron ●

Rhodes 1310–1522 ●

Fez 1450 ●

Mediterranean Sea

0   800 km
0   500 miles

N

Question Time

❶ Have you learned before today of any examples of Jews being treated differently or blamed for something in history?

❷ Explain two different ways in which Jews have been discriminated against

in past times. Give examples from the map on page 147 where you can.

❸ Why did Jewish immigration from eastern Europe possibly help to increase anti-Semitism in countries like Germany?

ANTI-SEMITISM 1933-9

There is nothing unusual about the children in the photograph (Source 2). Jewish children went to school with German children as Jewish families led normal lives in German towns and cities.

After Hitler came to power he and the Nazi Party began to make the Jewish people feel different. Hitler saw how a campaign against the Jews would help him strengthen his own power. He copied many of the actions that had been taken against the Jews in the past. And then he and his government went much further. Their policies became increasingly harsh. They started by identifying anyone of Jewish blood and then they drew up guidelines to define what made a person a Jew. Gradually they officially increased the restrictions on many aspects of Jews' lives, as the timeline shows.

SOURCE 1

Now the Jews serve as carriers of bacilli (germs) of the worst kind, and they infect souls everywhere. As is typical of all parasites, the Jew keeps enlarging his territory: he lives at the cost of his host and spreads like a dangerous baccilus.

Hitler's views on the Jews. An extract from Hitler's *Mein Kampf* (*My Struggle*) written in 1924, showing the strength of his anti-Semitism.

SOURCE 2

A school photograph of Jewish children in Germany. What is unusual about the children in the photograph?

German laws removing Jewish rights after Hitler became
Chancellor of the German Reich in January 1933

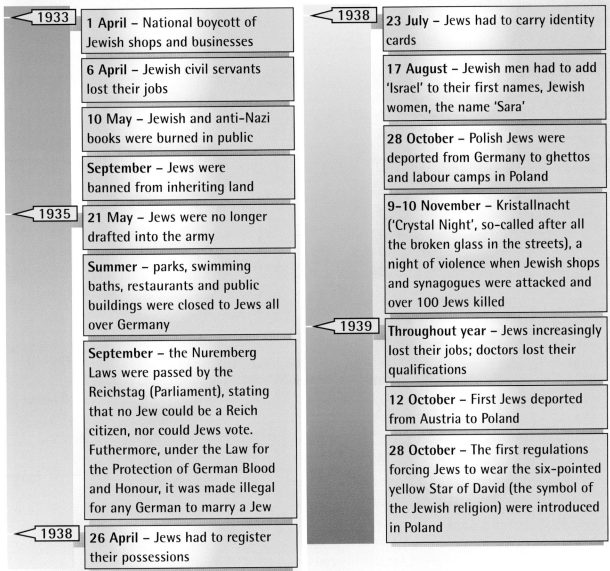

1933

1 April – National boycott of Jewish shops and businesses

6 April – Jewish civil servants lost their jobs

10 May – Jewish and anti-Nazi books were burned in public

September – Jews were banned from inheriting land

1935

21 May – Jews were no longer drafted into the army

Summer – parks, swimming baths, restaurants and public buildings were closed to Jews all over Germany

September – the Nuremberg Laws were passed by the Reichstag (Parliament), stating that no Jew could be a Reich citizen, nor could Jews vote. Futhermore, under the Law for the Protection of German Blood and Honour, it was made illegal for any German to marry a Jew

1938

26 April – Jews had to register their possessions

1938

23 July – Jews had to carry identity cards

17 August – Jewish men had to add 'Israel' to their first names, Jewish women, the name 'Sara'

28 October – Polish Jews were deported from Germany to ghettos and labour camps in Poland

9-10 November – Kristallnacht ('Crystal Night', so-called after all the broken glass in the streets), a night of violence when Jewish shops and synagogues were attacked and over 100 Jews killed

1939

Throughout year – Jews increasingly lost their jobs; doctors lost their qualifications

12 October – First Jews deported from Austria to Poland

28 October – The first regulations forcing Jews to wear the six-pointed yellow Star of David (the symbol of the Jewish religion) were introduced in Poland

WINNING PEOPLE'S MINDS

The Nazi Party did not just use the legal system and the police in its campaign against the Jewish people and other enemies of Germany. A powerful propaganda system was developed by Joseph Goebbels, Hitler's Minister of People's Enlightenment and Propaganda. He censored everything that was printed in Germany and all information about Hitler, the war and the Jews. Anti-Semitic messages were spread to the people of Germany using posters, films, speeches and many other methods. School timetables also included lessons about what makes a pure German citizen and the superiority of the Aryans. Hitler wanted to persuade the German people that the policies of the Nazi Party were the right policies for the country and that they must agree with them.

SOURCE 3

German children were taught in their school books to hate Jews. This cartoon shows a Jewish teacher and Jewish children being expelled from a German school.

Question Time

1 Study Source 1.
 a What image does Hitler give of the Jewish people?
 b Why is this a powerful description?

2 Chose four of the restrictions from the timeline and explain why you think that they were introduced.

3 'Hitler's anti-Semitic policies were not original – he just copied policies from the past'. Do you agree? Use the map on page 147 to help you decide.

4 Study Source 3.
 a What is the message of the cartoon?
 b Why were schoolbooks and lessons a clever way of spreading Nazi ideology (ideas) in Germany?

THE SITUATION INTENSIFIES – THE OUTBREAK OF WAR

War was declared in 1939 as Germany invaded Poland. Austria and Czechoslovakia were already under German control. Denmark, Norway, Belgium, Holland and France all fell to German armies by 1940. The USSR was invaded in 1941 and German expansion was at its peak. As Germany invaded Europe, Jews in other countries became the target for discrimination by the Germans. The Nazi armies of occupation quickly established the anti-Semitic policies already in place in Germany.

ANTI-SEMITIC POLICY AFTER 1939

In October 1939 a policy of enforced sterilisation of Jews was discussed among the Nazi leaders. It aimed to prevent Jewish children being born and was a step towards wiping out the Jewish race. With the outbreak of war, the Nazis were able to use the anti-Semitic campaign to force the Jews and other minorities to work for the war effort in the labour camps. In April 1940 the first ghetto was set up in Poland. A ghetto is a part of a town, usually near a railway line, where Jews are forced to live, crowded together and unable to leave. Ghettos were set up in major European cities, where the Jews were then isolated.

KEY

● Concentration camps

KEY
Numbers of Jews in each country based on Nazi reports

under 10,000
10,000 to 50,000
50,000 to 100,000
100,000 to 500,000
500,000 to 1 million
over 1 million
figures not known

THE FINAL SOLUTION

In 1941 the Nazis developed plans to deal with what they called the 'Jewish problem'. The plans were agreed at the Wannsee Conference in 1942 and were called the Final Solution. They were only known to a few people. The Final Solution involved the extermination of all Jewish people in Europe and was to be carried out in stages. Hitler believed that this would enable his control of Europe to be complete. On 31 July 1941 the first experimental gassing took place in Auschwitz, Poland. In December 1941 the first permanent extermination camp was established, also in Poland. By 1942, when the German advance was beginning to be beaten back, the Nazis became increasingly desperate to implement the Final Solution. The pace of the plan increased. Jews and other undesirables were to be shot by mobile murder units, called *Einsatzgruppen*, or sent to extermination camps.

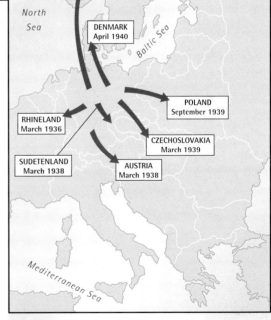

Hitler's invasion of Europe. The top map shows the number of Jews in each country, based on Nazi reports, and the locations of concentration camps. The lower map shows when Germany invaded other European countries.

Question Time

1. What rights and responsibilities had been denied the Jews by 1940? Look back at the timeline for help.

2. What was the main aim of Nazi anti-Semitic policy after 1941?

3. Why did the suffering of Jews increase as war broke out? Discuss this question in pairs and then answer it using these ideas to start you off:

- war was used as an excuse for persecution
- the need for labour
- the need for popular support
- the countries invaded by Germany brought more Jews under Nazi control, e.g. in the USSR and eastern Europe.

HOW AND WHY WERE GHETTOS SET UP AND WHAT WAS IT LIKE INSIDE THEM?

SOURCE 1

A Jewish mother and her children in the Warsaw ghetto.

SOURCE 2

All told, from various parts of the city 40,000 Jews were assembled and driven into the ghetto. When I passed through the wooden gates of the ghetto, I breathed a sigh of relief, for we were no longer being herded through the streets by Lithuanians and Germans. I thought that I had left my oppressors outside; how could I know that there was only an entrance to the ghetto – no exit!

As we entered, we were directed to a house that would have been occupied by a family of four to six people under normal conditions; now 25 or 30 of us were crammed in. Everybody was searching for a place to sleep. I was lucky, my mother found an empty space under a table and that became my bed ... Going to the synagogue, praying and studying about our religion were absolutely forbidden. The Germans wanted to break the Jewish spirit and morale. Many people lost their will to live, but I was too stubborn to give in.

A survivor remembers his first days in the Vilna ghetto in Poland.

Question Time

1 Study Sources 1–3. Make a list of all the information that they tell us and another list of all the questions that you would like to know about the sources.

SOURCE 3

The first step for the final aim (another code word, like solution) is the concentration of the Jews from the countryside into the large cities.

Reinhard Heydrich, the head of the Gestapo, talks to his special duty groups about how to put the Final Solution into action.

TRAPPED IN THE GHETTO

The ghettos were set up by members of the SS (the *Schutzstaffel* or security squad, who were very loyal to Hitler and the Nazis). Jews from country and town areas all over the new German Empire were rounded up and driven into the ghettos. These were in the slum areas of the major cities, surrounded by high walls and armed security guards. Jews were in effect kept prisoner there. The ghettos were very overcrowded – the Warsaw ghetto in Poland held 400,000 Jews in an area two per cent of the size of the city. Often there were raids and arrests by the authorities and Jews would be herded up and shot or deported.

People were taken away and never heard of again. Some sent postcards from new camps that they had been moved to, but many Jews were suspicious of these messages, thinking that the Germans probably forged them or forced someone to send them. Jews who were not deported often died from disease or starvation. Estimates suggest that 20 per cent of Jews died in this way.

Rations were deliberately tiny. The other way that the authorities tried to kill Jews 'naturally' was by working them to death. Groups of forced labourers were taken under armed guard to work on building projects where they would be beaten if they stopped work.

SOURCE 4

There are about 27,000 apartments with an average number of two and a half rooms. Occupancy therefore works out at 15.1 persons per apartment and six to seven persons per room.

The SS officer in charge of Warsaw ghetto reported these details to his superior.

SOURCE 5

The most fearful sight is of that of freezing children. Little children with bare feet, bare knees and torn clothing stand dumbly in the street weeping. Tonight ... I heard a tot of three or four yammering (crying). The child will probably be found frozen to death tomorrow morning, a few hours off.

An extract from *Notes from the Warsaw Ghetto* written by Emmanual Ringelblum, a Jewish writer who was confined there.

SOURCE 6

A street used by Germans ran through the Lodz ghetto in Poland. A bridge was built and guarded so that Jews were kept separate.

SOURCE 7

Some ghettos were surrounded by fences or barbed wire, as in Lodz, or by a wall, as in Warsaw – which the Jews had to pay a German firm to build. The ghetto wall in Cracow, Poland, was made of gravestones from the Jewish cemetery.

A modern historian describes the ghettos.

TRYING TO STAY ALIVE

Jews in ghettos grouped together and organised themselves to try to keep their sanity and stay alive. It was hard when they had to obey all the German orders and so many restrictions were enforced to try to defeat them. Secret lessons were held, as well as meetings, lectures and prayer meetings. A secret newspaper was produced and some Jews worked as couriers, travelling from ghetto to ghetto to pass on information. It was dangerous work. Children often became smugglers, escaping from the ghettos to scavenge for food.

Activity Time

You have been asked to prepare a talk for a history conference on 'The ghettos in the Second World War'. Your talk will need to be over 500 words. Mention sources where you can and include any extra research. Draw conclusions on these key questions:

a How and where were the ghettos set up?
b Why were the ghettos set up?
c How were Jewish men, women and children treated in the ghettos?

HOW WAS THE FINAL SOLUTION PUT INTO PLACE?

One of the most infamous images of the Holocaust is the front view of Auschwitz camp (see Source 1, page 156) with the railway track running through the front gate. It has become a symbol of what was to be the future of millions of Jews in concentration and extermination camps – a symbol of the unknown, of fear and of death. Details of the death camps show us the extent of the horrors of the Holocaust. There are some difficult facts to face.

There had been large scale killings across Germany since before the outbreak of war. Groups of 'enemies' were taken to forests, shot and piled into mass graves. Mobile extermination teams had the responsibility of killing large numbers of Jews. As the Final Solution developed it became more organised and systematic. Even though the German armies were losing ground in Africa and the USSR and needed more men, the German Government still put men and resources into removing its enemies. The Jews were considered to be the main 'enemy' to be dealt with.

WHO WAS THE ENEMY?

The German SS forces were responsible for the killing of approximately six million Jews in Europe during the Holocaust. In addition to this the Germans killed civilians, resistance workers and prisoners of war in Poland, the USSR, Yugoslavia and other countries they invaded. They also targeted the handicapped, homosexuals, Catholics, communists and gypsies. Political offenders were another main target. They could include teachers, writers and anyone who sheltered a Jewish person. Anyone considered to be an enemy of the Nazi Party could be shot, beaten to death or taken to a concentration camp.

Enemies of the Nazi Party or non-Ayrians were persecuted and often killed. It was the Jewish people who became the victims of genocide.

What does it mean?

Genocide
The extermination of a race of people.

SOURCE 1

The entrance to the Auschwitz camp.

WERE ALL THE CAMPS DEATH CAMPS?

After 1941 and the planning of the Final Solution, six camps were established just for the murder of Jews. These were all based in Poland. Over 20 other concentration camps had been running since 1933 as labour camps. In these Jews and non-Jews were starved, tortured and murdered in horrific conditions. Possibly the most notorious was Auschwitz concentration camp. It was really a series of camps including factories for making rubber oil and explosives as well as Auschwitz-Birkenau, the extermination death camp.

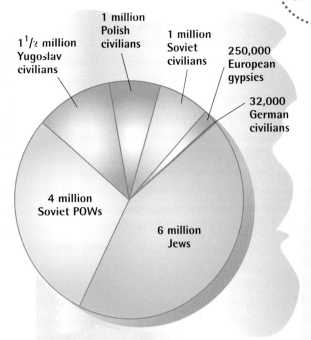

Estimates of the victims of Nazi occupation.

Pie chart labels: 1 million Polish civilians; 1½ million Yugoslav civilians; 1 million Soviet civilians; 250,000 European gypsies; 32,000 German civilians; 4 million Soviet POWs; 6 million Jews.

Activity Time

❶ Create a large spider diagram, as a class or in groups, with key words to sum up what you think the Final Solution involved. Include ideas even if you are unsure if they are fact or fiction. Think about what happened, using all your knowledge.

❷ Make a list of the questions that you would like asked about the Final Solution. Include questions even if you think that they are obvious. Other people may not know the answer either.

Question Time

❶ Why are all the statistics of the victims of Nazi occupation only estimates?

❷ Explain whether each of these statements is true or false:
a All concentration camps were extermination camps.
b Only Jews were killed in the extermination camps.
c All the Jews were killed using gas.
d Six million Jews were killed during the Holocaust.

FROM THE GHETTOS TO THE CONCENTRATION CAMPS

In the ghettos the Jews themselves were given the job of selecting people to fill the quotas for the German SS. Quotas were set for the numbers of Jews to be deported to concentration camps. Their goods were confiscated and sold to fund the process. In effect, Jews were made to pay for and organise many aspects of the Holocaust. They had little choice, and many would try to save a few people if they could. Some ghettos tried to resist. At the Warsaw ghetto Jews held out against the SS for several weeks but the ghetto was then burnt down. Once Jews were taken from the ghettos they were herded onto cattle wagons, often with no food or drink. Their personal details were recorded with great efficiency. It was a military operation.

SOURCE 2

On 2 April, we were taken to a train station, put into groups of sixty and crowded into freight cars. Each of us was given a bucket to serve as a toilet. We wondered where we were going and how long the journey would last. It was difficult to see outside because there was only one small window ... hours passed, the smell became unbearable. The lice spread to all of us, and weak people, one by one, were dying.

Errikos Sevillias was a Jew living in Athens when the German and Italian armies invaded. He was arrested and sent to Auschwitz where he survived by joining a working party.

ARRIVAL AND SELECTION

Old women, mothers with small children, pregnant women, and children under ten were usually taken immediately to be executed. Young boys would lie about their age and invent a skill or craft in order to be given work and stay alive.

SOURCE 4

As we huddled together, the SS quickly separated the men from the women. They took the old and the sick and put them in a special line. They asked for twins, but no one volunteered, even though there were twins among us. The doctor who examined me ... held my arm down on a table and tattooed it with the number 182699. My entire body was shaved, then I was given a shower and afterwards issued clothes which had huge red painted marks on them. This was so I could be easily spotted if I tried to escape.

Errikos Sevillias describes his arrival at Auschwitz.

DAY BY DAY

Prisoners were given varied jobs to do. Those who found themselves working in the kitchens had a greater chance of survival. Possibly the worst job was to deal with the bodies. They were taken from the gas chambers to the crematoria where they were burnt. The daily routine was strict, roll calls for several hours per day, before forced labour in mines or factories. Any offence would lead to beating, attack by dogs or shooting. Conditions were appalling. Food was deliberately scarce, a little bread and thin soup. As well as working their prisoners to death, the Nazis were starving them to death. Disease spread quickly. In many camps some victims were used in cruel medical experiments, mostly without anaesthetic. Doctors were experimenting to create the perfect Aryan type, for example by injecting blue dye into brown eyes.

THE FINAL SOLUTION

Prisoners not worked, starved or beaten to death faced the ultimate part in the Final Solution – death in the gas chambers. Carbon monoxide and Zyclon B gasses were both used to kill people on a large scale. The aim was to operate the Solution as efficiently as possible. At Treblinka and Belzec extermination camps 140,000 people had been killed per month by August 1942. People who were taken there were killed instantly unless they had special craft skills or could work as labourers around the camp. Most gas chambers were fitted out as showers so that the prisoners would not realise what was happening and panic. Bodies were burnt in ovens or left in mass pits. Richard Dimbleby, a BBC journalist was one of the first reporters to enter Belsen camp when it was liberated in 1945. He described one of the pits of bodies to be the size of a tennis court.

MAXIMUM EFFICIENCY

What happened to the possessions of the prisoners and their bodies indicates the extent to which the Nazi soldiers and camp officials treated the Final Solution as a military operation with no thought for human life. Gold fillings from teeth were removed from bodies and melted down to send back to Germany. Hair that had been cut was used to make mattresses. Even the ashes of the bodies was sometimes used as fertiliser. The Germans did not want evidence to be found – they had to get rid of all proof. People living near the sites of camps in Poland today can still see ash in the ground or in ponds.

SOURCE 5

In most cases the new arrivals did not know what awaited them. They were received with cold efficiency, but without brutality, invited to undress 'for the showers'. Sometimes they were handed soap and towels and promised hot coffee after their showers. The gas chambers were, in fact, camouflaged as shower rooms, with pipes, faucets, dressing rooms, clothes hooks, benches and so forth. If the prisoners showed the smallest signs of suspecting their fate, the SS and their collaborators used ... extreme brutality, with shouts, kicks, shots. They loosed their dogs, which were trained to tear prisoners to pieces, against people who were often confused, desperate, and weakened by five or ten days travelling in sealed railroad cars.

Primo Levi, an Italian Jew, describes why most prisoners did not try to escape from the gas chambers.

ESCAPE

Chances of escape were virtually non existent. Camps were guarded and surrounded by electric fencing and spotlights. Anyone who did try to escape was tortured then shot or hanged in public as a warning to the other prisoners. In 1943, 150 prisoners managed to escape from Treblinka and 300 escaped from Sobibor in the same year. At Auschwitz there was an unsuccessful attempt to escape.

SOURCE 6

The glasses of victims at Auschwitz.

Question Time

1. Why didn't prisoners try to escape or resist their treatment?

2. Why didn't prisoners know what would happen to them?

3. Return to your spider diagram on page 157. How many of the points have turned out to be true? Find any that are incorrect or too general and change them.

Activity Time

The Final Solution

1. In groups find out more about the Final Solution. Use ideas from these pages but also your own research. Your teacher will give you one topic to focus on.

2. Present your findings to the rest of the class, including one image and a summary. Explain what your image shows and why you have chosen this one rather than any other.

PEOPLE OF THE HOLOCAUST

Some people's stories of the Holocaust stand out as particularly famous. Oscar Schindler, Martin Niemöller, and Anne Frank are just three examples you may have heard of.

Oscar Schindler

Schindler was a wealthy Czechoslovakian industrialist who, as a member of the Nazi Party and a Nazi Intelligence Agent, made contacts with high ranking Nazi officials. He set up a factory near to a ghetto, using Jewish people as cheap labour. As the Final Solution was put into place he began to protect his workers, bribing Nazi officials and guards, smuggling in food and health supplies and forging documents. His factory made defective bullets for the German army, none of which ever passed quality tests and so were unused. Schindler was arrested several times but always released. His money and determination kept his workforce of 1200 Jews safe from the concentration and extermination camps. He was a controversial man, known for drinking and womanising and made famous in 1993 by the film *Schindler's List*. He was recognised by Jewish groups in 1960 as a 'Righteous Gentile' (a non-Jewish person who risked their life to save Jews during the Holocaust).

Pastor Martin Niemöller

Niemöller was a Protestant minister and theologian who campaigned against the Nazis treatment of the churches. He defended the right to speak out against the Party's control of the churches. He was Christian with a Jewish background. He sent Hitler a memo in 1936 and was arrested for resisting Nazi laws and sent to Dachau concentration camp. He was freed by the Allies in 1945.

Question Time

1. Why was it important that the bullets made in Schindler's factory were defective?

2. Schindler and Niemöller are both famous for helping Jews in different ways. Find another example of someone who acted or spoke out to help the Jews during the Holocaust.

SOURCE 7

A scene from the film *Schindler's List*, showing Oscar Schindler (centre) with his wife and his factory manager, Itzhak Stern.

ANNE FRANK'S DIARY

You will probably either recognise this person or have heard her name before. Anne Frank was Jewish, and became famous because she wrote a diary of her years in hiding before her family were captured by the German army in 1944. Her diary describes her experiences and what she saw happening in Holland during the Nazi occupation.

SOURCE 1

The Frank family in Amsterdam, 1941 – Margot, Otto, Anne and Edith.

WHAT WAS HAPPENING TO JEWS IN AMSTERDAM?

After the German armies invaded Holland in 1940 anti-Jewish laws were brought in. Jewish companies and managers had to register with the Nazi authorities. Jews had to wear a Star of David to let everyone know they were Jewish. They could only shop at certain shops and only be outside until certain times. One night before going into hiding Anne got into trouble from her father for being late home. He was worried that she might be arrested by the police for breaking the curfew. As increasing numbers of Jews were summoned to report for registration many businessmen stopped working so that they would not have to register. They knew that they would be taken to Westerbork transit camp and then on to labour camps in Germany. At the beginning of 1941 German police began arresting all the Jews in Holland.

Anne Frank's timeline

12 June 1929 Anne is born in Frankfurt, Germany

Jan 1933 The Frank family move to Holland

1934 Anne begins school in Amsterdam

1941 Anne and her older sister Margot start at a Jewish secondary school

Early July 1942 Margot Frank is ordered to report to the Nazi authorities for transfer to a labour camp

6 July 1942 Anne and her family move into their hiding place – the secret annexe. They are joined over the next ten days by the Van Daan family and Mr Dussel, who worked at Mr Frank's factory

4 August 1944 Anne and the occupants of the secret annexe are discovered, arrested by the Gestapo (secret police) and taken to a transportation camp, ready to move to a labour camp or a death camp in Poland

THE SECRET ANNEXE

Otto Frank (Anne's father) had been planning the secret annexe for some time. He had decided that hiding was the only chance of survival for his family. He prepared some attic rooms concealed behind his office as a hiding place for his family. He planned to move the family there on 16 July 1942. He had taken furniture and some basic possessions to the attic but when Margot received her call up from the Nazi authorities there was no time for further preparations. The family had to move at once from their home, wearing several layers of clothing and carrying all their belongings in one satchel and a shopping bag each. They had to be careful. Any suspicious behaviour might bring them to the attention of the police.

A plan of the secret annexe.

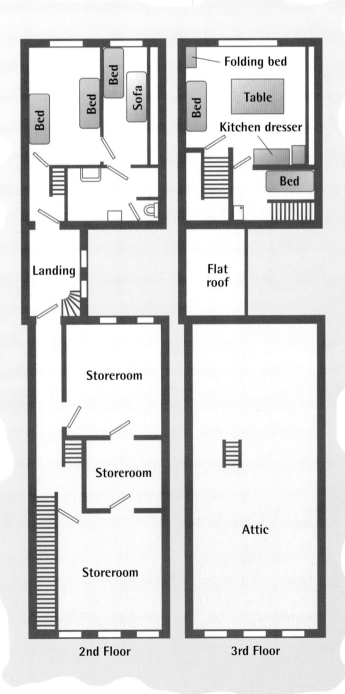

2nd Floor

3rd Floor

SOURCE 2

We have to whisper and tread lightly during the day, otherwise the people in the warehouse might hear us.

An entry from Anne's diary for 11 July 1942.

SOURCE 3

Ordinary people simply don't know what books mean to us, shut up here. Reading, learning and the radio are our amusements.

Anne's diary entry for 11 July 1943.

SOURCE 4

Our Jewish friends are being taken away by the dozen ... It is impossible to escape; most of the people in the camp (in Holland) are branded as inmates by their shaven heads. If it is as bad as this in Holland whatever will it be like in the barbarous regions they are sent to? ... The British radio speaks of their being gassed.

From Anne Frank's diary, 9 October 1942.

SOURCE 5

Evening after evening the grey and green army lorries trundle past. The Germans ring at every door to enquire if there are any Jews living in the house. If there are then the whole family has to go at once. If they don't find any they go onto the next house. No one has a chance of evading them unless they go into hiding.

From Anne Frank's diary, 19 November 1942.

DEAR KITTY

Anne writes each diary entry to 'Kitty' as if she were a close friend. Anne's diary tells us the fears of one victim of the Holocaust. It also shows the experiences of a teenage girl during the war. She pours out frustrations, moods and interests. She grumbles and jokes about the other people in the annexe and describes their day-to-day concerns – as well as their many arguments. She also writes about her feelings towards her parents and in particular about her increasingly close friendship with Peter van Daan. Anne decided that after the war she would publish her diary. Alongside the original she rewrote and edited passages and added bits which she thought would interest readers. These included events written from memory.

Question Time

❶ What rights were withdrawn from Anne and her family before they went into hiding?

❷ Make a list of the sorts of things that Anne could and could not do whilst she was in hiding.

❸ Why do you think that the Frank family:
a Went into hiding when they did?
b Went into hiding rather than escape from Holland?

ANNE'S DIARY IS PUBLISHED

After the war the diaries were passed to Anne's father by Miep Gies, who found them in the annexe. In 1947 he edited and published a shortened diary, suitable for teenagers to read. In 1989 a second edition of Anne's diary was published, containing more material and showing all sides of Anne's character, including her inner thoughts and dreams. Anne's diary has sold millions of copies in different languages and teaches people all over the world about some of the horrors of the Holocaust.

Question Time

① Why do you think that writing a diary was so important to Anne?

② Suggest some reasons why Anne's father did not include all of Anne's writing in the published diary.

③ Unlike many Jewish families the Frank family were able to survive for two years before being arrested. Why was this?

④ Try to find out about another Jewish person or family forced into hiding. Point out what was similar and what was different to about their story compared to Anne's.

SOURCE 6

Everyone thinks I'm showing off when I talk, ridiculous when I'm silent, insolent when I answer, cunning when I have a good idea, lazy when I'm tired, selfish when I eat one bite more than I should, stupid, cowardly, calculating, etc., etc. All day long I hear nothing but what an exasperating child I am, and although I laugh it off and pretend not to mind, I do mind ... More than once I've snapped at mother: 'I don't care what you say. Why don't you just wash your hands of me – I'm a hopeless case.'

Diary extract, 30 January 1943.

SUPPORT NETWORK

Anne and her family and friends could not survive in the annexe without food and help from outside. Five employees of Mr Frank agreed to help them. Forged ration cards were made by the Resistance in Holland (the underground organisation working against the Nazi invasion) to be used to buy food without too much suspicion. Miep Gies, her husband Jan, together with Mr Kraler, Mr Koophuis and Elli Vossen supported the hideaways for the two years until they were discovered.

THE END OF THE STORY

The occupants of the secret annexe were discovered and arrested on 4 August 1944. They were taken to Westerbork transportation camp before being moved to Auschwitz extermination camp in Poland. Mrs Frank died of starvation in Auschwitz. Mr Van Daan was gassed to death there. Mr Dussel died at Neuengamme camp near Hamburg. Peter Van Daan died in Mauthausen camp in Austria. Anne, Margot and Mrs Van Daan were moved to Bergen Belsen camp and died there. Anne and Margot died from typhus. A month after their deaths the camp was liberated by the Allies. Mr Frank survived the Holocaust.

SOURCE 7

Anne Frank's name is included on the last list of names of deportees from Westerbork transportation camp to Auschwitz camp in 1944.

JUDENTRANSPORT AUS DEN NIEDERLANDEN - LAGER WESTERBORK

Haeftlinge

301.✓Engers	Isidor — ✓30.4. 93 –	Kaufmann
302✓ Engers	Leonard	15.6. 20 -	Lamdarbeiter
303✓ Franco	Manfred - ✓1.5. 05 –	Verleger
304. Frank	Arthur	22.8. 81	Kaufmann
305. Frank ×	Isaac	✓29.11.87	Installateur
306. Frank	Margot	16.2. 26	ohne
307. Frank ✓	Otto	✓12.5. 89	Kaufmann
308.✓ Frank-Hollaender	Edith	16.1. 00	ohne
309. Frank	Anneliese 12.6. 29	ohne
310. v.Franck	Sara –	27.4. 02-	Typistin
311. Franken	Rozanna	16.5. 96-	Landarbeiter
312.✓ Franken-Weyand	Johanna	24.12.96▸	Landbauer
313. Franken	Hermann —✓12.5.34	ohne

WHAT HAPPENED WHEN PEOPLE FOUND OUT ABOUT THE HOLOCAUST?

SOURCE 1

Here are the facts about Belsen, the first concentration camp that the British soldiers have seen. Within its barbed wire fences, covering about fifteen acres, there are 40,000 men, women and children. They are German, Polish, Russian and six other nationalities besides this. Of the total, 4250 are acutely ill or dying of virulent disease. It is doubtful in the extreme if they can be saved. 25,600, of which three quarters are women, are ill from malnutrition or are actually dying from starvation. In the last few months the Germans have killed or allowed to die in the Belsen camp 30,000 more.

SOURCE 2

Such figures are staggering. It's something that we can hardly believe. But perhaps I can quote the young tommy gunner of the Eleventh Armoured Division, who was on sentry duty. He said 'now I believe every word I've heard about the Nazis'.

SOURCE 3

Let there be no mistake about it ... this day was the most horrible of my life. You will be glad to know that we have caught alive the commandant of the place, Kramer, and the whole of his SS guard who are now being made to carry the bodies. I have never seen British soldiers so moved to cold fury as the men who opened Belsen camp.

Richard Dimbleby was the first reporter to see the Belsen concentration camp in Germany when it was liberated in April 1945. Belsen was a prison camp, rather than an extermination camp, but had become horribly overcrowded as the SS moved prisoners into it away from the approaching Russian armies. Dimbleby broke down during the recording of what he saw. Although there had been news reports in England since 1942 of the mass killing of Jews, the BBC were reluctant to broadcast his report until they had checked that such horrendous information was correct. Sources 1–3 are extracts from his report.

Question Time

❶ Study Sources 1–3. What words can you find to describe Richard Dimbleby's feelings when he saw the Belsen concentration camp?

❷ How does Dimbleby show his attitude towards the Nazis?

❸ Belsen was not an extermination camp, so why had so many people died?

❹ What does the quote from the young British soldier suggest to us about attitudes towards:
a rumours about the Holocaust
b the Nazis?

❺ Why do you think that the BBC were cautious about broadcasting the report?

DID THE WORLD KNOW ABOUT THE HOLOCAUST BEFORE 1945?

Although the Nazis aimed to keep details of the Final Solution secret, a news report came from Poland to the Allies and to the Vatican as early as 1942. The British and American Governments condemned the extermination camps in a public statement in that year, but did not take action. A minute of silence was held in the British Parliament. In 1944 a Western Refugee Board was set up. British and American Governments allowed refugees into their countries, but in limited numbers. Conferences were held, but failed to take any decisive action. The Allies refused to bomb train lines or concentration camps. They did not want to believe the rumours and were concerned about the lack of direct proof of the Final Solution. Leaked Nazi reports spoke of 'removing' and 'resettling' the Jews and giving them 'special treatment', camouflaging what was happening.

Response from the Christian churches was also limited. The Pope called for more humane treatment of people during the war and gave his sympathy for what was happening. Religious leaders in western Europe spoke out, but in Germany priests and ministers did not oppose Nazi policy.

SOURCE 5

If we hadn't seen those ghastly skeletons and great heaps of emaciated bodies I don't think we would have believed it. Even now it doesn't seem possible that human behaviour could sink to such depths ...

George MacDonald Fraser, survivor of the war in Burma, reporter and novelist, saw newsreel footage of Belsen in a cinema.

SOURCE 4

So far three million have died. It is the greatest mass killing in recorded history; and it goes on daily, hourly, as regularly as the ticking of your watch. I have been lecturing Allied troops for three years now and their attitude is always the same. They don't believe it.

Arthur Koestler, an American journalist, writing in the *New York Times* in January 1944.

Question Time

1. Do Sources 4 and 5 help to explain one reason for lack of intervention by Allied governments?

2. Why do you think that newsreel footage of camps such as Belsen was shown in cinemas at the end of the war?

HOW DID PEOPLE REACT?

Many SS officers and commandants fled the camps as it became clear Germany was close to defeat. Local militias who had worked in the camps also left and hid in their villages. When Russian and British troops arrived at the camps they faced undeniable proof of the rumours. No one could have expected the extent of the murder. Some camp officials were caught alive and arrested. Local civilians were made to walk through the camps to see what had been happening in their neighbourhood. Many denied knowledge of what had been going on. Thousands of remaining bodies were buried as quickly as possible to prevent disease from spreading further.

When the Allies occupied Germany they made German people watch a film showing the details of the atrocities of the Holocaust.

SOURCE 6

Female SS guards at Bergen-Belsen camp in Germany are made to bury the bodies of those people they helped to kill.

Question Time

❶ Look at Source 6. Why are these women burying bodies?

❷ Why do you think that Allied soldiers made local civilians walk through the camps and help to bury many of the dead?

❸ What happened to Nazi camp leaders?

THE NEED FOR JUSTICE

The Allies were concerned to catch the leaders of the Holocaust and to see justice carried out. In 1945 a war crimes court was set up in Nuremberg. It tried 22 different Holocaust leaders, including Hoess, Eichmann and Göring. Hitler, Himmler and Göbbels had all committed suicide at the end of the war in Europe.

THE NUREMBERG TRIALS – VERDICT IN 1946

- The trial was organised by representatives from the USA, Britain, France and the USSR.
- The new charge of 'crimes against humanity' was introduced to deal with the Holocaust.
- Nineteen men were found guilty.
- Twelve men were hanged, three charged with life imprisonment, four charged with shorter prison sentences.
- There were many eye-witnesses and enormous amounts of detailed documentary evidence of the workings of the Final Solution. Diaries, log books, accounts, blue-prints for the gas chambers and many more pieces of evidence were brought together. The Nazis had been highly efficient in their record-keeping and this helped to prove the extent of their guilt.

SOURCE 7

Hans Heinrich Lamner, Hitler's right-hand man, at his trial in Nuremberg in 1947.

SUBSEQUENT TRIALS

Similar trials took place all over Europe and in the 20 years after the Holocaust over 20,000 people were taken to court for war crimes. One of the most famous is the trial of Adolf Eichmann, the commandant of Auschwitz, who fled to Argentina. He was discovered by the Israeli secret police, put on trial in Israel and hanged from the gallows that were used outside the kitchens at Auschwitz. Trials for war criminals from the Second World War still take place today.

DIFFICULT QUESTIONS

Since the Second World War it is not only the problem of war criminals that the world has had to face in the aftermath of war. Communities and countries have tried to come to terms with the events of the Holocaust. Many people, governments, organisations and churches helped or ignored the Final Solution, and many Germans felt shame or guilt at their involvement or that of their parents or country.

SOURCE 8

The wrongs we seek to condemn and punish have been so calculated, so malignant and so devastating, that civilisation cannot tolerate their being ignored because it cannot survive their being repeated.

Justice of the Supreme Court Robert Jackson, who represented the USA at the Nuremberg Trials said this during the trials of 1945-6.

SOURCE 9

Most of those accused of murder were not aware of the seriousness of their crimes. For instance, one man did not feel burdened in the least because, after all, he had only killed 5000. He said, ' Why am I being punished? It was only 5000. Ohlendorf killed 20,000, – that's something completely different'.

A commander of Soviet volunteers in the German army said this in an interview in 1989–90.

Activity Time

Here are some difficult questions. Discuss them in groups.

❶ Are owners of factories producing the gas Zyclon B guilty of mass murder?

❷ Are the camp guards as guilty as the commandants?

❸ Were Nazi SS guards just following orders and defending their country?

❹ Should war criminals be given sentences according to the number of people they killed?

❺ Should the industrialists who used prisoners as cheap labour also be taken to trial?

❻ The Allies knew of the mass murder well before the end of the war. Should they take some blame?

❼ Should survivors who have lost relatives receive compensation?

❽ Should survivors who had possessions removed receive compensation?

❾ War criminals can never get a fair trial. Do you agree?

❿ Should the people of Germany pay for their country's mistakes?

Question Time

1 What attitude does the judge in Source 8 take towards the accused war criminal?

2 Does the fact that the Holocaust happened over 50 years ago make any difference to the trials of Nazi war criminals today?

3 Why is it so difficult to establish blame and punishment for crimes like those described in Source 9?

4 'All that is necessary for evil to prosper is for good men to stand idle.' What does this quote suggest about the responsibility for the Holocaust?

5 Who do you think should accept responsibility for the war crimes – leaders, the army, groups like the UN, other governments, the civilians who watch it happen?

6 Can ordinary people take action to prevent atrocities like this from recurring?

Activity Time

Your teacher will split you into two groups. One group will consider answers to **a**, the other to **b**. Be prepared to present your case in a mini debate in front of the class.

a What arguments might people use to argue that Nazi war criminals should not be taken to court?

b What arguments might people use to argue that Nazi war criminals should always be put on trial?

WHAT HAPPENED TO SURVIVORS?

The survivors of the Holocaust had to begin to rebuild their lives. They had both practical and psychological problems to deal with. Immediately after liberation many ex-prisoners actually became more critically ill, as they seemed to stop fighting for survival. The ability of the body to cope with food after such malnutrition was limited. Disease continued to spread. Millions of people were homeless and without any family or friends to support them.

Displaced Persons (DPs)

About 30 million people in total lost their homes during the war. This figure included many POWs and labourers.

Taking action

Jewish organisations helped to trace living relatives and reunite families. Many children were orphaned. Some were given to Christian families or to churches to care for. Some remained with their foster families for the rest of their lives. The Red Cross and the Allied armies opened camps and shelters for the DPs. There was a desperate need for survivors to find work to earn a living, so for many all opportunity for education or training was lost. Many people left Europe to start new

Approximate figures for Displaced Persons

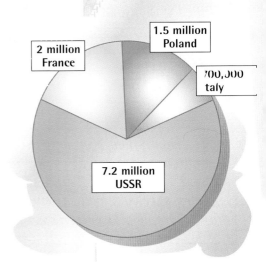

1.5 million
Poland

2 million
France

700,000
Italy

7.2 million
USSR

lives in Australia or Canada. Others moved around Europe and felt as thought they had lost their roots. For some Jews the creation of a Jewish homeland in Israel in 1948 was a healing step after the Holocaust. When Palestine was divided to make the Jewish homeland, many Arabs were forced to move and this has caused arguments over land ever since.

Activity Time

Copy a large version of this ripple diagram in order to build up a pattern of how the lives of survivors were affected.

Here are statements of different effects of the Holocaust on survivors. Make them into cards and place them on your ripple diagram to show how people were affected. Alternatively you could write them onto your diagram in pencil. Remember that the worst effect will be at the centre of your diagram. You could also divide your diagram into different sections, for example; psychological problems and practical issues, or long term and short term problems. Place each statement in the correct zone/s.

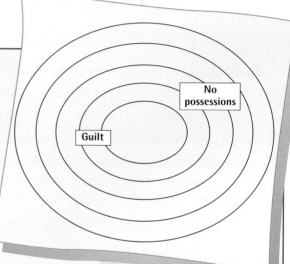

How did the Holocaust affect people's lives?

Survivors had no possessions

Survivors felt guilty that they had lived

Families and friends had been lost or separated

Memories of the Holocaust remained

Some Jews faced a hostile reception; in Poland locals killed a thousand Jews when they returned 'home'

Some Jews had their faith in God and/or man shattered

Survivors could not grieve properly – they had no graves to visit and no information about the circumstances in which friends or family died

Homes had been destroyed or taken over by civilians

Some survivors wanted revenge or justice, and for others to never forget the Holocaust

Health problems, caused by malnutrition, continued

EXPRESSIONS OF THE HOLOCAUST

Never Shall I Forget

Never shall I forget that night
The first night in the camp
Which has turned my life into one long night,
Seven times cursed and seven times sealed.

Never shall I forget that smoke.
Never shall I forget the little faces of the
  children
Whose bodies I saw turned into wreaths of
  smoke
Beneath a silent blue sky.

Never shall I forget those flames
Which consumed my faith for ever.
Never shall I forget the nocturnal silence
Which deprived me for all eternity of the
  desire to live.

Never shall I forget those moments
Which murdered my God and my soul
And turned my dreams into dust.

Never shall I forget these things,
Even if I am condemned to live
as long as God himself.

Never.

Elie Wiesel (born 1928)

Elie Wiesel was a Romanian Jew who was
sent to Auschwitz and Buchenwald labour
camps. His mother, father and sister died in
the Holocaust. He is a Professor in America
and won the Nobel Prize for Peace in 1986.

The Trains

Signed by Franz Paul Stangl, Commandant,
There is in Berlin a document,
An order of transmittal from Treblinka

248 freight cars of clothing,
400,000 gold watches,
25 freight cars of women's hair.

Some fine clothing was kept, some was
  pulped for paper.
The finest watches were never melted down.
All the women's hair was used for mattresses,
  or dolls.

Would these words like to use some of that
  same paper?
One of those watches may pulse in your own
  wrist.
Does someone you know collect dolls, or
sleep on human hair?

He is dead at last, Commandant Stangl of
  Treblinka,
But the camp's three syllables still sound like
  freight cars
Straining around a curve, Treblinka

Treblinka. Clothing, time in gold watches,
Women's hair for mattresses and dolls' heads.
Treblinka. The trains from Treblinka.

William Heyen (born 1940)

What does it mean?

Consumed – eaten up
Nocturnal - night time
Eternity - all time

Question Time

1 Why do you think that Elie Wiesel
repeats one phrase several times in the
poem *Never Shall I Forget*?

2 What does this poem suggest to us
about the effects of the Holocaust on
its survivors?

3 How does the poem make you feel?

4 Why do you think that William Heyen
writes about hair and gold and clothing
rather than about people?

5 Does it matter to historians that William
Heyen was not been part of the
Holocaust?

6 How could these sources be used by
historians?

EXPLORING THE HOLOCAUST – WHAT QUESTIONS AND ISSUES REMAIN?

The word 'Holocaust' came to be used for the deliberate murder of a whole race. It is an event which is difficult to understand and to come to terms with. Many questions that arise have not been answered and historians, Jewish groups and the general public disagree over different points.

Activity Time

1 Make a list of questions that you want answered about the Final Solution. Compare your list with the questions of the rest of the class. The Holocaust is such a complex event that there may well be questions that the class will want to discuss.

Here are some key questions to help you – you may have thought of some of these yourself:

a Why didn't the Jews resist?

b How did the Jews rebel in the Warsaw ghetto?

c What sort of people tried to help the Jews?

d Could Britain and the USA have done more to help the Jews?

e Why did the German people let it happen?

f Why didn't the Christian churches do more?

g What happened in lands that were occupied, like Holland and Czechoslovakia?

To start you off, here are some notes for an answer to **e** – can you add any more?

Why did the German people let it happen?

• The Nazis tried to keep it a secret, using code names.

• Effective propaganda.

• Fear – use of violence by SS.

2 Carry out some research to get nearer to an answer to one of the key questions. You will need to use books and the Internet if possible. Before you start your research note down what your group thinks might be the answer to the question – check back to see how correct you are at the end. Look for sources and information – you won't necessarily get a straightforward answer.

3 Present your findings to the rest of the group using a mixture of the following methods. *Role play, visual images, summary speeches, display of key points, fact file, bibliography, video, documentary, mini lesson.* All groups should give the rest of the class the chance to ask questions but don't worry if you do not have a final answer.

SO, HOW AND WHY DID THE HOLOCAUST HAPPEN?

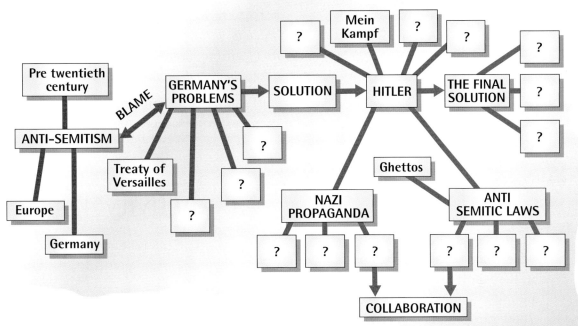

Design a concept map to help you answer the big question 'How and why did the Holocaust happen?' One is started above. Some of the key points are already included but add some more and design it in your own way. You could use the shape of a road map, a tree or a unique diagram to show what happened.

How and why did the Holocaust happen?

Make links between different points on your concept map by drawing arrows. One example is done for you – can you explain it to your partner?

Use the concept map as a framework for a report to answer the question. The map will give you different paragraph headings but follow this simple formula:

- Introduction – briefly state what you are going to discuss.
- Main body – step by step explain the main reasons, give details, evidence and link together ideas if you can.
- Conclusion – what do you think is the best answer we can give and why? What can't we answer? What do people disagree over and why?

THE LESSONS OF THE HOLOCAUST

In 1999 Anthony Sawoniuk, aged 78, was put on trial in Britain and sentenced to life imprisonment for murdering 18 Jewish people during the Second World War. His trial caused a lot of debate in Britain. People argued over whether such an old, ill man should be put on trial at all, and whether he should be imprisoned for life or given some hope of release. War crimes trials draw people's attention to events in history like the Holocaust. More recent examples of atrocities and genocide across the world mean that there are important lessons still to be learned.

SOURCE 1

The trial (of Sawoniuk) is a symbolic beacon, re-lighting memories of the hideous barbarity of the past. It reminded us of all the dangers that flow from allowing racist dictators to rule.

Lord Janner QC, commenting on the case.

SOURCE 2

The world has rightly been shocked by the news of killings in Kosovo, where maybe 5000 Albanians died in the whole province in just a few months. At Srebrenica more than 7000 were murdered in just a few days in July 1995 – mostly shot in the head before being dumped in mass graves...the responsibility lies with western powers that refused to help, repeatedly turning their faces away from a reality that stared them in the face...the UN admitted last week that the insufficient military response resulted from 'an inability to recognise the scope of the evil confronting us'...The ultimate criminals were, of course, the Serb and Bosnian leaders...

This article from the *Independent* newspaper appeared in November 1999. It refers to the extermination of a large number of Muslim men in Srebrenica. The area was supposed to be a UNO safe haven but Serbs took it over. The UNO took no action to prevent the shootings.

Activity Time

Use the following questions as discussion points for the class.

1. Do you think that war criminals should be put on trial for something that happened over 50 years ago?

2. Why does Lord Janner see the trial of Sawoniuk as so important?

3. What point is being made in Source 2?

4. Does the fact that there have been mass murders in countries around the world since 1945 mean that there is no point in studying the Holocaust?

5. What can prevent people from learning lessons from the past?

6. What do you think are the most important lessons to be learned form studying the Holocaust?

Unit 20: Twentieth-century medicine – how has it changed the lives of ordinary people?

BETTER HEALTH – LONGER LIFE: WHY?

In this unit, you will find out about the ways in which developments and discoveries in medicine have changed the lives of millions of ordinary people. You will also find out that these discoveries were not always and not necessarily for the better – and that they have not spread to all parts of the world.

WHAT KEEPS US HEALTHY?

Think for a few minutes about what makes and keeps us fit and well.

Drains and sewers

Vaccinating babies

Check-ups by school nurse

Good diet

Straightening crooked teeth

Taking out burst appendix

Clean water

Antibiotic drugs

Toilets

Spectacles

Setting a broken wrist

Taking out infected tonsils

Now add to these: think of as many things as possible that help to make and keep us fit and well. Make as long a list as you can. Think about:

- medicines and drugs
- operations and all kinds of surgery
- ways in which the government and local councils can help the public to live healthier lives
- what we can do to prevent diseases happening in the first place.

Sort your list under four headings: medicine, surgery, public health and preventative medicine, and fill in the table below. It has been started for you.

Medicine	Surgery	Public health	Preventative medicine
Antibiotic drugs	Taking out infected tonsils	Toilets	Flu jabs
	Fitting grommets in 'glue' ears	Clean water	Vaccinating babies
			Good diet

Activity Time

TWO FAMILIES – ONE HUNDRED YEARS APART

In 1900, the Dawson family lived in Whitefield, near Manchester

John Dawson	Aged 37	A grocer at the local Co-op store
Alice Dawson	Aged 35	Works part-time as a telephonist at the local telephone exchange
Harry Dawson	Aged 16	Apprenticed to a local electrical engineering company
Kathleen Dawson	Aged 14	Working as a shop assistant in a department store in Manchester
Jack Dawson	Aged 13	Working as an errand boy in the local bank
Ann Dawson	Aged 10	At school
Ellis Dawson	Aged 6	At school

Illnesses, accidents and the unexpected can hit any family at almost any time.

See if you can match the following happenings to the two families and to the people within the families.

The daughter has TB (tuberculosis – a killer disease that attacks the lungs). The doctor has said she should go to a health clinic in Switzerland where the air is clean.

The daughter has fallen off her bicycle and an ambulance has taken her to the nearest Accident and Emergency Unit. An X-ray has shown that her back is damaged and she has been taken to a special spinal unit.

The local council want to dig up the road and lay a sewer so that every house can have a flushing toilet connected to it.

The father has had a heart attack and needs open heart surgery. There is a waiting list of several months.

What does it mean?

Vaccination

Injection against diseases like smallpox and polio which, by introducing a minute sample of the disease, prevents it returning.

Antibiotic

A drug, like penicillin, produced by living things that can destroy or stop the growth of harmful bacteria and disease.

In 2000, the Freeman family lived in Norwich, Norfolk.

Michael Freeman	Aged 37	A manager in the local supermarket
Jennifer Freeman	Aged 35	Works as a part-time teacher in the local comprehensive school
Daniel Freeman	Aged 13	At school
Rachel Freeman	Aged 10	At school

Not all of these events happened to each family all at once, or even at all! But they are incidents that could have happened, and each incident would have presented problems to the family.

1 In groups, or with a partner, choose an event (or events) and the family which was affected. Work out what might have happened and how they would have coped with the outcomes.

2 Now present your findings to the class. You might use drama, a series of interviews, a wall display or 'family' scrapbooks. Remember to focus on medicine and what could or could not be done at the time.

The father has been knocked down by a runaway horse and has damaged his leg. Workmen have put him on a makeshift stretcher and taken him home. His wife has sent for the doctor.

The mother discovers she is pregnant and is worried that they cannot afford the cost of another baby.

The mother has kidney failure and is having complicated treatment every week while she waits for a kidney transplant.

The son has diphtheria. The doctor wants him to be injected with a new anti-poison drug that might cure him. (Diphtheria is a dangerous infection of the throat preventing breathing)

FREE AT THE POINT OF DELIVERY?

You have seen the differences in the health provision that was available to the Dawson family in 1900 and to the Freeman family in 2000. The Freeman family would go to their local GP, to their nearest Accident and Emergency Department or to a specialist consultant at their local hospital. Was it like this for the Dawson family in the early 1900s? Just how did people at the beginning of the twentieth century get their health care?

WHAT WAS THE SITUATION IN 1900?

In 1900, people had to pay the doctor directly if they needed to see him (most doctors were men) or if they wanted a home visit. Poor people and people on low incomes obviously found this difficult. Some joined a 'friendly society' where they would save a few pence a week and could get money out for medical help if they needed it. It was like an insurance against sickness. Many doctors started their own sick 'club' for poorer people to save for when they might need treatment.

As far as hospitals were concerned, most large towns such as Cardiff, Newcastle and Manchester had their own infirmaries, dating from around the middle of the nineteenth century. There were fever hospitals in the countryside for people with infectious diseases and some specialist hospitals for people with, say, spinal injuries. In country districts, local doctors joined together to run cottage hospitals that dealt with less serious problems which could not be dealt with at home.

But the main problem was poverty and how to pay for medical care. And there was almost nothing by way of preventative care i.e. trying to prevent people falling ill in the first place.

A big shock came for the government when the army turned down two out of every three young men who wanted to fight in the Boer War (1899–1902) because they were medically unfit.

LIBERAL GOVERNMENT REFORMS 1906–14

In 1906, the Liberal government came to power. It set about a whole range of reforms that were aimed at helping ordinary people lead healthier lives free from the worry of not being able to afford medical care, proper food and better housing.

The table below shows you some of the measures brought in by the Liberal government. Talk to a partner about how the things in the list on the left helped people to lead healthier lives. (You will probably need to ask your teacher or consult a reference book to find out the details of each item.) Then fill in the right hand column.

What?	When?	How did it help people lead healthier lives?
School Meals	1906	
School Medical Service	1907	
Children's Act	1908	
Old Age Pensions	1908	
Housing Act	1909	
National Insurance	1911	

There were few big changes affecting the health of ordinary people in the 1920s and 30s. From 1929 onwards, many people suffered increasing poverty as they struggled to survive in the economic troubles that were caused by the Great Depression. Meanwhile, the political storm clouds were gathering, and in 1939 the world was plunged into war again.

THE BEVERIDGE REPORT 1942

In 1941, during the Second World War, the government asked Sir William Beveridge, a senior civil servant, to suggest ways in which the government could help the sick, unemployed, low-paid workers and retired people. A year later, Beveridge produced a report that recommended far reaching reforms. He said that people should pay in every week to a government-run insurance scheme that would look after them 'from the cradle to the grave'. He was, he said, waging war on the five giants of Want, Ignorance, Squalor, Idleness and Disease.

We are going to look at how the war was waged on disease.

THE NATIONAL HEALTH SERVICE

In 1945, at the end of the war the British people elected a Labour government, and it was this government that introduced the National Health Service (NHS). The Minister for Health, Aneurin Bevan, masterminded this. The NHS was to provide medical services for everyone, these were to be free for people to use whenever they needed them and were to be paid for by the state. This was important. It meant that everyone, no matter how poor, could get medical treatment without having to worry about the cost. People spoke about the NHS being 'free at the point of delivery', which means that all medical treatment was free when it was given. People did, of course, pay for it through their rates and taxes.

- Hospitals were to come under the control of the state.
- Local authorities were to provide free ambulances, vaccination programmes, maternity clinics, district nurses and health visitors.
- Doctors, opticians and dentists were to provide their services free.

Doctors were the big stumbling block. They were afraid that the government would tell them where they had to work and would pay them a set salary. The British Medical Association spoke for the doctors. Their Secretary, Charles Hill, had many angry discussions with Aneurin Bevan. In the end, Bevan agreed that doctors would be paid an agreed sum for each patient registered with them and that the doctors would be allowed to treat private, fee-paying patients if they wanted to. By June 1948, 92 per cent of all doctors and nearly every hospital had agreed to work under the new National Health Service. Despite opposition, the National Health Service came into being on 5 July 1948.

SETTING UP THE NATIONAL HEALTH SERVICE

SOURCE 1

This cartoon was published in a newspaper, the *Daily Mirror*, in September 1945.

SOURCE 2

If the Bill is passed, no patient or doctor will feel safe from interference by some government rule or regulation.

From the *British Medical Journal*, 18 January 1946. This was the doctors' journal and linked to the British Medical Association, which spoke for the doctors.

SOURCE 3

The Bill threatens the independence of the general practitioner (GP). The doctors have a justifiable fear of becoming government servants.

From a newspaper, the *Daily Sketch*, 5 February 1946.

SOURCE 4

Medical treatment should be made available to rich and poor alike in accordance with medical need and nothing else. Worry about money in a time of sickness is a serious hindrance to recovery, apart from its unnecessary cruelty. The records show that it is the mother in the average family who suffers most from the absence of a full health service. In trying to balance her budget she puts her own needs last. No society can call itself civilised if a sick person is denied medical aid because of lack of means. The essence of a satisfactory health service is that the rich and poor are treated alike, that poverty is not a disability and that wealth is not an advantage.

This is part of a speech made by Aneurin Bevan in 1946, explaining why he wants Parliament to agree to the National Health Bill.

SOURCE 5

This cartoon was published in the magazine *Punch* in 1948. It shows Aneurin Bevan giving the doctors unpleasant medicine.

DOTHEBOYS HALL
"It still tastes awful."

Question Time

1 Read Source 4. Why did Aneurin Bevan believe the National Health Service was necessary?

2 Look at Source 1. What serious point is this cartoon making?

3 Study Sources 1–5.
Why did some people think the National Health Service was necessary?
Why did some people oppose the setting up of a National Health Service?

4 Look at Source 5.
What is the cartoonist saying about doctors' attitudes once the NHS had been set up?

5 What questions might an investigative journalist, in 1950, have asked Aneurin Bevan about the problems, pitfalls and successes he met in setting up the NHS?

6 It seems such a good thing to have free medical services for all. Why, then, were some people opposed to them?

WHAT DID IT ALL COST?

No one really knew what setting up the National Health Service would cost. It was providing free medical, dental and eye care treatment for everyone, but the problem was that no one could guess what demands people would put on it. By 1950 the NHS was costing the government £446 million a year – about twice what had originally been calculated. The money to pay for this came from people's taxes. This was all very well until an emergency came along, draining government money. One such emergency was the Korean War (1950-3). In order to fund this, in 1951 the government increased taxes. They also made people pay a certain amount for every prescription form they took to their chemist. Aneurin Bevan, who believed that the National Health Service should be 'free at the point of delivery', resigned in protest.

IS THERE A DOWN-SIDE TO MODERN SURGERY AND MEDICINE?

One of the problems with modern, hi-tech medicine is that there is now technology to keep people alive after horrific accidents, replace hearts and lungs in very ill children, and keep tiny babies alive when they are born after 24 weeks gestation, instead of 40. The chemical knowledge and ability to produce drugs that will control terrible diseases is there in the research laboratories and international drug companies. But the cost of doing this for everyone who asks is enormous, far greater than the government's ability to pay for it all on the NHS. So, choices have to be made and this is a very difficult thing to do.

The development of modern wonder drugs that seem to do everything has created problems as well. Some of them have side effects that no one realised at the time they were produced. Some of these side effects are totally non-acceptable (like the risk of giving birth to terribly damaged babies), whilst others may be acceptable to some people (like never being able to drink alcohol). Here, again, there are difficult choices to be made and risks to be measured.

Added on to these problems of risk taking and decision-making is the problem of cost. All NHS hospital trusts and departments within hospitals have to work within a budget. They cannot take on more work than can be paid for by the state, and this money comes from the taxes that everyone pays.

DIFFICULT DECISIONS

In every hospital in the country, hard choices have to be made. Some of these choices are to do with cost, because no hospital has unlimited funds. A large number of hip replacement operations can be done, for example, for the cost of one heart transplant operation. Some of these choices are to do with the quality of life the patient would have after the treatment. Others are to do with when a person's life is judged to have ended – this leads to the question of whether or not to switch off the life support machines.

Work through this next activity about 'difficult decisions' and as you do so, remember that there are no easy choices and no right answers.

Activity Time

Think about these imaginary people, all of whom have been diagnosed within a few weeks of each other as needing heart surgery if they are to lead normal lives. There is a waiting list at the NHS hospitals.

- A 22-year-old single mother, who has two children.

- A boy who is four years old.

- An 80-year-old woman who is a key fund-raiser for an AIDS charity.

- A single man, aged 45, who is a skilled surgeon.

- A 17-year-old girl who lives rough on the streets of London.

- A woman aged 40, who is an intrepid news reporter from the world's trouble spots.

- A man aged 65, who has worked hard all his life and is looking forward to a well-earned retirement.

- A 25-year-old man who has multiple sclerosis (a wasting disease of the muscles).

❶ Now put these people in order: who do you think should have the operation first? Second? Third? And so on until everyone has a place on your list.

❷ Compare your order with what other people in your class have done. Talk about why some people have a different order from you.

THE NHS AFTER FIFTY YEARS

These hard choices had to be made more and more often at the end of the twentieth century and the beginning of the twenty-first century. This is because high technology, powerful drugs and the skills of specialist surgeons and physicians have combined to give people access to treatments and procedures that were undreamed of in the early days of the National Health Service.

You read on page 184 that Aneurin Bevan resigned in protest when the government introduced prescription charges. Fifty years after the NHS was set up, most people were being charged directly for part of the cost of many drugs and treatments that once had been free. Millions of people, however, were exempt from paying charges because they did not earn enough or because they had long-term illnesses. Here are some examples, comparing 1948 with 2000.

1948	Cost?	2000	Cost?
Prescription	Free	Prescription	£6 per item
Eye test	Free	Eye test	£15.01 for a basic test
Glasses	Free	Glasses	From £35 for a child and £60 for an adult
Dental check-up	Free	Dental check-up	£4.76
A dental filling	Free	A dental filling	From £5.24
A set of false teeth	Free	A set of false teeth	From £100
A visit to or by the doctor	Free	A visit to or by the doctor	Free

In 1950, the first full year in which the NHS was up and running, it cost the government £446 million. In 2000, the NHS cost £49 billion.

A lot is spoken and written about private medicine. This when people pay the whole cost of medical help themselves. They do this mostly by paying regularly into an insurance policy in case they need medical treatment. In doing this they can often get treatment more quickly and usually in more comfortable and sometimes even luxurious surroundings. But even so, in the 1990s, 89 per cent of spending on health care in Britain was by the NHS.

Question Time

1 Look at the chart above. Do you think it is fair to compare things in this way?

2 Should the state keep on funding the NHS, no matter how much it costs?

LOOKING FOR THE 'MAGIC BULLET'

In 1900, Paul Erlich was looking for a 'magic bullet': a chemical drug that was man-made and which would work inside a person's body, killing off germs that were causing infectious illnesses. Scientists throughout the twentieth century followed this idea of finding chemical cures for diseases. Most of the outcomes were good, but some had mixed outcomes and some had outcomes that were terrible.

PAUL ERLICH

In 1909, Paul Erlich and his team developed the first magic bullet. This was Salvarsan 606. It was called '606' because the it was six hundredth and sixth arsenic compound the team had tested. It targeted the germ that caused syphilis and killed it, without harming the rest of the person's body. Syphilis is a sexually transmitted disease that at the beginning of the twentieth century killed thousands of people. Not everyone was pleased, though. Some doctors didn't like using the new drug. It wasn't very soluble and was difficult and painful to inject into people's veins. Doctors were also wary of injecting people with arsenic. Others thought that once people knew syphilis could be cured, they would become promiscuous.

GERHARD DAMAGK

Twenty years later, Gerhard Damagk found the second magic bullet. In 1932, he discovered that a red dye, called prontosil, stopped the streptococcus microbe from multiplying in mice. When his daughter was dying from blood poisoning, Damagk, with nothing to lose, gave her a massive dose of prontosil. She recovered. A team of French scientists found that the compound in the prontosil that acted on the germs was sulphonamide, which could be made from coal tar. Sulphonamide drugs were made that attacked the microbes causing tonsillitis, puerperal fever and scarlet fever. A British company, May and Baker, developed a sulphonamide drug that worked against pneumonia. But it wasn't all good news. Sulphonamide drugs sometimes caused damage to a person's liver and kidneys – and they could not attack some of the more virulent diseases.

What is it?

Streptococcus microbe
Harmful bacteria (cells) that cause disease and poisoning.

Puerperal fever
A dangerous fever caused by childbirth.

Pneumonia
Inflammation of the lungs – often a killer disease.

PENICILLIN

The most important magic bullet was found and developed by a team of scientists: Alexander Fleming, Howard Flory and Ernst Chain. In 1928, Fleming, who was working in St Mary's Hospital, London, discovered penicillin. His discovery was developed at Oxford University by Flory and Chain and in 1942 was put into mass production by the United States chemicals industry, so that it was available to troops during the Second World War. Penicillin was used, firstly, to combat deep infections caused by war wounds. After the war, it was used to fight a wide range of infectious illnesses. But some types of bacteria have become immune to antibiotics like penicillin and scientists have had to develop increasingly powerful antibiotics to defeat them. People who have been given penicillin many times have developed a resistance to it and doctors have to prescribe stronger and stronger drugs to help them fight disease.

MORE HARM THAN GOOD?

Drug companies have developed thousands of new drugs over the past 50 years. Some can be bought in chemist shops and some can only be prescribed by doctors. Drug companies usually work responsibly, but they need to make profits for their shareholders. Not all companies have always fully tested the drugs they produce before they put them on the market.

THALIDOMIDE AND LARGACTIL

In 1961, a German company produced a drug called thalidomide. It was an effective tranquilliser and was used by millions of people, some of whom were pregnant. The problem was that the drug had not been tested for possible effects on unborn babies. When these women had their babies, they were born with terrible deformities. Some had minute arms and legs; others had none at all. In 1964, the British Government set up a Committee on Safety of Drugs to screen all newly developed drugs.

In the 1980s, the drug Largactil was used to calm mentally ill patients. It was discovered that more than 25 million people throughout the world suffered irreversible brain damage because of the drug.

PROZAC

In the 1990s, Prozac was one of the most widely prescribed drugs for people needing to cope with problems in their everyday life. Many people called it their 'happy pill'. But later it was found it could cause schizophrenia and depression and even lead to suicide.

ALTERNATIVE AND COMPLEMENTARY MEDICINE

Many people have decided to have nothing to do with drugs and are turning to other kinds of medicine to cure their illnesses and keep themselves healthy. This is called alternative medicine. Others use different sorts of treatments side-by-side with standard medical treatment; this is called complementary medicine.

Question Time

❶ Make a 'temperature graph' of the pluses and minuses of modern medicine. Do the 'pluses' outweigh the 'minuses'?

❷ Use this temperature graph to help you answer the question 'Does change always mean progress?'

Factfile

Acupuncture

The ancient Chinese believed that there were pathways, called meridians, in a person's body through which energy (ch'i) flows. These meridians, they believed, link a series of points where energy and blood meet. Disease happens when energy is blocked from flowing along a meridian. To be in a healthy state, a person's ch'i has to flow freely. Thousands of people believe this today. An acupuncturist will first find the point where a sick person's ch'i is blocked, and insert a needle into the place. Sometimes a lot of needles are inserted along a meridian line. The depth of the needle, the length of time it stays there and the number of needles used depend on the extent of the disease.

Aromatherapy

This dates from the time of the Ancient Egyptians who used aromatic oils, such as eucalyptus, lavender and cloves to cure skin disorders. Today, aromatherapists massage essential oils into their clients and claim that a number of conditions, from emotional stress to dry skin, can be treated successfully.

Chiropractic

Chiropractic is a system of therapy, based on the theory that a person's health is determined by their muscles, skeleton and nervous system. Chiropractors will never treat their patients with drugs or surgery, but instead use diet and physiotherapy, manipulating the spine and other joints.

Herbal medicine

This form of medicine has been used for thousands of years. Herbalists use seeds, fruit, flowers, leaves, stems and the bark of plants and herbs to make either an infusion or a tincture. Infusions are drunk, like tea, and tinctures are painted on the affected part of a person's body. The most commonly treated illnesses nowadays are colds and 'flu, sleep problems, nausea and vomiting.

Homeopathy

The treatments prescribed by a homeopathic doctor will be based upon the idea that the body has the power to heal itself through its own vital, natural force. Homeopathic doctors dilute drugs to achieve the smallest possible dose that seems necessary to control the symptoms of the patient. They will only prescribe one pure drug at a time, never in a mixture that could contain harmful components.

Osteopathy

An osteopath uses all the usual kinds of medicine, but looks more at the links between a patient's internal organs, muscles and skeleton.

Reflexology

Reflexologists believe that energy flows through the body along pathways that end in the feet. By massaging the point in a person's foot that corresponds to the part of their body that is affected by illness or pain, then the condition will be eased.

Question time

❶ Why do you think some people turn away from accepted medical treatments?

❷ Why do you think some doctors are opposed to alternative sorts of medicine?

HEALTH FOR ALL?

You have been looking at the ways in which medicine and surgery has affected the lives of ordinary people in the rich, western world. What about people in other parts of the world? How do people who live in drought-stricken areas of Africa or India, where living conditions are poor, manage when they fall ill? What about families who were used to a good standard of health care, but for whom natural disasters like earthquakes, or man-made disasters like civil wars, tore their worlds apart?

There are international organisations that exist to provide immediate, emergency help in time of disaster, and long term support as well.

Factfile

The World Health Organisation

This is one of the organisations that is part of the United Nations. It is responsible for helping the people of the world to become as healthy as possible.

The WHO advises on the training of doctors, nurses and paramedics; it gives people information about sicknesses like malaria and tuberculosis (TB), venereal diseases and AIDS; it gives governments advice on population control, the health of babies and children, and sanitation.

The WHO undertakes research on things like the control of epidemics and the ways in which diseases are spread, and publishes technical papers by medical scientists.

The International Red Cross and Red Crescent

This is an international humanitarian organisation. In times of war, it helps wounded soldiers, civilians and prisoners of war. In peacetime, it gives medical aid and other help to people affected by major disasters like floods, earthquakes, epidemics and famines.

United Nations Children's Fund

This is one of the organisations that is part of the United Nations and is concerned with the care and welfare of children. It aims to set up programmes that give long term benefits to children everywhere such as basic health care and advice about nutrition. One of its main programmes is Universal Child Immunization. Together with the WHO, it has vaccinated 80 per cent of the world's children against diphtheria, measles, polio, tetanus, TB and whooping cough.

Medicins sans Frontières

This is the world's largest medical charity. It gives medical help to the victims of conflict, famine and natural disasters and aims to cover urgent needs such as medical and surgical care, vaccination, and the provision of clean water and sanitation.

What is it?

United Nations Organisation
This was set up before the end of the Second World War to try and keep peace in areas of war and conflict, and to help, through its agencies, to combat disease and poverty worldwide. Most countries in the world have joined the UN.

Governments in all countries, rich or poor, torn apart by civil war, earthquake or famine, try to provide health care for their people. This is often complicated by factors other than their wealth or poverty, or the particular disaster they are facing. Examples of these factors are:

- **National pride** Many countries in the world, particularly in Africa, were once run by western European powers. Their governments do not always want to accept help from former colonial powers. They want to look after their own people in their own way.

- **Priorities** Some countries where health aid is needed are busy fighting their own civil wars. They do not consider it important to deliver health aid until their main priorities have been sorted out. Sometimes medical supplies, like bandages and drugs, are accepted for government or rebel forces.

- **Conflicting interests** Sometimes groups and companies within a country want to supply aid even though outside agencies could supply what is needed faster. Aid organisations often quarrel amongst themselves about who should give aid and what that aid should be.

Activity Time

❶ Working in groups, create two imaginary families of parents and children, as well as other relatives who might live with them or near them; give them names and ages that are appropriate for where they live.
- One family lives in Ethiopia, in a small village 80 kilometres from the nearest small town. They have no electricity and the only water comes from a tap in the village street. There are no flushing toilets and no sewerage system. There are no doctors or nurses and the nearest hospital is 200 kilometres away.
- One family lives in eastern Turkey. An earthquake has virtually destroyed their small town. All the water mains and sewerage systems have been destroyed and communications with the outside world are poor.

❷ Now work out the health risks that each family faces.

❸ Think about your two imaginary families. What help do they need? Where will they get this help? How can they make sure they stay healthy in the years to come?
Draw a flow chart to show the situation of each family, the help they will need, where they will get this help and how they can stay healthy.
Use all the information in this section to help you.

HEALTH FOR ALL BY 2000?

The constitution of the World Health Organisation contains a statement about everyone's right to health:

The enjoyment of the highest attainable standard of health is one of the fundamental rights of every human being without distinction of race, religion, political belief, economic or social condition.

In 1981, 158 member countries of the World Health Organisation agreed that they would work for a 'Health for All' policy. They listed eight goals that they intended to achieve by the year 2000:

- Treatment of common diseases and injuries
- Prevention and control of the main local diseases
- Provision of essential drugs
- Promotion of food supply and proper nutrition
- Safe water supplies and basic sanitation
- Mother and child health care, including family planning
- Immunisation against the major infectious diseases
- Education about health problems

Question Time

❶ Use all the information in this unit to plan an answer to the question – is 'Health for All' really possible? Write up your answer, using your plan. Remember to put actual examples into your writing to support what you are saying.

Unit 21: From Aristotle to the atom – scientific discoveries that changed the world?

In this unit we will look at discoveries that have changed the world for good or for ill. We will start with the big picture – the universe and the solar system – and gradually get smaller, considering mankind's place in the universe and then smaller still, looking at microbes and atoms.

SOURCE 1

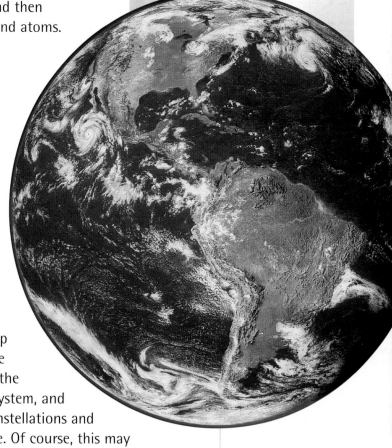

SOURCE 1

The Earth as seen from space.

WHERE IS THE WORLD?

Today, we know where the world is. Or at least we think we do! Astronomers and other scientists have told us that our world is one of nine planets that circle the Sun; they have told us that our Sun is just one of thousands of stars that make up a constellation we call the Milky Way, and that the Milky Way is just one constellation amid the (probable) thousands that make up the universe. Mathematicians have calculated the distances between the planets and the Sun in our solar system, and between some of the different constellations and galaxies that make up the universe. Of course, this may all change when astronomers make more discoveries as they look out into deep space. But, for the moment, at this point in the twenty-first century, we know where we are.

WHAT DID EARLIER PEOPLE KNOW ABOUT THE UNIVERSE?

It wasn't always like this. Thousand of years ago, men and women looked up into the heavens and wondered. They knew that the pattern of the stars at night changed; they knew that the Sun rose in

SOURCE 2

Stonehenge was built over several thousands of years and was finished around 2200BC. No one knows why it was built, although most archaeologists agree that it was built for religious, ceremonial or astronomical uses. The mid-summer sunrise and the mid-winter sunset shine directly through two of the archways. Fifty-three post holes across the entrance line up with the mid-winter risings of the moon.

one place on the horizon and set in another. But what was moving and what was stationary? They didn't have the scientific instruments of later ages; they didn't have the knowledge of past generations on which to build. But people thought about what they saw and they worked out their own explanations for what they saw happening. The way they used their observations differed between different peoples in different parts of the world, and they were changed and refined as time passed.

SOURCE 3

The ancient Babylonians worked out a sophisticated calendar. About 400BC they worked out how to predict when a new moon would appear and so when the first day of a new month would come.

Question Time

1 Study Sources 1-4. What does each source tell you about people's ideas of the universe at that time?

SOURCE 4

The American Indians who lived on the plains of North America believed that the Sun, the Moon and the Earth were round and that they moved in circles. Because of this, they believed the power of the Earth worked in circles. This is a photograph of an enormous circle built by Indians on Medicine Mountain in Wyoming.

ENTER ARISTOTLE!

Aristotle was a Greek philosopher who lived between 384 and 322BC. Like all philosophers, he had a lot to say about everything. But we are interested in what he had to say about the Sun, the stars and the planets. Aristotle, like ancient peoples before him, knew that the stars appeared in patterns and that, although they moved through the sky, these patterns never changed. The Sun and Moon moved in a set path across the sky, too. But there were some 'stars' that did not seem to follow any particular path. The Greeks called these 'planets', the Greek word for wanderer. Any explanation of how the universe worked had to include them.

Aristotle came up with an explanation that seemed to fit the facts as people observed them and understood them. He put the Earth at the centre of the solar system and said it was stationary. He made the planets and stars go round the Earth in different orbits. This explained the way the planets seemed to move and fitted astronomers' calculations about the distances away from the Earth of the planets and the stars.

Aristotle, we now know, got it wrong. Some Greeks at the time thought he had got it wrong, too. But Aristotle was such a well-respected teacher and philosopher that most people believed what he said. His model of the universe was accepted for over a thousand years.

Most importantly, once the Christian Church was established, it accepted Aristotle's model of the universe. After all, it put the Earth (and therefore mankind, God's creation) at the centre of all things. It was going to be very difficult to shift peoples' beliefs.

This is the way Aristotle thought the universe worked. It is called a 'geocentric' universe because the Earth is at its centre.

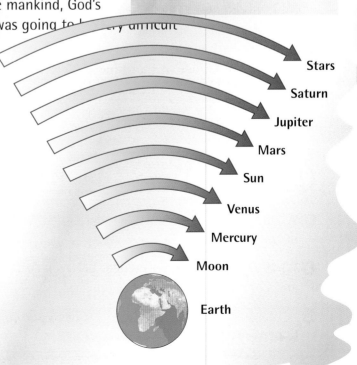

Stars
Saturn
Jupiter
Mars
Sun
Venus
Mercury
Moon
Earth

COPERNICUS' CHALLENGE

Nicolaus Copernicus (1473–1543) was a Polish astronomer. What he observed in the skies and the conclusions he drew were so dramatic that people later called it the Copernican Revolution. Copernicus suggested that the Earth moved, just like the other planets and that, just like the other planets, it went round the Sun. In Copernicus' model, the Earth rotated on its axis once every 24 hours and went round the Sun once every year. This explained things like the Sun seeming to rise in the east in the morning and set in the west in the evening; it explained the movements of the planets because it put them at different distances from the Sun. Copernicus, however, thought that the Sun and the stars were fixed and did not move.

Copernicus' heliocentric model of the universe was published in 1543, the year of his death. At one point in his life, Copernicus had worked as a church administrator; he knew about Catholic teachings and, along with most people in Europe at that time, had lived his life as a Catholic. Maybe, before he died, he had guessed at some of the problems his theory would cause.

This is the way Copernicus thought the universe worked. It is called 'heliocentric' because the Sun is at its centre. This illustration has been re-drawn from a picture in Copernicus' book *De Revolutionibus Commentariolus*, which means 'On the Revolutions of the Celestial Spheres'.

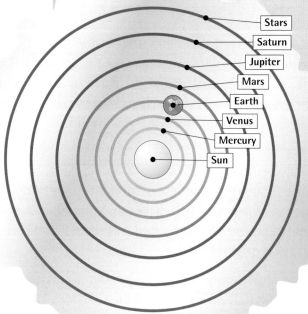

Stars
Saturn
Jupiter
Mars
Earth
Venus
Mercury
Sun

Question Time

❶ What scientific observations underpinned Aristotle's model of the universe?

❷ What were the basic differences between Aristotle's model and Copernicus' model of the universe?

❸ Why would the Catholic Church be likely to oppose Copernicus' model of the universe?

GALILEO GALILEI GETS IT RIGHT, TOO

In 1606 an Italian, Galileo Galilei (1564–1642), was the first person to build and use a telescope for making observations of the Sun, Moon, stars and planets. Three years after he had built the first telescope, he built an even more powerful one. What he saw convinced him that Copernicus was right. He saw the moons of Jupiter circling their planet. This proved that not everything orbited the Earth, as Aristotle had supposed. Most importantly of all, he was able to observe the planet Venus. For hundreds of years, people had seen that the shape of Venus changed from week to week. Galileo saw that it only *seemed* to change and that this was because people on Earth saw different amounts of light falling on it in different weeks. The only way this could happen was if Venus went behind the Sun. This was still more proof that Copernicus was right. Galileo published what he had discovered in *Sidereus Nuncius*, which means 'Starry Messenger', and quickly became court mathematician and philosopher in Florence.

THE CATHOLIC CHURCH SUPPORTS ARISTOTLE!

But Galileo was soon in big trouble. A professor at Pisa told the Medici family (who ruled Florence and were Galileo's employers) that Galileo's belief that the Earth moved went against the teachings of the Catholic Church. Galileo immediately wrote a pamphlet explaining the relationship between science and church teaching. The situation grew worse and worse, with argument following argument and pamphlet following pamphlet. In 1616 Galileo travelled from Florence to Rome, where he tried to convince the leaders of the Catholic Church that the Copernicum system was correct. All he succeeded in doing was having Copernicus' writings put on the list (index) of banned books and was himself forbidden from teaching anything that might indicate that the Earth went round the Sun! Galileo and other mathematicians and astronomers were allowed to used Copernicus' theories when they were making calculations, as long as they didn't give any indication that they believed them to be true.

GALILEO ALLOWED TO WRITE

Then, in 1624, Galileo began writing a book he was going to call *Dialogue on the Tides*. This involved writing about the Moon and its relationship to the Earth and so Galileo had to get a special licence from the Catholic Church to write it. The Catholic censors in Rome gave him a licence, but changed the title to *Discourses Concerning Two New Sciences*.

GALILEO FOUND GUILTY OF HERESY

When the book was published, Galileo was in even deeper trouble than before. Though he had tried to be even handed, the book was clearly supporting Copernicus and the observations that led him to the theory of a heliocentred universe. In 1632, Galileo was summoned to appear before the Inquisition in Rome. He was tried, found guilty of heresy and made to swear the Earth was the centre of the universe, and that it didn't move. There is a legend that, as he was led away, he whispered 'But it does, all the same.' Sentenced to life imprisonment, (later changed to permanent house arrest), the Catholic Church forbade Galileo to publish anything in Italy. So, six years later, he published *Two New Sciences* in the Netherlands!

Many Catholic churchmen believed Galileo was right and most scientists knew he was. The Catholic Church had, after all, used Copernicus' system to calculate the new calendar used by all Christians from 1582 – the Gregorian calendar. But it was not until 1992 that the Catholic Church formally re-opened the Galileo case, issued an apology and 'rehabilitated' him.

What does it mean?

The Inquisition

A group of Catholic churchmen appointed by the Pope to make sure everyone obeyed the teachings of the Catholic Church. They questioned people who were accused of speaking or writing against the Church's teaching and could punish those found guilty or condemn them to death. The Inquisition was much feared throughout the Catholic world.

Heresy

Saying, writing or doing anything that was contrary to the teachings of the Catholic Church.

SOURCE 5

This is a nineteenth-century painting of Galileo's trial at the Vatican, in Rome.

Question Time

❶ Why did the Catholic Church try Galileo for heresy?

❷ What do you think happened at Galileo's trial? Write an account that might have been written either for a pro-Catholic journal or for a scientific journal.

❸ Look carefully at the painting (Source 5). It was painted about 300 years after the trial of Galileo. What 'message' is the artist giving us? How can we be sure the trial really looked like this?

Why do you think that, after 300 years, people were still interested in what happened at Galileo's trial?

❹ How important were Galileo's ideas to people living at the time? Think carefully: would a peasant, a fisherman or a washerwoman have been affected by them? Why were they important?

❺ Make a list of the things today that need a knowledge of a heliocentred universe before they can be done.

THE SCIENTIFIC REVOLUTION: WHAT IS A REVOLUTION?

THINKING ABOUT REVOLUTIONS

- Look back to the ideas and theories of Copernicus. What made them revolutionary?
- Think back to the work you did on the English Civil War. This is sometimes called the English Revolution. Can you work out why?
- The time when William and his wife Mary became king and queen of England is called the Glorious Revolution. Why was this a revolution?
- Think about any other revolutions you may have studied in history. You may, for example, have learned about the American, the French, the agricultural or the industrial revolutions. What made people call these 'revolutions'?
- Make a list of all the things that revolutions have in common. Make sure everyone else in your class agrees.

You now have a list of agreed **criteria** that you should be able to apply to any event or movement to help you decide whether or not it is a revolution.

Historians talk about the **scientific revolution** of the seventeenth century. As you work through the next few pages, see whether or not you agree with them.

ISAAC NEWTON (1642-1727): A BOY PLAYING ON THE SEASHORE?

If you have heard anything at all about Isaac Newton, it is probably the story about the apple. It goes something like this: when he was a young man he was sitting under a tree when an apple fell on his head. Newton wondered why it fell on his head and didn't float off into space. In explaining why the apple behaved in this way, he wrote the theory of gravity. It didn't happen quite like this, but the story is almost true.

When Newton was a Professor of Mathematics at Cambridge University, a young astronomer called Edmund Halley asked Newton for help in working out the orbit of some planets. Newton had worked them out once, but had lost his calculations, and so he did them all over again. This was the start of Newton's greatest and most important book *Mathematical Principles of Natural Philosophy*. In it, he explained why the planets did not fall out of the sky, crash into each other or into the Sun. He showed that the same force, which he called gravity, that made apples fall to the ground on the Earth, attracted planets to each other and to the Sun. This kept them together in the solar system.

The most important thing about Newton's theory was that it was universal: it could be applied to all moving objects, anywhere. The same forces controlled falling apples, swinging pendulums and orbiting planets.

Newton's work was important in two other main ways:
- Other scientists began to look for universal, fundamental laws that underpinned the particular branch of science in which they were working.
- He showed scientists how to work, by insisting that any experiment which seemed to point to a theory or conclusion being correct, must be repeated again and again before they could be sure. This is called scientific method.

Isaac Newton made many other discoveries, like calculating the speed of sound waves, and many inventions, like a reflecting telescope in which light

Question Time

1. Copernicus discovered that the planets went round (orbited) the Sun. Newton explained why they did this. Which is the more important: to discover that something happens or to be able to explain why it happens?

2. In groups, research the life and work of other people who played a part in the scientific revolution of the seventeenth century: Francis Bacon, Richard Lower, William Harvey, Robert Hooke, Robert Boyle and Charles II. You need to find out about the importance of their discoveries and inventions, and the impact they had on people at the time and later. Work out how to present your findings to your class.

3. Can you find any connections between the work of the people you have all researched?

4. What is a revolution? Do you think there was a scientific revolution in the seventeenth century?

is concentrated by a special mirror. Shortly before he died in 1727, he said 'I do not know how I may appear to the world, but to myself I seem only to have been a boy playing on the seashore, while the great ocean of truth lay all undiscovered before me'.

MAKING CONNECTIONS

Aristotle, Copernicus and Newton were all concerned with the movement of the planets, the stars, the Sun and the Moon – and about where the Earth was in all of this. Test yourself by finishing off the table below:

PERSON	DISCOVERY	THEORY
	Planets move in orbits	Geocentric universe
Copernicus		
	Planets were kept in their place by two forces	

CHARLES DARWIN: ARE PEOPLE JUST ANOTHER SPECIES?

Nineteenth century Britain was one of great contrasts, as you will have found out.

Look at the two images that follow:

SOURCE 1

This picture from the time shows the engine (*The Rocket*), built by George and Robert Stephenson, winning the Rainhill trials in 1829. After this, steam locomotives were used on the the Liverpool to Manchester railway, except for the last, steep climb into Liverpool where fixed engines were used.

SOURCE 2

In 1851 the Great Exhibition was held in the Crystal Palace, London. It was an international exhibition, designed to celebrate achievements and point the way to future developments. This is a picture of the British section.

(Insert pic 21.10)

Question Time

What words would you use to describe the people who lived in a society like this? Choose two words from the ones below and explain why.

enterprising   adventurous   curious   clever   technical

dangerous   inventive   brave   creative   rich

Now look at Sources 3, 4 and 5:

SOURCE 3

The cover of a book about the life and achievements of Dr David Livingstone (1813-73), missionary and explorer.

SOURCE 4

An engraving of the Temple Church in about 1830. The Temple Church was a fashionable London church at that time. You won't see any poor people in this picture!

SOURCE 5

This is a photograph of Hastings in about 1888. You can see a line of bathing machines along the edge of the sea. Women used these to change into swimsuits and then the bathing machines were pushed out into the sea. In this way, women could swim without anyone seeing their bare arms or legs.

Question Time

What words would you use to describe people who lived in a society like this? Choose two words from the ones below and explain why.

conservative   rigid   conformist   proud
conventional   traditional   respectable
sensible   strait-laced   proper

THE VOYAGE OF THE BEAGLE

On 27 December 1831, HMS Beagle, under the command of Captain Robert Fitzroy, left England to chart the coast of South America. On board was a young naturalist, Charles Darwin (1809–82). What he saw during the voyage and what he worked out afterwards, were to change forever the way most people regarded the human race.

Before we start looking at what Darwin worked out, it is important to understand what most geologists, in the early years of the nineteenth century, believed about living things on Earth and how some people's ideas were beginning to change.

- Most geologists believed in the **catastrophe theory**. This meant that they thought there had been a series of creations of animal and plant life (the dinosaurs, for example) and that each one had been destroyed by a sudden catastrophe. The final catastrophe had been Noah's flood, as described in the Bible. These geologists believed that animals and plants were individually created and remained unchanged until they were wiped out.
- Charles Lyell, a British geologist, agreed that animals and plants were individually created. However, he was beginning to work out that perhaps the Earth's surface was going through constant change and that this change, called *evolution*, had been going on since God created the world.

Charles Darwin was given a copy of Lyell's first book when he set out on the *Beagle*. Lyell's second and third books were sent out to Darwin when he was in South America. So he had a basis on which to work and the security of the feeling that another professional was working and thinking along the same lines.

On the voyage of the *Beagle*, Darwin filled many notebooks with his sketches and observations. He packed these up, with various specimens, and sent them home to England at regular intervals. He was particularly interested in the animal life he found on the Galapagos Islands, 1000 km off the coast of Ecuador. Here, he found that, while each island had its own type of tortoise, finch and mockingbird (for example), they were very alike. He began to think about links between the species.

ON THE ORIGIN OF THE SPECIES, 1859

This is the title of the book written by Charles Darwin, which created one of the greatest sensations ever. In it, Charles Darwin said some important things:

- There is not enough food for every animal that is born or seed that germinates. They will therefore struggle to survive.
- The ones that are successful in this struggle will be those who have special variations – longer necks or stronger beaks, for example. Because they survive, they will pass on these variations to their offspring.
- Those who are unsuccessful will be weeded out and will die off.
- This process happens slowly over thousands of years.

Darwin called this 'natural selection' and other people said he was writing about 'the survival of the fittest'.

WHY DID THIS CAUSE SUCH AN UPSET IN VICTORIAN BRITAIN?

What Charles Darwin had worked out about natural selection upset many Christians, especially those who believed that every word of the Bible was true. Darwin's views challenged people's accepted beliefs in three main ways:

- The Bible says that God created the world and everything in it in six days. By showing that species of plants and animals evolved over thousands of years, Darwin was saying that the Bible's account of creation was wrong.
- The Christian God is shown as a caring, just and compassionate God. But Darwin's picture of evolution involves struggle, waste and the death of the weakest. This was hardly the work of a loving God.
- Darwin never said that his theory of natural selection applied to human beings – but people could work that one out for themselves! This, therefore, must mean that human beings were the same as the other animals and had not been specially made by God. In 1871 Darwin wrote a book called *The Descent of Man* which explained this.

Who were they?

Samuel Wilberforce (1805-73) was the son of William Wilberforce, the famous campaigner for the abolition of slavery. Samuel was chaplain to Prince Albert, husband of Queen Victoria, and his views were therefore influential. However, his various charms and desire to rise high in people's opinion earned him the nickname of 'Soapy Sam'.

Charles Kingsley (1819-75) was a Professor and churchman and much interested in the movement for reform in the middle of the nineteenth century. He wrote many books, among them, *The Water Babies*, *Westward Ho!* and *The Heroes* – a retelling of the Greek and Roman legends.

WHAT WERE VICTORIAN PEOPLE'S ATTITUDES TO DARWIN AND HIS THEORIES?

Look at the next three sources. What attitude to Darwin's theories does each source show? What do you think were the reasons for people reacting in this way?

SOURCE 6

Man's supremacy over the Earth; man's power of sensible speech; man's gift of reason; man's free-will and responsibility ... all cannot be matched up with the degrading idea that man, who was made in the image of God, had brute beginnings.

This is how Samuel Wilberforce, the Bishop of Oxford, reacted to Darwin's *On the Origin of the Species*. This is adapted from a review he wrote for the journal *Quarterly Review*.

SOURCE 7

This cartoon was published in 1874. It is called 'As others see us'.

THE LONDON SKETCH BOOK.

PROF. DARWIN.

This is the ape of form.
Love's Labor Lost, act 5, scene 2.

Some four or five descents since.
All's Well that Ends Well, act 3, sc. 7.

SOURCE 8

I have gradually learned to see that it is as possible to believe in a God who has created animals and plants capable of developing, as it is to believe in a God who made each species separately.

The Reverend Charles Kingsley took a different point of view after reading *On the Origin of Species*. This is adapted from a letter he wrote to Charles Darwin.

Question Time

Look back to Sources 1–5 and the work you did on them. All the sources, as you know, relate to Victorian Britain. What impact do you think Darwin's ideas would have had on these people?

MIASMA OR GERMS: HOW IS DISEASE SPREAD?

Think back to two frightening killer diseases you have learned about: the Black Death and cholera. Try to remember what happened (you can look things up if you can't remember) and fill in the table below:

	When?	Where?	Symptoms?
Black Death			
Cholera			

What did these terrible diseases have in common? They both spread very quickly, they both had frightening symptoms and they both killed quickly and in large numbers. But the most important thing that linked them was that nobody knew what caused the diseases and nobody knew how they spread. Until people knew what caused diseases and how they spread, they could neither prevent them nor cure them. This was true of all diseases, not just the Black Death and cholera.

HOW DID PEOPLE THINK DISEASE SPREAD?

The following sources will give you some idea of what people thought were the causes of disease.

SOURCE 1

First we had to bathe Plutus in the sea. Then we entered the temple where we placed our offerings to the gods on the altar. There were many sick people present, with many kinds of illnesses. Soon the temple priest put out the light and told us all to go to sleep and not to speak, no matter what noises we heard. The god sat down by Plutus. First he wiped the patient's head, then with a cloth of clean linen he wiped Plutus' eyelids a number of times. Next, Panacea (the god's daughter) covered his face and head with a scarlet drape. The god whistled and two huge snakes appeared. They crept under the cloth and licked his eyelids. Then Plutus sat up and could see again, but the god, his helpers and the serpents had vanished.

From *Plutus*, a play written by Aristophanes. Aristophanes was a Greek playwright who died in 388BC. Plutus had gone to a special Greek temple, called an Asclepion, to be cured.

SOURCE 4

Plague sores are contagious because the humours of the body are infected and the reek of these sores poisons and corrupts the air. So it is best to flee from such infected persons. In times of plague, people should not crowd together, because someone may be infected. All four stinks should be avoided – the stable, stinking fields, ways or streets, carcasses and stinking waters. Let your house be clean and make a clear fire of flaming wood. Fumigate it with herbs – leaves of bay, juniper, oregano, woodworm, etc.

Written in 1485 by the Bishop of Aarhus, in Denmark.

SOURCE 2

Here is the great remedy. Come! You who drive evil things from my stomach and my limbs. He who drinks this shall be cured, just as the gods above were cured.

This is a spell from the *Papyrus Ebers*, which was made about 1500BC. The Egyptian doctor was supposed to chant this spell while giving medicine to the patient.

SOURCE 3

If the pain is under the diaphragm, clear the bowels with a medicine made from black hellebore, cumin or other fragrant herbs. A bath will help pneumonia as it soothes the pain and brings up phlegm. But the bather must be quiet. He must do nothing himself but leave the pouring of water and rubbing to others.

The Greek philosopher and doctor, Hippocrates (460-377BC) believed that a person's body had to be in perfect balance, if they were to be healthy. This extract comes from one of his writings, *On the treatment for acute diseases*.

Activity Time

Work in groups, or with a partner. Take each of the sources about the causes and cures of disease in turn (Sources 1–4). For each source, decide what the 'cure' is, and what the illness was that it was trying to cure. Then work out whether the 'cure' would be likely to work, and what it tells us about medical knowledge at the time.

HOW DID DISEASE SPREAD?

People had known for thousands of years that people caught diseases from other people. Some diseases spread quickly and some slowly. There were all sorts of explanations as to how disease spread. By 1800, the most common theories were:

- Miasmas: invisible gases that caused and spread disease through the air.
- Spontaneous generation: decaying matter turned into maggots and micro-organisms that spread disease.

Some scientists looked carefully at the theory of spontaneous generation. It was true that maggots seemed to grow out of rotting meat. Improved microscopes meant that they could see that dead flesh was teeming with micro-organisms. But what if it was the other way round? What if these micro-organisms (which we now call germs) were the cause of the decay, not the result of it?

ENTER LOUIS PASTEUR

Louis Pasteur (1822-95) was Professor of Chemistry at Lille University, in France. He did many investigations for manufacturing businesses, when they had problems with chemical processes in their production runs. In 1857, a local brewery asked him to help sort out a problem with their fermentation process that seemed to have gone wrong. Pasteur found large numbers of micro-organisms in their vats, and set up a series of experiments to find out how they got there. He discovered that the micro-organisms were carried in the air and entered the vats because they were open to the air. Pasteur had followed Isaac Newton's scientific method: his experiments that proved this could be carried out again and again, and always with the same result: germs were carried in the air and caused the fermenting liquid to go bad. It was not the bad liquid that produced the germs.

SOURCE 5

I place some liquid in a flask with a long neck. I boil it and let it cool. In a few days, little animals will grow in it. If I repeat the experiment, but draw the neck into a curve, but still open, the liquid will remain pure for three or four years. What difference is there between them? They both contain the same liquid and they both contain air. It is that in one, the dust in the air and the germs in it can fall in. In the other, they cannot. I have kept germs out of it and therefore I have kept life from it. Life is a germ and a germ is life.

Pasteur describes the experiment he carried out in public at the University of Paris on 7 April 1864.

In 1865, Pasteur carried this one step further. He had already made the link between germs and decay. Now, by investigating a disease called pebrine that had broken out amongst silkworms, he showed that it was caused by germs. He had made the link between germs and disease.

KOCH CONTINUES THE WORK

Robert Koch (1843-1910) was a German doctor and a scientific researcher. He read about Pasteur's work that showed germs caused disease. He decided that he wanted to try to find the particular germs that caused particular diseases. In 1872 he began to study anthrax, a terrible disease that affected cows and sheep and which could spread to humans. He studied the blood of sick and well animals, and after three years had identified the actual microbe that caused anthrax.

He went on to try to find the germ that caused septicæmia (blood poisoning). In order to do this he had to use new technology. He developed a way of using industrial dyes to stain the microbes so that they could be seen. He connected a new lens to his microscope so that he could photograph them. He then carried out thorough and detailed tests so that he could isolate and identify the germ that caused septicæmia.

In 1882 he identified the germs that caused tuberculosis and, in 1883, the germ that caused cholera. By 1900, he and his students had identified the germs causing 21 separate diseases. This meant that cures for specific diseases were now possible.

SOURCE 6

In the twentieth century, the government published a lot of information posters like this one.

MINISTRY OF HEALTH SAYS—

COUGHS AND SNEEZ SPREAD DISEASES—

trap the germs in your handkerchief

HELP TO KEEP THE NATION FIGHTING

Question Time

❶ What was the 'spontaneous generation' theory?

❷ In what way did Pasteur's 'germ theory' show that the 'spontaneous generation' theory was wrong?

❸ Some people, even after Pasteur had shown that germs caused disease, carried on believing in the spontaneous generation theory. Why do you think this was?

❹ What did Pasteur mean when he said that 'Life is a germ and a germ is life'

❺ Do you think that Pasteur or Koch was the more important in the fight against disease?

❻ Why was the germ theory so important?

Activity Time

Make a poster that could have come from the 1880s and which is aimed to encourage people to protect themselves from the spread of disease by germs.

SPLITTING THE ATOM: FOR GOOD OR ILL?

WHERE DID THIS ENORMOUS POWER COME FROM?

The power of an atomic bomb comes from the splitting (or fission) of the nucleus of certain types of uranium or plutonium. This splitting, because it happens so quickly in a chain reaction, results in a huge and devastating explosion.

WHO SPLIT THE ATOM AND WHEN WAS THE ATOMIC BOMB DEVELOPED?

1919 Ernest Rutherford's team at Cambridge University found that an atom's nucleus could be changed.

1932 John Cockcroft and Ernest Walton split the atom.

1938 Hahn and Fritz Strassmann discovered fission reaction. Many of Europe's leading atomic scientists, like the Danish physicist, Niels Bohr and the Italian, Enrico Fermi, fled to Britain or the USA as war approached.

1942 Enrico Fermi made the first nuclear chain reaction.

1942 Top secret Manhattan Project, directed by the American physicist, J Robert Oppenheimer, was a $2 billion programme which designed and built the first atomic bomb. Most of the work was done in Los Alamos in New Mexico.
BUT
The Allies knew German nuclear scientists were working on a nuclear bomb, too.

SOURCE 1

In 1945, three atomic bombs were exploded. The first was a test explosion in the USA on 16 July, the second was on the Japanese city of Hiroshima on 6 August and the third was on the Japanese city of Nagasaki on 9 August. This is a photograph of the last atomic bomb to be dropped.

All scientists working in nuclear physics realised the strength and the power of the energy released by splitting the atom. One of them, Albert Einstein, wrote to the President of the USA, Franklin D Roosevelt, in 1939 to tell him about his concerns:

SOURCE 2

Some recent work leads me to expect that uranium may be turned into a new and important source of energy in the immediate future. Certain aspects of the situation seem to call for watchfulness and, if necessary, quick action.

This recent work could lead to the construction of bombs. In view of this, you may think it desirable to keep in close contact between government and the physicists who are working on a nuclear chain reaction.

I understand that Germany has stopped the sale of uranium from Czechoslovakian mines that she has taken over, and that in Berlin some of the American work on uranium is being repeated.

Part of a letter from Albert Einstein to Franklin D Roosevelt, written on 2 August 1939.

The first atomic bomb was tested in New Mexico on 16 July 1945. Some of the scientists who saw the explosion were so horrified at its tremendous destructive power that they urged the politicians never to use it against people. Most, however, thought it should be used if it would end the war quickly.

Question Time

① Read Source 2. What is Albert Einstein saying about an atomic bomb? What is he saying about Germany?

② What would you guess Roosevelt's reaction to be? (Hint: look at the date and think about the Second World War!)

③ Usually, scientists make the discoveries and politicians make the decisions about how these discoveries should be used. Do you think this is right?

WHY DID ALLIED LEADERS DECIDE TO DROP THE ATOMIC BOMB IN 1945?

Read the following sources and try to decide why.

SOURCE 3

To quell Japanese resistance man by man and to conquer the country yard by yard might well require the loss of a million American lives and half that number of British, if we could get them there; for we were resolved to share the agony. I thought immediately of how the Japanese people, whose courage I had always admired, might find in the apparition of this almost supernatural weapon an excuse which would save their honour and release them from the obligation of being killed to the last fighting man.

This explanation for dropping the bomb was given by Winston Churchill in 1945.

SOURCE 4

I voiced to him my grave misgivings, first on the basis of my belief that Japan was already defeated and that dropping the bomb was completely unnecessary, and secondly because I thought that our country should avoid shocking world opinion by the use of a weapon which was, I thought, no longer essential as a measure to save American lives. It was my belief that Japan was, at that very moment, looking for a way to surrender without loss of 'face'.

General Eisenhower, Supreme Allied Commander in Europe, gave his reaction to the decision of President Truman (President of the USA) to drop the atomic bomb on Japan.

SOURCE 5

We thought of the fighting men who were set for an invasion that would be very costly in both American and Japanese lives. We were determined to find, if we could, some effective way of demonstrating the power of an atomic bomb without loss of life that would impress Japanese war lords. If only this could be done.

Arthur Compton was a member of the 'Interim Committee' formed to look at US weapons policy. This Committee made three important recommendations: i) that the atomic bomb should be used against Japan, ii) that the target should be a military one surrounded by a civilian population and iii) that the bomb should be dropped without any warning.

SOURCE 6

The common belief is that the question is closed, and President Truman's explanation is correct:'The dropping of the bomb stopped the war and saved millions of lives' My own view is that the evidence we have shows the atomic bomb was not needed to end the war or save lives – and that this was understood by American leaders at the time. By June, it was clear to American leaders that either a Russian declaration of war on Japan or a change in the surrender terms was likely to bring surrender. Almost certainly both measures, together, would stop the fighting immediately.

Adapted from Gar Alperovitz, *Atomic Diplomacy: Hiroshima and Potsdam*, published in 1965.

Question Time

❶ Read Sources 3–6. What reasons do the writers of the sources give to support the idea of dropping the bomb on Japan? What reasons do the writers of the sources give to reject the idea of dropping the bomb on Japan?

❷ Now look at the people who wrote the sources and when they were written. Can you think why they thought what they did, when they did?

❸ Do you think that the decision to drop the atomic bomb was the correct one to take at the time?

NUCLEAR POWER: FOR OR AGAINST?

The knowledge of how to split the atom and of the enormous power this splitting generated could not be lost or forgotten.

NUCLEAR WEAPONS

The USA invented nuclear weapons because it feared that Nazi Germany would build them first. The USSR developed nuclear weapons to offset the American advantage. Britain and France built nuclear weapons to deter the USSR. This 'arms race' dominated what was known as the 'Cold War' between the super powers, the USA and the USSR in the second half of the twentieth century.

During this time nuclear weapons that are far more powerful than the first atom bombs were developed. Many people believe that the possession of nuclear weapons makes the world a safer place because, if everyone has them, no one will use them because they will be afraid of retaliation. Other people argue that, when more and more countries have nuclear weapons, the world will become a much more dangerous place.

NUCLEAR POWER IN DAILY LIFE

After the end of the Second World War, scientists worked to harness this power to peaceful ends. The British scientists who worked on the Manhattan Project returned from the USA in 1946 and began to develop nuclear power for generating electricity. But not everybody thought they were right to do so. Many people today are worried about the ways in which nuclear power has developed since the Second World War. However, other people welcome the development of nuclear power because of the way it provides cheap, clean energy.

As you study the sources that follow, try to think through the arguments for and against the peaceful development of nuclear power.

SOURCE 7

The Sizewell nuclear power plant in Suffolk, England. In Britain, the first full-scale nuclear power plants began operating in 1956. It is a 'clean' source of energy because it does not produce carbon dioxide (one of the main gases responsible for global warming). It does not use any of the world's resources of fossil fuel (coal, gas and oil).

SOURCE 8

On 25 April 1986 the nuclear power station at Chernobyl in the USSR exploded. 31 workers and fire fighters died from radiation burns and 50,000 square kilometres of surrounding land was contaminated. The nuclear fall-out reached 20 countries, including Britain. Scientists estimated that up to 5,000,000 deaths, worldwide, will eventually result. This picture shows trucks containing decontamination fluid on their way to the power station.

SOURCE 9

Many people object to the very existence of nuclear weapons. The Campaign for Nuclear Disarmament provides information and organises marches and protests.

Question Time

❶ Work in groups or with a partner. You are going to research the ways in which people have developed and used nuclear power since 1945. Use Sources 7–9 as your starting point. When you have enough information, use it to make out a case either for or against the use of nuclear power in the twenty-first century.

❷ Decide how you are going to present your case to others. You could, for example, design a website, write a magazine article, make a poster or design and print a leaflet, using computer-aided design.

WHICH DISCOVERIES CHANGED THE WORLD THE MOST?

Activity Time

ENTER THE BALLOON – AND LEAVE IT!

You have spent a lot of time looking at some discoveries that, for better or worse, changed the world. Which one does your class think was the most important?

In order to find out, your class is going to hold a balloon debate. A balloon debate is one where several people are (in your imagination!) put in a hot air balloon. Unfortunately the balloon begins to sink towards the ground and people have to be thrown out to keep it airborne. Each 'person' in the imaginary balloon has to argue fiercely for being the last one to be left in!

Work in groups and choose one person from this unit whom you think made the most important discovery of all time. Make sure your group hasn't chosen the same person as any other group. Now prepare a case to support that person being the last one left in the balloon. Choose one person from your group to argue strongly in front of the class for your historical person surviving.

Now hold your debate – argue – and decide!

Unit 22: The role of the individual – for good or ill?

WHY ARE CERTAIN PEOPLE 'FAMOUS'?

History is about people and how they saw their world and how they lived inside that world. While you have been learning about the past, you have been finding out about the lives of people we would call 'famous'. This raises some interesting questions:

- Why are some people famous while others are not?
- Why do we remember particular individuals but forget others?
- How do we remember these people?
- How have our interpretations of them changed over time?
- Why do different generations and cultures have different views of particular people?
- Why do societies need to have 'heroes' and 'heroines' at all?

In this introductory section, you will explore some of these ideas about famous people before going on to study three particular individuals who will always have a place in history.

Activity Time

THINKING ABOUT BEING FAMOUS

Famous people of the twenty-first century

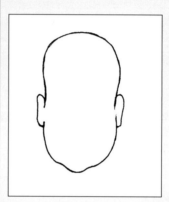 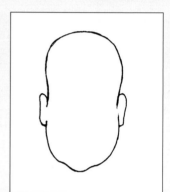

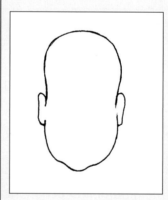 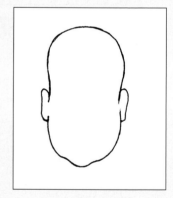

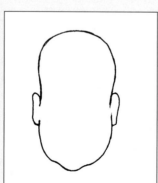 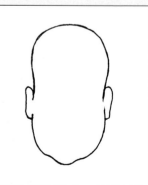

You will notice that there are no pictures in the boxes under the heading 'Famous people in the twenty-first century'. This is because you are going to choose them.

1 a Make six cards like the ones shown and write down the names of six famous people who are alive today. Think carefully about your choices, and ask yourself why you have selected them. Will they still be famous in 50 years time?

b In small groups, compare your lists of famous people of today. How many different ways can you categorise the cards? For example, you could group together famous people according to:

• occupation – are they pop stars, politicians, religious leaders, sporting personalities, freedom fighters, scientists, IT experts, writers, leaders of nations?

• racial background

• good things they have done

• bad things they have done.

Can you think of other categories?

c Now fill in your chosen faces (if you can!) and write underneath their names, occupations and the main reason why you think they are famous.

d Did you have any disagreements about what is meant by famous? Make a list of arguments that were used to justify or challenge someone being called a famous person.

2 a Now make a list of six famous people from the past.

b Carry out the same analysis of these six people as you did for famous people of today.

c What similarities do you notice?

d What differences do you notice?

3 All your choices of famous people say something about you and your society. Use the questions below to discuss what your choices say about you:

• What kind of people are valued and admired in your culture?

• What sort of things (race, sex, occupation) make a difference to who becomes famous?

• What does the choice of these people say about the values and attitudes in your society?

4 To show how the answers to these questions can change from generation to generation, now ask an older person (you decide how old!) to write down the names of three famous people from today and three from the past.

a Ask them for the reasons for their choices.

b What similarities are there to your choices and why?

c What differences are there?

d How can you explain these differences?

You are now going to find out about three famous people, one from the Middle Ages, one from the eighteenth century and one from the twentieth century. We will look first at Eleanor of Aquitaine.

WHO WAS ELEANOR OF AQUITAINE?

The life of Eleanor of Aquitaine is a story of power, ambition, sex and culture.

PERSONNEL FILE

Birth	1122 at the Chateau de Belin in Bordeaux, France.
Education	At her father's court Eleanor learned to read and write in Latin as well as speaking several European languages.
Marriage	1137 Eleanor married Louis, heir to the French throne. After giving birth to two daughters, Eleanor's marriage to Louis was annulled in 1152. In 1152 Eleanor married Henry of Anjou who became Henry II of England. They had five sons and three daughters.
Occupation	Queen to two of the most powerful kings in Europe. Mother of two English kings – Richard the Lionheart and John. Patron of poets and writers. Power builder for herself and her family.
Famous events in life	At the age of 15, Eleanor became a very wealthy heiress and ruler of half of France. Through marriage Eleanor became a queen twice, and played a major part in government and the politics of Europe alongside her husbands. While Queen of France Eleanor went on the Second Crusade with her husband King Louis. It was almost unheard of for a woman to go on Crusade. Rumours spread that Eleanor murdered her husband Henry's lover, Rosamund Clifford, with a cup of poison. Rumours also spread that Eleanor had lovers of her own, including the Muslim leader Salah Al-Deen. In the 1170s Eleanor plotted with her children to overthrow and possibly even murder Henry II. She was caught and imprisoned by Henry II for 16 years until his death. In her sixties, and a free woman again, Eleanor supported and built up the power of her sons, Richard and John.
Death	In 1204 at the age of 82 at the Abbey of Fontevrault.

Her life story touches upon many aspects of medieval life – royal governments, politics, conventions of marriage and courtly love, travel around Europe, contact with the Arabs, the Crusades, religious life and retreat, music, song and poetry. Eleanor was an exceptional person and an exceptional woman for her time.

SOURCE 1

Eleanor's tomb at Fontevrault Abbey. To the left lie Henry II and Richard I.

Question Time

❶ What impression of Eleanor's character do you gain from her Personnel File?

❷ Using the Personnel File, make a list of the ways in which you think Eleanor might have been an 'exceptional woman' for her time.

EARLY LIFE OF ELEANOR

At the age of 15 when her father died, Eleanor's life changed dramatically. She became ruler of the Duchy of Aquitaine and Poitiers, one of the greatest kingdoms in medieval Europe. Stretching from the River Loire to the Pyrenees, her kingdom covered half of present day France. In the same year Eleanor became wife to Louis, heir to the French throne, and when she entered Paris for the first time with her new husband, it was as Queen of France.

Eleanor's contemporaries at the French court commented on her intelligence, beauty and high spirits. Although we cannot be certain exactly what Eleanor looked like, she was often described as having long dark hair and bright, sparkling eyes. In contrast, her husband Louis was described as a dull man, lacking his wife's sense of adventure. When the Second Crusade began, Eleanor insisted on going with her husband to the Middle East and also took with her 300 of her woman servants. This decision shocked her contemporaries and the Pope was so horrified that he forbade any women to join the next expedition.

LOVE AFFAIRS

It was while on Crusade that rumours started to spread that Eleanor had lovers. Most of the rumours centred on the relationship between Eleanor and her Uncle Raymond, who was described as handsome, elegant and cultured. According to the medieval chronicler, John of Salisbury, Louis was very jealous and suspicious of the amount of time the two spent together.

However, while in the Holy Land there were even more rumours about Eleanor taking lovers, including the Arab leader Salah Al-Deen. It was at this point that Eleanor started to make enquires about annulling her marriage. It seemed clear that she and her husband were not a good match. According to the chronicler William of Newburgh, Eleanor used to often complain: 'I have married not a king, but a monk!'

Although Eleanor gave birth to two daughters soon after her return to Paris, the marriage was annulled and Eleanor left her daughters to be brought up at the French court. Such behaviour was not unusual at the time. Babies of the nobility were not close to their mothers, but usually raised by 'wet nurses' who breast fed them and cared for them. Boys were often sent to another court to be brought up.

Question Time

❶ Do you think the marriage between Eleanor and Louis failed because:
• Rumours began that Eleanor had lovers?
• Eleanor gave birth to daughters and not sons?
• Eleanor and Louis had different ideas and personalities?

❷ Why do you think Eleanor left her children at Louis' court?

ELEANOR AND HENRY II

Eleanor rapidly found herself a new husband, Henry of Anjou. She was 30 and he was 19 when they met. Henry was far from monkish in his character! He was dashing, handsome and well educated. He was also highly ambitious – determined to increase his power and wealth. They married months after Eleanor's marriage to Louis was annulled, and thereby dealt France a severe blow as Eleanor's French kingdom would now be ruled by Louis' great rival, Henry. After the death of Stephen in 1154, Henry became Henry II, the King of England, and on 8 December, Eleanor arrived in England as Queen.

They lived mostly in Westminster Palace but Henry had a restless spirit and much time was spent travelling around their kingdom. Henry also spent time in France, Wales and Ireland on campaigns to expand his kingdom and his power. During his absences, Eleanor ruled as regent. In the first 13 years of their marriage, she also gave birth to five sons and three daughters. Eleanor often travelled while she was pregnant, giving birth in different royal residences, for example, Westminster in London, Winchester and Oxford.

SOURCE 2

As the future King of England, she saw him as a lusty, youthful adventurer. He saw in her a chance for a brilliant political alliance as she owned more than half of France.

A modern historian commenting on the marriage of Eleanor and Henry.

A map of Europe and the Holy Land showing important places in Eleanor's life.

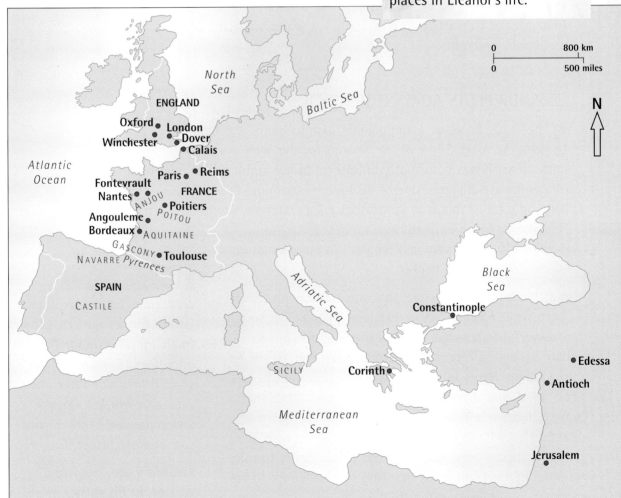

Question Time

Look at the map on page 225.

1 Why do you think Henry wanted to marry Eleanor?

2 Why do you think Eleanor wanted to marry Henry?

3 Why do you think Eleanor's marriage to Henry survived while her marriage to Louis did not?

ELEANOR: A WOMAN OF POWER

Eleanor's experience of politics in the French court of Louis had served her well. She was particularly determined to protect and promote the power of her sons and she proved to be a shrewd politician. Together Eleanor and Henry built up their land and power through the conquest of Ireland and parts of France. They also built up their power through marriages arranged for their children. In 1160, Henry arranged for their five-year-old son, Henry, to be married to the two-year-old Margaret of France (daughter of Eleanor's first husband!), – a young marriage even by medieval standards.

ELEANOR PLOTS AGAINST HENRY II

By the 1170s, however, Eleanor's marriage to Henry was heading towards the rocks. Some of the reasons for this were personal ones. Henry II was notoriously unfaithful to her and had a number of illegitimate children. One of his lovers, Rosamund Clifford, was living in a set of rooms in Woodstock Palace, Oxford, where Eleanor had given birth to her youngest child, John. Henry II also had a very bad temper – remember what happened to Thomas Becket.

In 1173 Henry II lit the fuse that was to blow his family apart. While Eleanor was determined to make her sons as powerful as possible, Henry II found it difficult to share his power, especially with his oldest son, Henry. As the younger Henry grew into adulthood, quarrels began over what lands father and son should rule. While the young Henry was keen to build up his own kingdom in France, Henry II did not want challenges to his own power. Instead of giving land to the young Henry to rule, he upset him even more by granting land in France to his younger brother John, still a child.

SOURCE 3

Dost thou not know, that it is our proper nature, planted in us by inheritance from our ancestors that none of us should love the other, but that ever brother should strive against brother, and son against father?

Eleanor's son, Geoffrey, writing to his father, Henry II.

In the power struggle that followed, Eleanor sided with her sons against their father. In March 1173 the young Henry rebelled against his father and took refuge with his mother Eleanor. It seems that she was more than eager to support him and, at the age of 50, Eleanor led a rebellion of her sons against their father.

For Eleanor the rebellion was to be short lived. Some time later, we cannot be sure exactly when, Eleanor was captured, apparently while disguised as a man, and was kept a prisoner by Henry II for the next 16 years. The rebellion of her sons against their father continued without her. Over the next ten years there were outbreaks of fighting until the rebellion was eventually put down by Henry II.

Question Time

1 Why do you think Eleanor led a rebellion against her husband? Write your ideas in note form and organise them into ideas to do with:
- revenge
- power.

2 How do Geoffrey's words in Source 3 help us to understand the causes of the rebellion against Henry II by his wife and sons?

3 Write a two minute news report about the rebellion against Henry II.
Think about:
- What role did Eleanor play?
- What were her motives?
- What other key points could be included?

ELEANOR: EUROPEAN WOMAN

In 1189 Henry II died and was succeeded by Richard I, third and favourite son to Eleanor. Released from captivity and still energetic and vigorous at the age of 63, this was the start of a new and exciting phase in Eleanor's life. Between 1190 and 1194, she ruled England for Richard while he was on Crusade. When Richard was captured and imprisoned on his way home from the Holy Land, it was Eleanor who organised the huge ransom for his release.

As well as managing her affairs in England and France, defending her land, managing her estates and income, Eleanor continued to promote the power of her family. She travelled to Castile in Spain to fetch her granddaughter, Blanche, and took her back to France. Blanche married Louis VIII, grandson of Eleanor's first husband, and was soon competing with Eleanor for political power and influence in Europe. It was Eleanor who chose Berengaria, daughter of King Sancho of Navarre to be a suitable wife for her beloved son, Richard. She rode over the Pyrenees mountains at the age of 70 to collect Berengaria and take her to Richard in Sicily.

In 1204 Eleanor died while on religious retreat at the Abbey at Fontevrault. She was 82 and had lived a full and adventurous life up to the very last minute.

Activity Time

❶ Make a sketch of the map on page 225. Select information from this section to plot on your map the journeys that Eleanor made during her lifetime.

❷ You are a Hollywood film producer who thinks Eleanor's life history would make a great story for a film. You need to find sponsorship to pay for the film.
a Select events from the information in this unit that will convince sponsors that it would be a blockbuster. You could do this by creating an eight frame storyboard of Eleanor's life. You will need to select eight events. Use drawings and text in the frame to illustrate each event.
b Finally, write a paragraph explaining why people today will be interested in the story. Will they find her story inspiring / exciting / moving / tragic / important, and so on.

HOW HAS ELEANOR BEEN PORTRAYED?

According to a recent biography of Eleanor by the historian D D Owen, Eleanor attracted legends to herself like metal to a magnet. In other words, Eleanor was the type of woman who people talked about both during her lifetime and long after her death. Although not all of these stories are true, they are still interesting and important to historians. Here are just a few of the legends about Eleanor.

Why do you think legends are important to historians even though they are not completely true?

ELEANOR THE AMAZON WOMAN

You will remember that when Eleanor decided to go on Crusade with her husband Louis and 300 of her women servants, she shocked the world. Both at the time and later, Eleanor was compared to an Amazon woman while on Crusade. 'Amazon' referred to a fabulous race of women warriors reputed to have lived in ancient Greece. According to mythology, these tall, strong and athletic women removed their right breast in order be able to use their bow and arrows more efficiently.

SOURCE 1

A picture of Eleanor of Aquitaine entering Constantinople in 1147, from a book published in 1989.

SOURCE 2

Even women travelled in their ranks, boldly sitting astride in their saddles as men do, dressed in male clothes and, with their lances and armour, looking just like men. With their warlike looks, they behaved in an even more masculine way than the Amazons.

An account written soon after the end of the Second Crusade of the arrival of Crusaders in Constantinople.

Soon after the Second Crusade ended, a Greek chronicler called Nicetas Choniates wrote a description of the arrival of the Crusaders in Constantinople. Although he does not mention Eleanor by name, it is very likely that the description refers to her and her servants (see Source 2).

The Victorian female historian, Agnes Strickland, also wrote about the event (see Source 3). As you read the extract think about Agnes' tone and attitude - does she sound as if she approves of Eleanor or not?

SOURCE 3

Queen Eleanor put on the dress of an Amazon; and her ladies, all in a frenzy, surrounded her and practised Amazonian exercises. On the Crusade King Louis showed great ability and courage ... but nothing he did could counteract the misfortune of being saddled with this army of fantastic women. The freaks of Queen Eleanor and her female warriors were the cause of all the misfortunes that happened to Louis and his army. For example, the King was slowed down by the huge amount of baggage which Eleanor and her servants insisted on taking on Crusade.

Agnes Strickland's account of Eleanor on Crusade.

Question Time

1 When was Source 1 published? How reliable do you think it is as a source of information about Eleanor's appearance on Crusade?

2 There is no reliable evidence that Eleanor and her women servants did dress as Amazons while on Crusade. How does Source 2 help to explain why the legend exists?

3 Read Source 3 by Agnes Strickland and use phrases from the extract to support your answers.

a Who does Agnes blame for Louis' failure to beat the Arabs?
b What is her attitude towards Eleanor?

4 Agnes was writing her history in Victorian times. She was against the growing movement for women's rights and instead supported Victorian ideas about the role of women. How does this information about Agnes help us to understand her view of Eleanor's behaviour?

ELEANOR AND SALAH AL-DEEN – A MEDIEVAL SCANDAL!

One of the best stories about Eleanor that circulated at the time was about an alleged affair between her and Salah al-Deen, the great Arab prince, poet and army commander. In 1186, Salah al-Deen proclaimed Holy War and captured Jerusalem the following year.

Why did people at the time think it was a good story?

In the Middle Ages, Arabic culture had a huge influence on European life. Sicily in Italy, for example, was a leading place for Arabic learning. This was despite the fact that while on Crusade, the Arabs and the Christians were enemies. Eleanor, in particular, had a reputation for being fascinated with Arabic literature and poetry. The courts of Europe were intrigued by any stories that came from the Middle East, especially a story that literally united the West and the East in one alleged love affair!

Question Time

1 Look at the dates of Salah al-Deen's campaigns and the dates of Eleanor's life. Why is it unlikely that the story is true?

2 Can you think of any other reasons why it is unlikely to be a true story?

3 Can you think of any other reasons why it would make a good story at the time?

4 What sort of people do we gossip about in Britain today? Royalty, film stars, politicians, explorers, scientists? Can you think of any others? How different is this to Eleanor's time?

ELEANOR: WOMAN OF CULTURE

Eleanor has not just been portrayed as a scandalous woman and as a woman hungry for power, but also as a great cultural figure of her time. She was a patron of poetry, music and song. During her lifetime Eleanor's court in Aquitaine became a famous centre, particularly for the troubadours. Troubadours were the poets of 'courtly love' – the code of behaviour that laid down how a man should talk, look at and act towards a woman. Almost all troubadours were men, but Eleanor encouraged women poets at her court, such as the woman who wrote the poem in Source 4.

SOURCE 4

Fair, sweet lover, how will you endure your great ache for me out on the salty sea,

When nothing that exists could ever tell the deep grief that has come into my heart?

When I think of your gentle, sparkling face that I used to kiss and caress,

It is a great miracle that I am not deranged ...

These lyrics were written by a woman whose lover had gone on Crusade.

Question Time

❶ Both during her lifetime and after her death people wrote and continue to write about Eleanor. Suggest why this is so, looking back through your work on Eleanor before writing your ideas in note form using the following headings:

- Eleanor's private life
- Eleanor's cultural life
- Eleanor's political life.

❷ What ideas do you have from this section about how legends are made?

WHAT IMPACT DID ELEANOR HAVE BOTH DURING HER LIFETIME AND AFTER?

Eleanor experienced more than most people of her time and certainly more than most medieval women. This was partly because of Eleanor's wealthy and privileged background, but also because of her determined and adventurous character.

What ideas did people have about women in the twelfth century?
At the start of the twelfth century, the importance of women was regarded as being largely as the bearers of children and, if wealthy, as the bearers of a dowry. Ideas about how women should behave were strongly influenced by the religious figures of Eve, the first woman,

and of the Virgin Mary. According to religious teaching at the time, Eve was responsible for the sin of men in tempting Adam to eat the forbidden apple and so, said the church, men must beware of women. On the other hand, the Virgin Mary was seen as pure and good, a woman to be worshipped and looked up to. At the same time, the idea of 'chivalry' became a strong part of European culture, and women were seen to inspire love, devotion and heroic deeds.

Women in the Middle Ages, therefore, were not considered to be suited for power, adventure or travel. These pursuits were for men. It was only very exceptionally that women played a major role in politics. Matilda, mother of Henry II, had been one of these exceptions and Eleanor was another.

Question Time

❶ How did the medieval church view women?

❷ Eleanor's life was not typical of that of other medieval women. Think of three ways in which Eleanor's life challenged medieval ideas about women.

❸ Using the notes you have made during this study, and looking back to your storyboard on her life, write down as many ways as you can in which you think Eleanor had an impact on the events of her time.

WHO WAS DICK TURPIN? WAS HIS STORY FACT OR FICTION?

Every society has its folk heroes whose stories are handed down from generation to generation. These stories are not always handed down accurately but often change as they are retold. We do not just remember people who have done good things in our society. We also remember people for being famously bad! Our national 'baddies' sometimes become even greater heroes than good people or, at any rate, are more fascinating.

Source 1 shows a famous late-twentieth-century 'baddie'. He was a robber and in 1963 he and his 'gang' robbed a train, stealing £2,600,000.

SOURCE 1

Ronnie Biggs holding the poster published by the British police after the train robbery. The picture was taken in Brazil, January 1994.

At first they got away with it, but then they were caught, put on trial and imprisoned. After less than six months in prison. Ronnie Biggs escaped and went to live in South America. The money has still not been recovered. Why do you think the story of Ronnie Biggs is a popular one? Ronnie Biggs is a thief, an escaped convict and he owes Britain a lot of money. Why do you think some people find his story fascinating?

In the future, our society may continue to remember Ronnie Biggs through stories, film, songs, and poems. Dick Turpin is a 'baddie' from the past who has been remembered in this way. He is a legendary folk figure. This means that we know about him because ordinary people have preserved his story.

PERSONNEL FILE

Birth	1706 in Hempstead, Essex.
Education	Trained as a butcher.
Marriage	To Mary Millington.
Occupation	Butcher, thief, murderer and highwayman!
Famous events in life	1734 Turpin was a member of the Gregory Gang. With the gang, Turpin took part in violent robberies of isolated farmhouses.
	1735 The Gregory Gang collapsed after several members were arrested and hanged.
	1737 *February* Turpin teamed up with highwayman Tom King and carried out a series of robberies in the south of England.
	1737 *April* As Tom King was being arrested, Turpin fired at a constable, but hit Tom King instead. Tom later died of his injuries. Turpin went into hiding in Epping forest.
	1737 *May* Turpin shot a gamekeeper to avoid being caught. He fled to the north of England. According to legend, he covered 190 miles in less than 24 hours on his horse 'Black Bess'. He settled in Yorkshire under the name of 'John Palmer'.
	1738 'John Palmer' was arrested for disturbing the peace.
	1739 When it was discovered that 'John Palmer' was really Dick Turpin, he was tried on two charges of horse theft and sentenced to death.
Death	1739 *April* Dick Turpin was executed in York.

Dick Turpin on his horse, Black Bess. The story of Turpin's daring ride from London to York is the most famous one about him.

DICK TURPIN *Clearing the Old Hornsey toll bar* GATE,
TO THE SURPRISE OF HIS PURSUERS.

THE LIFE OF A HIGHWAYMAN IN THE EIGHTEENTH CENTURY

The eighteenth century was a good time to be a highwayman. England was becoming one of the wealthiest countries in the world. More people had more money and they were carrying it around with them. Travel was becoming easier because roads were improving, and many people were building fine houses all over the country. In addition, England was still full of large forests which made it much easier for a highwayman to creep up on innocent travellers and to disappear quickly afterwards!

Question Time

❶ Why was the eighteenth century a good time to be a highwayman?

❷ Can you think of any other information about life in the eighteenth century that might be relevant? For example, how might thinking about law and order help to answer the question: Why was the eighteenth century a good time to be a highwaymen?

❸ What impression do you get of Dick Turpin from Source 2?

❹ Do you think Dick Turpin's life has 'the ingredients' of a good story? What might those ingredients be?

MORE ABOUT DICK TURPIN

Dick Turpin was born in Hempstead in Essex in 1706. As a young man he trained as a butcher and set up a shop in Whitechapel, London. It was there that his life of crime began when he started to receive deer stolen by poachers. When he was caught stealing cattle, he ran away and hid in the Essex countryside. By his thirties he was part of a gang known as the 'Gregory Gang'. They broke into isolated farmhouses, terrorising the people inside until they gave up their money. At Loughton in Essex, Dick Turpin broke into the house of an old woman because he had heard that she had £700 in the house. When she refused to tell him where it was, he hung her over the fire until she told him.

By 1735, the *London Evening Post* had regular reports on Turpin and his gang and the King offered a reward of £50 for their capture. In February 1736, the gang committed one of their most horrible crimes. They broke into the house of a wealthy farmer at Mary-Le-Bone and beat his wife and daughter until he gave them his treasures. Eventually two of the gang were captured, but Turpin escaped by jumping out of a window.

Turpin hid in the countryside of East Anglia and there met another famous highwayman called Tom King. The two criminals joined forces and started robbing travellers. They used a cave in Epping Forest as their hideaway. In 1737, soon after Tom King was captured, Turpin shot dead a gamekeeper in Epping Forest. Turpin then went to Yorkshire where he called himself 'John Palmer' and was eventually caught - for disturbing the peace after stealing a cockerel!

While he was in custody as 'John Palmer' he wrote a letter to his brother asking him to 'get hold of any evidence from London that could give me a (good) character that would go a great way towards my being set free'. This was not a good idea! At the Post Office in London someone who knew Turpin spotted the letter and recognised his handwriting. He took the letter to the authorities and it didn't take them long to realise that Turpin and Palmer were the same person.

Turpin was convicted and sentenced to death. His father pleaded for transportation rather than execution, but his pleas were ignored. Turpin gave his belongings to friends, including a married woman in Lincolnshire. On 19 April 1739 he was taken through the streets of York in an open cart to be hanged. Then he climbed to the gibbet in front of a large crowd. Without help from the executioner, he threw himself off the ladder, and was dead in a few minutes.

SOURCE 3

All the way Turpin bowed repeatedly and with the most astonishing calmness and courage. Arriving at the fatal spot he talked for some time to the hangman and presented him with a small ivory whistle.

An eyewitness report on what happened when Dick Turpin was taken to be executed.

Activity Time

Use the information you have just read to produce an eight frame storyboard of Dick Turpin's life. You will need to select eight events. Use drawings and text in the frame to illustrate each event.

1 a Pick out the event or events which you think would have made him famous in his own life time. Give reasons for your choice.
b Pick out the event or events which may have ensured that he was remembered after his death. Give reasons for your choice.
c Is there anything in the story of Dick Turpin that you have read so far that indicates that he, as an individual, had any influence on an event or events at the time?
d Is he similar or different to Eleanor of Aquitaine in this way?

HOW HAS DICK TURPIN BEEN PORTRAYED: GLAMOROUS HIGHWAYMAN OR NASTY VILLAIN?

Much of the story of Dick Turpin is a legend. A legend is a mixture of facts and stories that people want to hear. Only a good story will be passed down whether about a good person or a bad person!

Dick Turpin and Black Bess: fact or fiction?

There was another legend about a ride from London to York:
'Early one morning in 1676 a daring and fearless highwayman called John 'Nick' Nevins robbed a sailor on the road outside Gads Hill in Kent. But he needed an alibi to avoid arrest and conviction. So he rode 190 miles in about 15 hours and by eight o'clock that evening, he was playing bowls on a green in York. He even played a few rounds with the local mayor. When rumours spread of his amazing ride across England, he became known as 'Swift Nick'.

This is how the story of the ride was told until the publication of a novel called

SOURCE 1

And the highwayman came riding, riding, riding,
The highwayman came riding, up to the old inn door.

He'd a French cocked hat on his forehead, a bunch of lace at his chin,
A coat of the claret velvet, and breeches of brown doe skin.

Over the cobbles he clattered and clashed in the dark inn-yard,
He tapped with his whip on the shutters, but all was locked and barred,
He whistled a tune to the window, and who should be waiting there
But the landlord's black-eyed daughter, Bess, landlord's daughter,
Plaiting a dark red love-knot into her long black hair.

A poem by Alfred Noyes written in 1913.

Rookwood by Harrison Ainsworth in 1834. A secondary character in the novel is a highwayman called Dick Turpin who makes a daring and very fast journey on horseback from London to York. The novel was a bestseller.

SOURCE 2

An eighteenth-century woodcut showing Dick Turpin fleeing from the authorities.

George Cruikshank.

SOURCE 3

Only at the very end of his life, while waiting to be hanged at York racecourse, did Turpin show any of the swaggering, devil-may-care heroism or derring-do usually attributed to him. Before that, both his existence and his criminal activities had been squalid, to say the least.

A modern historian writing about the behaviour of Dick Turpin just before he was hanged.

Question Time

❶ How do these stories help us to understand the stages by which the legend of Dick Turpin developed?

❷ Look at Source 2. Dick Turpin is portrayed in this image as a dashing and exciting figure. Now read the poem in Source 1. What image of the highwayman is given?

❸ a How many of the following ingredients does the Turpin story have: romance, bravery, freedom, glamour, evil, money, rebelliousness, adultery?
b Can you think of any other 'ingredients' that make it a good story?

❹ There is plenty of evidence that Dick Turpin was a nasty criminal who tortured and robbed people.
a What view of Turpin's life was shown in your storyboard - for example, hero, villain, glamorous, nasty?
b Do you think people in the eighteenth century would have agreed with you? Give reasons why or why not.

❺ Read Source 3, written by a modern historian. Does the source explain why Dick Turpin became a famous figure?

❻ Looking at all the sources, what has been the impact of the story of Dick Turpin over the years?

WINSTON CHURCHILL

WHO WAS WINSTON CHURCHILL?

In a few words, write down why you think Churchill is famous. Compare your ideas to those of others in the class. What do you notice about all your ideas? Do you all agree or are there different ideas? How many of you were sure and how many were guessing?

PERSONNEL FILE

Birth	1874 in Blenheim Palace, Woodstock, Oxfordshire. Son of Lord Randolph Churchill.
Education	Harrow School and the Royal Military College, Sandhurst.
Marriage	To Clementine Hozier, 1908.
Occupation	Politician, journalist, soldier, author and artist, war leader.
Famous Events in Life	1898 Churchill is in the cavalry charge at Omdurman, Sudan.

1899 Churchill is captured while he is a newspaper reporter during the Boer War (1899-1902) in South Africa, but he escapes and returns to England.

1900 Churchill becomes Conservative MP. In 1904 he joins the Liberal Party instead. In 1922 he rejoins the Conservatives.

1917 Churchill supports the anti-communist 'Whites' who are trying to end the Bolshevik Revolution in Russia.

1926 General Strike in Britain. Churchill edits the government newspaper the British Gazette.

1939 Churchill takes over the Admiralty on the outbreak of war.

1940 Churchill becomes Prime Minister at head of an 'all-party' coalition government set up for the war and leads Britain to victory in 1945.

PERSONNEL FILE

Continued

1945 Defeated by Labour Party in General Election.

1946 Churchill visits America and makes anti-communist 'Iron Curtain' speech.

1951 Becomes Prime Minister of Conservative Government until he retires from government in 1955.

1948-54 Churchill publishes a six-volume set of books *The Second World War* for which he is awarded the Nobel Prize for Literature.

Death

1965 On 24 January after a series of strokes.

Question Time

Think back to the answers you wrote at the beginning of this section. It is likely that you have heard of Churchill as leader of Britain during the Second World War. However, as you have found out from his Personnel File, Churchill took on many different roles during his lifetime. Apart from war leader, what other 'jobs' did he have?

1 a List the 'jobs' Churchill held during his lifetime.
b Rank them according to which made him most famous.

2 What impression do you get of Churchill's attitudes and skills from his Personnel File?

LIFE AND WORK UP TO 1938 – WHAT MOTIVATED CHURCHILL?

CHURCHILL'S EARLY LIFE

Born into an aristocratic and wealthy family, Churchill had a privileged start in life. His father had been a Conservative MP and his mother, Jennie Jerome, was American and a writer. As a trained army officer Churchill commanded men on the Western Front in the First World War. For part of the war, he was Minister of Munitions in charge of the production of aeroplanes, guns, shells and tanks.

SOURCE 1

Churchill cannot visualise Britain without an empire, or the empire without wars of acquisition (conquest) and defence. A hundred years ago he might ... have affected the shaping of our country's history. Now, the impulses of peace and internationalism, and the education and equality of the working classes, leave him unmoved.

An extract from a book by J. R. Clynes published in 1937.

CHURCHILL AND EMPIRE

The colonies of Canada, Australia, New Zealand and South Africa, had by the time of the First World War become effectively independent from Britain. In the 1920s and 30s, under the leadership of Mahatma Gandhi, India came to demand self-rule. Gandhi, a lawyer with a degree from London University, used non-violent protest to fight for Indian independence. In 1931 the British Government invited Gandhi and other Indian leaders to discussions on independence for India. Unlike many of his contemporaries, Churchill did not support independence for India or any other colony. He believed that British rule of its Empire should continue.

Question Time

1 In Source 1 Clynes is suggesting that Churchill was born a hundred years too late and that his attitudes and values belonged in the nineteenth, not the twentieth, century. Do you think Clynes is making a good point about Churchill? How can it help us to understand what Churchill believed in?

CHURCHILL AND COMMUNISM

During 1917, the communist Bolsheviks seized power in Russia from the traditional ruler, the Tsar. The Bolsheviks, led by Lenin, believed in rule by the Bolshevik party on behalf on the peasants and the workers. They were against wealth and privilege, and supported equality for all. Not everyone agreed with them and in 1918 opposition to Bolshevik rule escalated into civil war. Those groups who opposed the Bolsheviks, and wanted to bring back the monarchy, were known as 'Whites'. Churchill was against the Bolshevik Revolution and supported the Whites.

CHURCHILL AND THE WORKERS

In the summer of 1910 there was a wave of strikes across Britain by trade unions. The strikes happened partly because, while the profits of industry had risen in the years before, the wages of many workers had fallen. Churchill, as Home Secretary in the Liberal Government in 1910, was against the strikes. In Tonypandy, Wales, a local mining dispute turned into a riot. Responsible for public order, Churchill sent in troops to break it up. The miners were not at all happy and criticised Churchill for his decision.

The conflict between workers and their employers continued. By the mid-1920s unemployment was rising. In South Wales and the north of England, in particular, mines had closed and communities were becoming poorer. Mine owners demanded that miners work longer hours for lower wages. In 1926 the miners went on strike and asked all other workers in trade unions to support them. More than two million workers in industry and transport came out on strike in sympathy. It became known as the General Strike. As a result there were no workers to run power stations, drive trains and buses, or unload food arriving on ships in British docks. Britain was in danger of grinding to a standstill.

When the General Strike began, Churchill was given the task of editing a special government newspaper, the *British Gazette*. As editor, Churchill was determined that the strike would be broken without giving in to any demands made by the miners. Source 2 is an extract from this newspaper.

After nine days, the Trade Union Council called off the strike. Churchill and his colleagues in government had won this struggle with the unions.

SOURCE 2

... there can be no question of compromise of any kind. Either the country will break the General Strike or the General Strike will break the country. His Majesty's government will not flinch from the issue ...

An extract from the *British Gazette*, 6 May 1926.

SOURCE 3

Winston Churchill assured me that we both wanted the same thing, only we had different notions of how to get it. The richer the rich became, the more able they would be to help the poor ... That was his theme ...

Jennie Lee speaking about events in 1926. She became a Labour MP in 1928 and supported policies that took money from upper classes and used it to help the working classes.

Question Time

1 What was Churchill's attitude towards communism?

2 What was Churchill's attitude towards the British Empire?

3 What was Churchill's attitude towards trade unions and strikes?

4 How do you think Churchill's background might help us to understand his attitudes and values?

CHURCHILL AND THE SECOND WORLD WAR

CHURCHILL AND HITLER

In 1938 Hitler was preparing to invade Czechoslovakia. The situation was very tense. Hitler had already rearmed Germany and occupied the Rhineland. Both of these actions were against the agreements made at the end of the First World War in the Treaty of Versailles, but no country had done anything to try and stop him.

Neville Chamberlain, Prime Minister of Britain, wanted to stop war happening by giving in to Hitler's demands. This policy was called 'appeasement'. He flew to Germany to talk to Hitler. Hitler told him that Germany only wanted to take over the Sudetenland, a region of Czechoslovakia that had been part of Germany before the First World War. The Sudetenland, said Hitler, was his 'last territorial demand'. Chamberlain believed him, but Churchill did not. On the contrary, Churchill was very critical of Chamberlain's policy of appeasement. In criticising appeasement, Churchill was very much in the minority in Britain. Most British people, and most politicians, were against any action that could lead to war. At a conference in Munich, it was agreed that Hitler could take over the Sudetenland.

Hitler took over the Sudetenland and in the following spring, seized the rest of Czechoslovakia. Chamberlain and other appeasers were now very worried. It looked as if Poland might be next. Britain and France had promised to help Poland if Hitler invaded. On 1 September, German armies marched into Poland. Two days later Britain declared war against Germany.

CHURCHILL AS WAR LEADER

In May 1940 the King, George VI, asked Churchill to become Prime Minister of Britain at the head of an all-party coalition government. When Churchill took over as Prime Minister in May 1940, the war was going badly for Britain. During that spring, Hitler invaded Denmark, Norway, Holland, Belgium, Luxemburg and France. By June they had all been defeated. Britain was the last remaining country in western Europe that was prepared and able to fight back. It was crucial, therefore, that the morale of the British people was high.

SOURCE 1

We have sustained a total ... defeat ... Do not suppose that this is the end. It is only the beginning.

Winston Churchill speaking during a Commons debate after the Munich Conference, October 1938.

SOURCE 2

A poster from 1940.

"LET US GO FORWARD TOGETHER"

One important way to raise morale was the use of propaganda. Images like the one in Source 2 encouraged men and women throughout the Britain and the Empire to support the war effort. Churchill also made speeches that were broadcast by radio throughout the British Empire.

Here are some extracts from speeches made by Churchill. As you read them, think about how Churchill's skills as a wrter and speaker helped Britain to win the war.

Question Time

❶ Look at Source 2. Use the image of Churchill, background images and the wording in the poster to explain why this poster was made.

❷ Do you think it would have served its purpose well?

❸ What impression of Churchill do you get from the poster?

I would say to the House, as I said to those who have joined this government: I have nothing to offer but blood, toil, tears and sweat.

Speech in Commons, 13 May 1940.

Arm yourselves, and be ye men of valour (courage) and be in readiness for the conflict; for it is better for us to perish in battle than to look upon the outrage of our nation and our altar."

BBC broadcast (his first as Prime Minister), 19 May 1940.

We shall fight on the beaches. We shall fight on the landing grounds. We shall fight in the fields, and in the streets, we shall fight in the hills. We shall never surrender!

Speech in Commons, 4 June 1940.

Let us therefore brace ourselves to our duties, and so bear ourselves that if the British Empire and commonwealth last for a thousand years, men will still say, 'This was their finest hour'.

Speech in Commons, 18 June 1940.

The gratitude of every home in our island, in our Empire and indeed throughout the world ... goes out to the British airmen who are turning the tide of world war by their prowess and their devotion. Never before in the field of human conflict was so much owed by so many to so few.

Speech in Commons, 20 August 1940.

Speech to the Canadian Parliament, 30 December 1941.

We have not journeyed across the centuries, across the oceans, across the mountains, across the prairies, because we are made of sugar candy.

Question Time

❶ In his speeches, Churchill was trying to appeal to different emotions and qualities in the British people. Choose three speeches. What emotions and qualities is he appealing to in each of the speeches you have chosen?
- Faith and religion
- Patriotism
- Pride in achievements
- Sense of duty
- Determination
- Courage
- Self-sacrifice

❷ Churchill was very successful in raising the morale of the British people. However, the speeches he made were not only directed at people in Britain. Who else was he appealing to? Why was it so important to do this? Is this consistent or inconsistent with what you know about his attitudes before 1939?

TURNING THE TIDE: GETTING THE USA'S SUPPORT FOR THE WAR

Churchill thought it was very important to get support from the USA against Germany. Think about what you know about the USA. Why do you think it was so important to get their support?

However, most Americans were against going to war in Europe. Churchill had to work hard to get their support.

A meeting with President Roosevelt led to the 'Lend-Lease Act' being passed in April 1941. As a result of the Act, Britain and the USSR received huge amounts of war materials from the USA.

Activity Time

Use the information on pages 238 to 242 to produce an eight frame storyboard of Churchill's life to 1945.

You will need to select eight events. Use drawings and text in the frame to illustrate each event.

HOW HAS CHURCHILL BEEN PORTRAYED?

Look at the people in the cartoon in Source 1. Which one is Winston Churchill? The cartoon was drawn by David Low.

SOURCE 1

This cartoon was drawn to commemorate the eightieth birthday of Sir Winston Churchill. It shows a room full of many 'Winston Churchills' who are all toasting the 80-year-old Churchill sitting in his armchair. In fact, all the people in the cartoon are Winston Churchill! The main message of the cartoon is that Churchill had a long and interesting life with many different roles.

From 1919 to 1962, David Low drew political cartoons for British newspapers. Many of those cartoons were of Churchill. Look again at the cartoon and the information on why it was drawn. What impression do you get of Low's feelings for Churchill? These feelings had not always been warm or affectionate! Up to about 1938, Low was a great critic of Churchill in his cartoons. Low was from Australia, a former British colony. He supported independence for nations and was against colonialism. He was also a supporter of trade unions and sympathetic with communism.

Look back at pages 238 – 242 about Churchill up to 1939. How does the information about Low's background and political beliefs help to explain why he was critical of Churchill up to 1938?

From 1929 to 1939 Churchill did not have an important position in government. Many at the time thought his political career was over. Apart from cartoons making fun of Churchill's views on independence for India, Churchill did not appear in Low's cartoons.

This was to change dramatically in 1939 when Churchill became the 'star' of many of Low's cartoons. During the 1930s Low had been anti-Hitler and anti-appeasement, and as we have seen, this was very much a minority view. Throughout the war, he supported Churchill with images like the one in Source 2 and others with similar slogans, such as 'We are all behind you, Winston'. When war broke out in September 1939, Low's cartoons portrayed Churchill as the only man capable of leading Britain to victory over Germany. This was very different from the messages sent by earlier cartoons when Low had made fun of Churchill's anti-communist, anti-trade union, pro-British Empire views. Low was not the only person to change his mind about Churchill during the 1930s and 40s, as Source 3 shows.

SOURCE 2

A cartoon of Churchill, by David Low, shown in the *Evening Standard*.

Bring us the tools ... we will finish the job

LOW

SOURCE 3

I then (1926) regarded him as the most dangerous of all politicians. He combined brilliance with the most foolish and antiquated views, which would have condemned us without hope of reprieve to war between classes and nations; he had tried to make war with Russia in 1919, and he waged successful war against the workers in 1926 ... and would have carried on a disgracing war in India. All the more remarkable that I was to become his admirer in the later thirties and to write a eulogy of him as our indispensable leader in 1940.

Kingsley Martin writing in 1966 about Churchill.

Question Time

❶ Look at Source 2. How would the cartoon have helped Churchill?

❷ Look at Source 1. Which of the figures of Churchill would Low have approved of? Why?

❸ a Why did Kingsley Martin think Churchill was the 'most dangerous of all politicians' in 1926?
b When did he change his mind about Churchill?

❹ Why did people such as Martin and Low change their minds about Churchill in the late 1930s?

WAS CHURCHILL'S IMPACT FOR 'GOOD' OR 'ILL'?

Activity Time

❶ Draw two spidergrams. One with 'good' at the centre and one with 'ill'. Fill your spidergram with ideas about Churchill's impact on home and world events during his life time.

❷ Write an obituary of Churchill. An obituary is written just after someone's death. It is an account of their life and achievements. You could use the Personnel File to help organise your writing. Your obituary will be published in a newspaper and needs a headline. What headline could you use to sum up his achievement?

❸ Now imagine that Churchill had died in 1939. How would the obituary and headline be different?

❹ Imagine that the obituary had been written by someone with strong feelings for or against Churchill, for example, a trade union leader or British citizen during the defence of Britain. How would the obituary and headline be different?

Index

Witchcraft!
Medieval toilets!
Exploding rats!

It can only be:

digging deeper **① BRITAIN 1066-1500**
ALAN BROOKS-TYREMAN   JANE SHUTER   KATE SMITH
Heinemann

Digging Deeper

A range of supplementary books for Key Stage 3 History

- A book per Compulsory Study Unit means they slot in alongside your existing resources, whatever your Scheme of Work.

- Cheaper than buying a whole new series of core textbooks, *Digging Deeper* refreshes your lessons without the expense of adopting a new course.

- Lively colour spreads cover the History students <u>really</u> want to learn about, while the use of overarching themes helps them to think like Historians.

Book 1: Britain 1066-1500
0 435 32771 2

Book 2: Britain 1500-1750
0 435 32770 4

Book 3: Britain 1750-1900
0 435 32773 9

Book 4: The Twentieth Century World
0 435 32772 0

See them FREE for 60 days -
call Customer Services on
01865 888080 NOW!

digging deeper **② BRITAIN 1500-1750**
ALAN BROOKS-TYREMAN   JANE SHUTER   KATE SMITH
Heinemann

digging deeper **③ BRITAIN 1750-1900**
ALAN BROOKS-TYREMAN   JANE SHUTER   KATE SMITH

Heinemann

digging deeper **④ THE TWENTIETH CENTURY WORLD**
ALAN BROOKS-TYREMAN   JANE SHUTER   KATE SMITH
Heinemann

S 999 ADV 08

F054